Beatrix
From Royal Court to Cookstove

© Copyright 2003 Rodney H. Pain. All rights reserved.

No part of this publication may be reproduced, stored in a retrieval system, or transmitted, in any form or by any means, electronic, mechanical, photocopying, recording, or otherwise, without the written prior permission of the author.

Printed in Victoria, Canada

Design of cover and inside pages by Jean Compton.

```
National Library of Canada Cataloguing in Publication

Pain, Rodney H.
      Beatrix : from royal court to cookstove / Rodney H. Pain.

ISBN 1-4120-0482-9

      1. Pain, Beatrix.  2. San Diego (Calif.)—Biography.  3.
Upper class women—England—Biography.  I. Title.

F869.S22P33 2003       979.4'985052'092        C2003-903154-3
```

TRAFFORD

This book was published *on-demand* in cooperation with Trafford Publishing. On-demand publishing is a unique process and service of making a book available for retail sale to the public taking advantage of on-demand manufacturing and Internet marketing. **On-demand publishing** includes promotions, retail sales, manufacturing, order fulfilment, accounting and collecting royalties on behalf of the author.

Suite 6E, 2333 Government St., Victoria, B.C. V8T 4P4, CANADA
Phone   250-383-6864   Toll-free   1-888-232-4444 (Canada & US)
Fax   250-383-6804   E-mail   sales@trafford.com
Web site www.trafford.com   TRAFFORD PUBLISHING IS A DIVISION OF TRAFFORD HOLDINGS LTD.
Trafford Catalogue #03-0851   www.trafford.com/robots/03-0851.html

10   9   8   7   6   5   4   3

Beatrix
From Royal Court to Cookstove

Rodney H. Pain

I am grateful to Frances Linenthal who, with the help of Lincoln Pain, provided a new perspective on Beatrix' life, and to Jean Compton, Hume Compton and Mary Shakespeare for their unparalleled editorial help.

Beatrix

From Royal Court to Cookstove

CHAPTER ONE

O to be in England
Now that April's there,
And whoever wakes in England
Sees, some morning, unaware,
That the lowest boughs and the brushwood sheaf
Round the elm–tree bole are in tiny leaf,
While the chaffinch sings on the orchard bough
In England—now!

—Robert Browning, 1812—1889

London was hushed when Beatrix was born. Straw was strewn from cross street to cross street to quiet the noise of horse traffic. That was the way it was done, if your family had money.

One week later, on June 18, 1884, the little Minchin baby, her parents, godparents, the priest, family and friends gathered by the font in Edgewater Gate Church. The white–gloved ladies could not touch anything because London in the 1800s was very sooty. The ladies' prayer books, bound in white kid leather with white kid slipcases, was carried by a footman or maid.

Scents of heliotrope, lilies of the valley, lavender and violets wafted luxuriously through the granite chamber of the church.

The men wore afternoon dress—cutaway tails and spats—and carried an aura of eau-de-Cologne, dabbed on white handkerchiefs stuffed in their cuffs. Their hats, walking sticks and umbrellas were left by the front door. Dean Farrah of Durham Cathedral was as resplendent as the ladies, with lawn linen sprouting, almost gushing, from his collar and cuffs. He wore gaiters, buttoned up the side, and his hat brim was suspended from the rim by four chaste little strings, a sartorial gesture of unknown provenance.

The nanny handed the Minchin baby, dressed in a long white embroidered christening robe, to her mother. As the great copper lid of the font was pushed aside, the ritual of the High Church of England commenced:

"Grant to this child the inward grace
While we the outward sign impart..."

As the holy water was poured from a small cruet onto the baby's head, she started to cry. Her father, James, remarked:

"Only a week in this world and she's complaining!"

Her mother retorted:

"What would you say if they poured cold water on your head?"

James marked his wife's contentious tone.

After a reading from the Gospel of Saint Mark and recitation of the Lord's Prayer, the new godparents, relatives and friends raggedly intoned the child's name, "Beatrix Mary" and all renounced "the Devil and all his works, covetous desires and carnal desires in Beatrix's name." They answered tentatively and unevenly, being more certain of Beatrix's name than the renunciation of the Devil. Dean Farrah, in good conscience, added in pulpit tones, "We do renounce them all." With further exhortations, they baptized Beatrix Mary and crossed her forehead with holy oil. Beatrix's christening, as her birth, rang a high social note, reveled in by her mother, Mary Dickson Minchin.

~~~~~~

In 1852, James Innes Minchin had marked Mary McLeod, seeing her beauty across the wide street from the balcony of his club in Madras. As she drove by in her father's carriage, he was smitten and resolved to his companion: "I'll marry that girl."

As a junior official in the Honourable East India Company, James was a promising suitor and, with the blessing and permission of her father, James married the beautiful Mary. She kept his company through twenty–five years of Indian heat, hundreds of miles of travel by palanquin, horseback, carriage, rickshaw, and train. From Bombay to Calcutta, from Madras to Darjeeling, from the coast to the Himalayas, she followed his postings, with the children and their whole entourage—amahs, cooks, punka pullers and curry grinders. She started as a young bride, beloved by James. The climate, the diseases, the postings, seven pregnancies, and the wretchedness of losing three children exhausted her. She died in 1879, in Madras, India, where she had been born.

That was the cruel India, rich–beyond–dreaming India, falling–down–poor India, a country which made you, broke you, killed you, or launched you into glorious battle, giving you a rich career of opportunity and responsibilities. It was India that made a Queen an Empress, and gave a country an empire. It also gave a short, vivid and elaborate life to Mary McLeod. James mourned her. He mourned her as an Englishman did, hiding his grief.

Some of the English in India kept their traditions for generations; they spoke of England as "home," though Britain for them was a mirage of a mirage. Though he was born in Madras, James Innes was a man of two lands. India called him and at the same time England called with its stag hunts, the "Old Queen's" levees and roasted chestnuts on the Mall. His family called too, though they would treat him as though he had been born in Devon, not Madras.

He decided to close up his Indian life with its pomp, office and prestige. He packed his dress clothes—the formal Diplomatic Corps uniform embroidered with gold oak leaves, his straight sword, and gold-trimmed, cocked hat for court visits. His house in Madras and his racehorses were sold; he resigned his club memberships, said goodbyes and set sail for Britain, as he had many times before. This time the trip was three weeks on a fast P&O liner round the Cape of Good Hope, faster by far than his first time when the *Indiaman* took six weeks to sail to London.

James wanted to see his family and start a new life in London society, near the Queen he had served from such a distance for more than three decades. At 59, he did not feel old. He was slender and bearded, a retired civil servant, sportsman and gentleman athlete. At home, family tradition was strong. They would welcome him and call him a widower. He would call himself a bachelor.

As he steamed to England, memories of other trips home came to his mind. How miserable he had been when he had to leave his parents to go off to school. He had wondered what the boys and the schoolmasters would think of him. Would they see him as a tanned boy or an

Indian? Would anyone speak Hindustani? Would they expect him to speak Latin?

His mind flitted back and forth through the years with his young wife, Mary McLeod, remembering elaborate picnics in fitted wicker hampers served by turbaned servants, suppers with Mary in England during the long leave, and the Derby with his old friend, Lord Bentink.

He thought of his blackguard preacher brother who scandalized him from the pulpit, abetted by another black clad brother–in–law preacher who likewise disreputed James' freethinking. For all their conventional piety, these two relatives could not alleviate poor Mary's distress when she lost their babies, all buried there in India.

Why did these images so bewilder him who was accustomed to making clearheaded, important, quick decisions? The visions gave no satisfaction. He sighed and turned into the saloon bar on the main deck of the liner.

What would he have? Would it a gin and it, pink gin with quinine water? No, he no longer needed quinine for malaria. No, this drink would be a toast, a toast to past experiences and a toast to a hoped for augury.

"Johnny Walker, please, with water."

He'd take his cue from jaunty Johnny, pictured on the label in day–time finery—a stylish beaver hat, coat cut high at the front, tails flipping almost to the knee, cream coloured skin–tight riding britches, jockey boots with revers just below the knee, loose top and yellow facings. What style!

"Yes indeed, almost my shadow, '*Johnny Walker, born in 1820, still going strong!*' It is a better motto than the Minchin family's *Regarde la Mort*. I never liked that. After all, Johnny is just five years older than I am and I'm still going strong."

Chuckling, he returned to his whiskey.

During his career he had relished year–long leaves in England, where his brothers and sisters lived. He had reveled in London and the greenness of English countryside, the plays, libraries, newspapers, the European chess masters and restaurants. England was home, even for an Anglo–Indian. He had worked himself through an arduous career and had his fill of India, though it had provided him with prestige and position.

"I put in 39 years of intense effort. My first assignment as a green eighteen–year–old apprentice designated to run a cholera–ridden province, sink or swim. Then to another province, which had run out of water. My early days with the Honourable East India Company were nothing but challenges —diseases, man–killing tigers, politics, famine, and those early days of solitude. Then the Mutiny! If it hadn't been for that amah—I should remember her name—who carried our son through the sewer tunnel to save him from the mutineers…"

By huge good luck James was assigned to a distant posting during the Mutiny, to an area with a hundred square miles of jungle, with more tigers than people, and too much solitude and time on his hands. During the years of enforced solitude James spent a year translating Dante's *Divine Comedy* into English verse. He then laid it aside until he might find an English editor.

"I survived everything—the assignments and the long, gradual climb to ministerial level. Now I'm leaving it, leaving Mary and our three infants buried there. How will it be different in England? Will I follow horse racing and gambling? Will I need a stable of polo ponies with a crew of staff jockeys? Should I take up writing again, and poetry? Should I take up Society, and perhaps seek out the title I turned down, perhaps a belated career playing chess, with all the concentration that it entails? How many of the perquisites of office had become habits?"

The crowded images jostled and gave no hint the future.

In India he had been British Resident to Travancore, the Old Queen's personal emissary and plenipotentiary to a maharajah who was responsible to him. And as a representative of the British Raj, he had to look princely, even when he wore black broadcloth and a cocked hat amidst their jeweled tunics and turbans. How much of that would he want, or need? His puritan, Roundhead forbearers despised luxury, pride and pomp.

"If necessary I can live at the club, with the Mahrattee cook preparing the curries for me."

He would need some thrills to liven his retirement. His pension of 1,000 pounds a year was not extravagant, but would provide a very comfortable life with the 30,000 pounds he had saved, despite the money spent on horse-breeding and racing.

He allowed himself one boast: he had won *The Governor's Cup*, the top achievement for a horse breeder in India. He relished the prospect of displaying the trophy on his sideboard.

He would miss riding such fine horseflesh, particularly *The Queen of the Night*, his traveling mare. His sais used to bring her to his tent before supper, and the horse would nuzzle through the door hangings for a lump of sugar or a flap of native bread. But, he allowed, he wouldn't miss the mounted Sepoy guard that, in late years, shadowed him whenever he appeared in public.

"Damned nuisance, all that clatter, stamping and shouting of orders, and no way of getting round it. It was so much a part of it all!"

He felt himself a very modern man in every sense of the word, living on the cusp of the most modern time. He was ready. He was going home to pick up the thread of the times, with the advantages of money and prestige earned in India.

~~~~~~

James bought an estate in Devon, near his daughter Alice, who was known as "Dolly" to her family. He joined his daughter on the local stag hunts, taking part in breakneck meets. He enjoyed the high life of the big and the rich, yachting with his son-in-law, Henry Dumas, a member of the Royal Yacht Club. The Royal Yacht Squadron was in the Solent, not far from Devon by fast train. He joined the London Chess Club and a gambling club.

One day, the eye that could spot a stag in a thicket across a wide field spotted Mary Dickson, as plump and sleek as a partridge, half his age and with lovely brown hair. She had the right quartering on her crest. Her family, Dicksons of Scotland, were landed gentry with regimental connections and Ind Coop brewers, and were, according to James' solicitors, to Minchin standards. In the atmosphere of the stag hunt, their acquaintance matured to an attachment, and progressed to an engagement. James took Mary Dickson to hunt breakfasts and the hunt dinners with the cream of Devonian huntsmen and their families. He found she was happiest when he invited her to official banquets in London where she could wear clothes to match his court uniform. She was charming and made sure she did not seem dazzled.

The courtship was not protracted or overblown, although the strict protocol of middle-aged courtship with a mature single woman was followed. Their train trips from Devon to London included at least one of Mary Dickson's close women friends. James and Mary were married quietly in Devon, James with the heat of India still in his body and Mary with the need to make a showing after so long as a spinster. She had heard the whispered gossip "she almost missed the train!" A decorous honeymoon in Italy preceded their installation at 8 Westbourne Gardens, Park Place, London, reasonably fashionable, not far from the Churchill residence. Mary Dickson wished silently for more.

The selfish union of an aging father and a fervid, older woman was not promising. In 1882, Violet was born. Not long after, in 1884, London church bells rang and straw muffled the street noise for the birth of Beatrix. She was sturdy, rachitic and plain. Her birth was hard because her large head and shoulders tore her mother. Mary Dickson blamed Beatrix, and transferred this feeling into hateful acts through much of Beatrix's young life.

James very much wanted to please his new wife. Before Violet was christened, he told his wife:

"Mary, I want you to name this our first child, our joy, born so long after all the rest of my children."

But Violet? James kept his council. It could have been worse; it could have been a virtue, such as Prudence. After all, his younger brother John William and his wife, Julia had six children—Humphrey, then Violet, Lily, Rose, Ivy and Primrose. James deplored this sentimental Victorian bathos, naming children after a row of flowers.

When their second child was born, he said, "This child is mine to name. She will be named Beatrix after the heroine of huge drama."

9

That year, James published his translation of Dante's *Divine Comedy*, which he had translated into English verse years before, during the Mutiny.

"What an accomplishment! To have another daughter, Beatrix, and publish the *Divine Comedy* simultaneously."

With the arrogance of a young author, James noted in the introduction to his translation that the vernacular pronunciation *Beatriss* was anathema to him, an error he cured by writing Beatrix.

"Proper names must be pronounced in Italian to keep the harmony of the verse. Beatrice must be pronounced with four syllables, 'Beatreechee', unless it is spelled 'Beatrix'."

So Beatrix's private war with her mother and pretty sister, Violet was established. As a plain child, Beatrix needed the help of a society-wise mother to launch her with the style befitting the child of prestigious parents. She would need help and guidance to negotiate the social shoals of her future.

CHAPTER TWO

"The family name depends very much upon you, Samivel, and I hope you'll do wot's right by it.
Upon little points o' breedin', I know I may trust you as vell as my own self...
If you gets up'ards of fifty, and feels disposed to go amarryin ...pison yourself... Hangin's wulgar."

—Charles Dickens, *Pickwick Papers*

"No more of that nonsense, James!"

It was in the privacy of Mary and James' third floor bedroom with its Louis Quinze furnishings and balcony gay with marguerites, that Mary defined, and defied, James' sexual efforts. She had made up her mind after the christening.

The servants recognized this Victorian contraceptive when a light van with a steady trotter, a Suffolk punch, delivered two beds. The old double bed was dismantled and stored in the attic.

Soon after, the servants discussed the event in their little sitting room off the kitchen. Pansy, Mary Dickson's ladies maid, led the discussion, as it was she who made the beds and laid out Mary Dickson's night clothing.

"Well, if you are h'asking, and I know you ain't, I can say almost for a certain that there will be no more

Minchin children in this famb'ly. No more at all, poor Mr. Minchin."

Their Cockney was broad – below stairs they didn't have to speak proper.

"I know you 'ave to be discreet Pansy, but 'ow can youse be certain?"

"Well I wasn't born yesterday, or the day before, an' towels don't lie. I used to be hired out to a publican, who rented bedrooms for very special purposes, if you get my meaning, sometimes several times a day, an' I know me towels."

"I for one 'ate to see Mr. Minchin treated that way."

The cook and the rest of the staff agreed, as they sat round the Rockingham teapot full of hot water with two teaspoons of strong servants' tea swirling in it.

"Don't pour it yet, or you'll kill the pot!"

"Don't tell me 'ow to m'ike tea."

The cook, on firm ground, added:

"He'll find a lady love, you wait."

"Not 'im," said Albert, "E's as straight as an arrow. He'll just put up wi' 'er nonsense."

James put up with it, and set about the ordering of Beatrix's mind, which for him was more interesting than pleasing his wife. He would take the time to educate Beatrix to prepare her for her future.

Beatrix was born into privilege and into the world of nannies, who became their teachers, guardians, confidantes, nurses, and surrogate mothers. Nannies were expected, if necessary, to run through fires to save their charges. Well-to-do mothers bore, but did not raise, the dozen children expected of well off mothers. Nannies allowed them to satisfy their husbands, allowing their "due" in bed, a child a year, but no active child rearing and none of that nonsense, breast feedings through the night.

Beatrix's nanny dressed in a grey uniform with tailored coat, long skirt, and a bonnet with a veil from crown to shoulders. Every day, except Sunday, she took the baby out in the huge perambulator, safe in the nearby streets of London. Beatrix was cocooned in this swaying, deeply sprung, rubber tyred, striped and polished, varnished and hooded vehicle with parking brake and bicycle bell. All it lacked was the size and lamps to challenge family coaches in the street.

The nanny could open the gate into the nearby park with a key the like of which the nearby elite kept in drawers in their hall coat stands. These keys kept the park as a privilege of the elite, preventing the lower orders from entering the park. When Beatrix, her nanny and the family dog joined the other nannies, their employers' rank determined who would first greet the other before they sat down. The pram was rocked to soothe little Beatrix, while her nanny gossiped and knitted with her colleagues. These fresh air outings were considered essential for proper growth. But for Beatrix, despite the outings with thin rays of sun through the perennial London smog, she did not get enough to create the vitamin D she needed to prevent the rickety bowlegs

Her baby years passed, in the nursery with well-chosen nannies, addressed as "Miss Clark" or "Mrs. Smith," not by their Christian names. For Beatrix, the servants were dear friends, friends who had offered affection and tenderness to replace her mother's coolness.

While Beatrix learned to love her nanny, she learned to respect her mother. The nannies instinctively mothered the babies. In these times, the mothers settled for socially adapted forms of affection or responsibility. That was the

Victorian way. Minchin children learned to respect their relatives and to respect other human beings, with a special consideration for prestige. They also developed a tender conscience for most animals, with the exception of foxes, pheasants and rabbits. Swans were considered to be royal, almost holy.

There was a rule for all behaviour. Shoes were polished de rigueur for "whom might we meet." Voices were kept low to avoid inconvenience or not to draw attention. Girls were to cover their hair in church and carry small linen pocket-handkerchiefs, and to dab their noses daintily. Boys were bareheaded in church; their hankies were larger, with permission for some noise. On the street, a funeral cortege for a perfect stranger brought men and boys to attention, hats in hand.

Even rules had rules, "Well bred people do it that way." In many households women servants bobbed a curtsey before and after taking an order.

Mary was no slave to her children. In her daily visit with Beatrix she made no opportunity to dandle her, or, heaven forbid, speak baby talk. She called her Trix, when James was not listening. In front of servants it was always Beatrix or Miss Beatrix, and in front of the servants the Minchins spoke a special lingua franca or French if they did not want the servants to understand. James had only women in his household, except the coachman, who slept in the stable.

The new parents only saw the baby when the nanny brought down the wee thing in fresh clothes smelling of lavender, shown "on the arm." When the nanny had Beatrix to herself, she would dandle her and coo, and speak in broad Cockney to her heart's content, not in the proper English she was expected to speak.

The nanny was responsible for Beatrix. The parlour maid climbed the four flights of stairs to carry meals to the nursery. Hot water for baths was brought up stairs and waste carried down in chamber pots covered with a towel. Many hours of work from the downstairs staff helped the nanny as she cared for the children. Some nannies, in the family for generations, stayed on after retiring on half pay, doing made work, and ended their lives in the service of old employers.

Beatrix had the one sister, Violet. Her other siblings, born to James' first wife, Mary McLeod, were her half brother James Cotton, who was thirty-three when Beatrix was born, Alice, known as Dolly, who was twenty-three, Florimel and Hamilton. Mary, Frederick, and Arthur had died in India.

It was a wonderful decade for the upper classes in England. Beatrix was entering them in the best years of her life.

She delighted in the church bells of London, each church bell tower and peal distinct and unique, the sound of Bow Bells named her proudly a Cockney, though she had the practiced, careful and tuneful diction of the well-born.

The bells of London were tuneful peals, a chromatic cascade from littlest and shrillest down to the deep *bourdons*, one hurrying bell at a time, a note in a magical tumble of shrill to tenor to bass followed again with sequence changes of single bells hunting up and down the cascade, the whole enchanting stair of sound varying peal by peal. The tune was stated, answered, stated, and answered, cascades of sound ringing through changes, an enchantment she would always remember.

Although James was no longer in Imperial India, he

was accustomed to having his own way. He was a scholar, with half a dozen European languages at his command, and another half a dozen Indian dialects. His first English ancestor was Chambray Minchin, a Norman from a noble family in William the Conqueror's court at Caen, Normandy. He owned the Gloucestershire estate of Avening and a second estate, soon called Minchinhampton, and became an Englishman by right of conquest.

Chambray had come from Brittany in 1066 with William the Conqueror. He planted the *Minchin Oak* in Southwark, a village across the Thames from London, and left his name, Minchin, a female monk, to his descendants. Fifty generations of English men and women between Chambray and Beatrix carried the name Minchin, to James Innes Minchin and the Minchin baby.

~~~~~~

In the next eighteen years, James saw to it that Beatrix's life was filled with poetry and classical prose, with even an occasional word of Hindustani. He truly wanted her to have his mind, to have his intelligence and information, to have his thoughts; though he would have denied wanting to influence her thoughts.

"The idea! I would not force something on her mind, but I'd die before I failed to introduce her to the wonders of the intellect."

Books were the vines that laced their lives, carried the two of them afield and abroad. He collected books and treasured them. He invested in expensive bindings, boards, fine calf backings, gold leaf titles, expensive, bespoke clothe vestments, with colours corresponding to their classification. The library with deep maroon mahogany shelves defined James as an educated, selective and visible scholar.

Beatrix learned to love and care for the books.

"Don't let books fall on the floor, dear, they are such wonderful friends."

"A stiff new book needs to be read first with careful cutting of pages, then creasing them to open the back, without breaking it."

"A book with uncut pages is an adventure waiting to happen."

CHAPTER THREE

For knighthood is not in feats of warre,
As for to fight in quarrel right or wrong,
But in a cause which truth can not defarre:
He ought himself for to make sure and strong,
Justice to keep mixt with mercy among:
And no quarrel a knight ought to take
But for a truth, or for the common's sake.

—Stephan Hawes, *The True Knight,* 1523

Mary Dickson put her stamp on the household. It took on a modish London style, rather than the Anglo–Indian caravansarai it would have been without her. When her husband's taste in condiments continued to offend her nose, she complained:

"No amount of airing cures curry!"

She tried to rule her rebellious daughter as she ruled the house, but Beatrix and her father were inseparable. They loved playing games, particularly pick–up–sticks, played on the library carpet. The sticks—rounded and tapered with a fancy finial on one end and a sharp point at the other—were carved from beef bones. Some had a delicate ring cut from the same bone, which might serve or frustrate a key pick.

The sticks were carved by French prisoners of war, who were housed in retired warships anchored on the Thames. It was considered a tony thing to go to view the French prisoners. The pick–up–sticks, an innocent memento of international violence, gave James a chance to talk about the morality of war.

"Bring Miss Beatrix down after her nap, please, Miss McNair."

James could so easily demand his daughter's company because at an early age her behaviour was thoroughly schooled and her company decorous. She had been taught the "right way" of "a good family", the behaviour of upper class English in their skein of life. She had a well–ordered life, a life with the events and the best things money could buy, the cost never discussed. In this well–ordered and outwardly harmonious reality, *Time and Place set the scene*, as Tennyson put it in *Crossing the Bar*, for the two scholars, old and young, to live together.

Often when James went out for a horse ride, Beatrix followed on her pony or in the trap behind the donkey. One day, as Beatrix galloped her donkey cart at an indecorous speed, the cart hit a pile of road metal and turned over. She was knocked senseless and lay unconscious for two days. When she woke, her father was by the bed.

"What would you like me to read to you, my dear?"

As she recuperated, James read Prescott's *History of the Conquest of Peru* to her.

"Father, will we ever go to India?"

"Although it is now a shorter voyage than when I was your age—six weeks by Indiaman—it would be impossible to take your mother away from her social life. But, we can read about India. For instance, this new author, Kipling, writes about India almost like a native. Let's see what he has written."

The woven–together couple lived life through their books. They rode with Quentin Durwood, dressed head to foot in plate armor. They felt the heave and shudder as the pirate brig crashed across the ocean to Treasure Island, and eagerly compared Crusoe's Island and Prescott's Peru. When school or sickness interfered, the pair picked up where they had left off. They read together until bedtime.

To Beatrix, her father was her prince without fault, her Preux Chevalier—her True Knight. His grace, humanity, ingenious scholarship, rectitude with flexibility and generousness of spirit were her delight. His knowledge and beliefs became hers.

Beatrix also shared the household with her sister Violet, hearing the cries of London as the pushcart men served the neighbourhood, crying their products and services at the kerb.

"Vi, do you realize that Father has a terrible cold, and the doctor ordered him stay in bed for two days. And you remember when Father has to stay in his bed, he orders a hot bath in front of a big fire. Maybe he will invite us in for hot muffins and strawberry jam and strong tea."

"Yes, and fun to see him looking a bit Turkish, with the hot bath steaming, wearing all those towels and his embroidered skullcap. He's positively imperial. I always love it when he gets a bad cold."

"Me too. I heard the bell stop when the cook called out to the muffin man this morning. I wonder if he lives on Drury Lane."

"Let's ask Father to sing *Muffin Man* with us!"

On Sundays, horses were given a day of rest so the family walked to Edgewater Gate Church by Hyde Park. After the service, they stopped at the Albert Memorial where James told histories of the heroes.

Sunday lunch was special—the girls were allowed to eat in the dining room with their parents. They wore clean pinafores, white socks and their "Alice in Wonderland" shoes with narrow straps buttoned over the instep. Their long hair was brushed until it was shiny and tied with a ribbon bow. Nanny stood silently behind each girl to ensure their behavior through the meal, enduring a silent appraisal of her care of the girls.

When the girls could handle food neatly they had breakfast with their parents in the dining room. And that treat might, if they were very well behaved, include making toast at the morning fire, with pronged toasting forks made of stiff brass wire with an ingenious sliding centre to lengthen the fork if the coal fire got too hot.

When Beatrix could add to fifteen, her father called her to the library. She approached these visits with pleasant anticipation, looking forward to the nutty aroma of Cuban cigars and her father's greeting:

"I have something to show you, Beatrix," he said, taking a pack of cards from a drawer under the oval table with the green billiard felt top.

"Oh I know those cards Father! Nurse taught us to play *snap*."

"Yes," James said quietly, not wanting to acknowledge *snap* as a card game.

"I think you and I will have even more fun with cribbage. This is your hand. Hold it so I don't see your pips."

"Oh, we always hold our cards close so Vi wouldn't cheat."

"She doesn't cheat, Beatrix. It's your business to keep

your cards private. If she inadvertently shows you her cards, look away."

James took pains to use large words with his children, knowing instinctively that his choice of words, as well as his personal morality, were important to his daughters' education. Beatrix's face shone with her desire to understand. She showed, inadvertently, the unspoken tokens of her upbringing, the awe and respect that she felt for him.

Indeed, everyone who came into the house was to be treated with respect, regardless of whether they were social equals, whether they came in to the house via the area way, through the kitchen, or up the front steps past the bottle-shaped stone pillars on either side of the front door and through the wall that quietly but formidably held the private world in and the outer world away. The uniform Corinthian facades along Westbourne Park Place, with their generous landings and ten granite steps, read established gentility, the values of the bourgeoisie, the Queen and empire. Although these pillared facades defined the *us* from the *them*, for the Minchin family, everyone was to be treated with equal respect.

James kept a tight ship about manners, respect and the myriad perspectives governing behavior. Beatrix observed and stored his words and gestures:

"Why do you tip your hat to the charwoman, Father?"

"I tip my hat to everyone I know, and some I don't know, as common courtesy. I acknowledge them. They acknowledge me. I suppose it started with knights meeting and taking off their helmets to show friendliness. Think of the knights, where a lesser greeting might court disaster! You have only to smile and nod."

Understanding, awe, respect, and an opportunity to

demonstrate virtue in words came easily to Beatrix. Beatrix knew many family servants, barrow men and shopkeepers; some she held in awe. But to not respect each one would be considered vile and most ill bred.

In the card games between father and daughter, cribbage replaced Parcheesi, and then bezique replaced cribbage. The battle between whist (too simple a game) and the new card game, called bridge, was played out in the library. But they never played chess, perhaps because James did not want to risk finding her a poor player. James had learned to play chess by reading a chess journal while traveling in India by palanquin. He became an accomplished player, challenging the top echelon of players in India and Europe. He now felt he had to play the ancient game with experts.

James usually chose the family's travel plans.

"We'll go to Ostend this summer, Mary. Tell Nanny and the chambermaid to get ready. Put the staff on half pay and the horse out to pasture. We can have fun at the casino, the children can fish, play at the beach and practice their French."

"Oh James, perhaps we will see the royal family. I must get some new gowns."

"Don't be such a goose, Mary. Who cares for their royalty? We can have fun at the Kursaal; the music will be wonderful. Get the servants going on it soon."

Although Ostend was the more prestigious and fashionable resort, the sisters preferred Dinant with its spooky grotto, *La Merveilleuse* and the ascenseur up the cliffs. It also had their favourite pastries, couques de Dinant. "Pack the hamper with the girls' things, Nanny."

The hamper just fitted into the big slipper bathtub, which was shaped with a wide horn on one side to keep bath water from splashing on the carpet. In French and

Belgian hotels, which often lacked bathtubs and hot water in their suites, the porter would haul up pairs of huge copper ewers with the hot water for the bath, and later haul the dirty water down. Sometimes James and the children, servants and Spider, the Yorkshire terrier, traveled via the boat, riding mixed cargo at a lower cost from Greenwich across the English Channel. Beatrix preferred the adventure of riding mixed cargo, meals with the valets, nurses and ladies' maids and Scottish nannies, and coachmen whose unguarded talk, intonations and accents were more than she usually heard. The girls were always kept close to their nanny, protected from the untoward, and taken to their cabin much too early.

When traveling without the girls, James and Mary would embark on the boat train for Dover with Mary's ladies maid and their toy terrier, Mephisto. They bought tickets on the luxurious Dover Packet to Calais from Thomas Cook and Sons. Thomas Cook, still alive, now sold tickets for the traveling public instead of the religious pilgrimages of his youth. The train went through the Kent countryside, green with hops, willow brakes, spiked with oast houses, smooth rolling prelude to the tossing crossing to Calais.

After the trying channel trip, known to disturb all but the most seasoned sailors, the Minchins, father, mother, children, dogs and servants disembarked to the stone dockside, walked the short distance to the railroad station, the great steel tracery arching over the tracks. At the French railroad cafe they bought ham sandwiches, finding the ham in the bun thin to transparency. But the rough crossing had disposed of a meal or two so they needed sustenance.

Ostend had good hotels, food and gaming for the nobs of English society. Gambling, dancing, and, for lively men, the girls, could be pursued with a freedom hard to match in England. Gambling clubs of London, such as James' club, Whites, were not open to women. In Belgium, women and men mixed with less than Puritanical propriety, enjoying the elegance of the Kursaal, the casino. Everyone, even the croupiers, wore evening dress. Ladies in evening gowns with bustles, with fashionable hourglass figures, wagered their money alongside the men. And Beatrix took it all in, undismayed by foreign travel or public gambling.

After the two-week holiday, life took up again in the stately Georgian, Number 8, Westbourne Gardens Park and the careful London routine.

James was a privately divided man. On one hand, a conventional Victorian gentleman, a servant of his esteemed Queen, but also cosmopolitan and socially advanced, privately a free-thinker, and a questioner of religious strictures. He disagreed with his government over Indian policy.

His independence led him to enjoy and support a wide variety of friends, including the Marks family. When he heard that their son, Leon, was to be blackballed at his club, James rebelled.

"Young Marks was nominated for membership at my club, but the private consensus was that he would be blackballed because he was a Jew. Can you believe it, for being a Jew! What about Disraeli who got India for Queen and Country? I told the club that either Marks was in, or I was out."

Marks was accepted.

Through the years Beatrix and Vi enjoyed the Marks family—their grand parties, and visits to their Toy Emporiums.

James' years in India had taught him a personal liberalism his colleagues could not understand. When James' coachman sported the white cockade of the rival Liberal candidate on his whip, James' Tory friends tut-tutted: "He will support Gladstone next, if you don't take a stand!"

"Never you mind. He takes care of the horses and gear. My coachman can choose the colour of a cockade to sport!"

James, in another departure from the conservative conventions of the day, insisted that his wife and daughters wear the latest swimwear from southern France. The bathing costume was svelte, without sweatered arms and legs, with no overlaid skirt or stockings. Violet and Beatrix did not enjoy these modern costumes, which were criticized by their friends.

Though James felt that most sports were too rough for women, he taught his daughters the speed-swimming stroke of the day, the over-arm sidestroke. During family holidays, most days were spent with the nanny—walking on the sand dunes, swimming and being rolled in the warm dry sand to dry off, and making little fires to heat the tea.

At the beach there were no beachside changing rooms. Instead bathing machines afforded privacy—little cabanas with roofs like cottages, shafts at one end, a short flight of wooden steps and a door at the other, the whole rolling on two large wooden wheels. The bathing machine was just large enough to change in. Not liking to be seen cowering at the water's edge, Victorian ladies climbed fully dressed into bathing machines, undressed and swathed themselves in decent black wool suits, with sleeves to cover any trace of armpit hair, skirts to hide human bulges, stockings to hide womanly leg hair. Victorians disliked the sight of body hair, except when made into jewelry, and picture frames.

A horse, hairy as a yak from the brisk air and cold water, harnessed to the shafts pushed the machine backwards into the water. When Vi and Beatrix opened the door, a burly, laconic woman waited to take each of them and dip them into the water, leaving them to swim at large until they were ready to return to the beach in the bathing machine.

During those early, carefree years, James and Mary had lavish, elaborate Christmas parties for their two daughters. Parties meant Punch and Judy shows on a little ornate stage, which fit into a corner of the parlor. The raucous lines and action astounded the girls.

"Oh the poor Judy! How Punch hit her, with the cricket bat!"

"Not so fast, Trix, didn't she hit Punch just before?"

"But not with the bat; the frying pan! Father, they are so violent!"

"Punch and Judy were once Puncinello and Puncinella. They acted out rowdy little dramas as part of the Commedia del Arte of Renaissance Italy." said James, "The poor supported these plays with a farthing here and a farthing there, which the street artists collected in a hat. The acts had to resemble the lives of the onlookers, made vivid by exaggeration. The audience related to the action of the family fights and they got them in a mood to contribute a little money. Street actors could never succeed as mountebanks by being kind and pious. Piety was made fun of, with a really nasty priest figure, a nasty professor who ridiculed learned men, and so on. There was nothing kind or gentle about Commedia del Arte, I'm afraid. This is pantomime."

Christmas festivities were lavish. The twelve-foot parlour ceilings barely cleared the biggest Christmas tree. As Nanny brought the boxes of balls down from the box room under the roof, the sisters cried:

"Take care, please don't drop them!"

"Please let me unwrap them."

The spheres were magical, some with gilt spirals or springs, some with molded finials, gilded or silvered. The really old ones were revered beyond their ragged appearance - blown glass ephemera living past their normal life.

"Please let me fix the hooks!"

"No, you dropped too many last year."

"Only one broke!"

"Will you help me on this bough? Hold it down until I hook these balls on it."

The tree was decorated with Christmas balls, and punctuated top to bottom with white exclamation mark candles. Each candlestick was set clear of twigs and branches to avoid fire, the little spring clamp with sharp teeth setting at just the right angle so the socket would be up and down, making the candle properly vertical so it would not dribble wax. A bucket of water was always at hand in case of fire.

Nanny stood by, ready to deal with any extremes of excitement or emotion—extremes were so ill bred. The girls ached to see the candles lit, but they had to wait. No candles until Christmas day.

Presents arrived, wrapped in light brown paper. There were Postal Service parcels, tied with kitchen string making hot cross bun shapes front and back, sometimes knotted and sealed with sealing wax for extra security. All the packages— stamps, cancellations, names of sender and receiver—were checked and rechecked by the sisters. Each was well shaken, but no clues. The wrapping paper gave a sandbar colour to the pile. Some of the wrappings turned out to be parcel paper from a previous Christmas, turned like a frayed shirt collar, often by a great-aunt who was peculiar about economy.

Stockings were hung Christmas Eve. The fattest, deepest stockings were pinned to the day nursery mantelpiece. Nanny would lay a meager fire, meant to go out before Father Christmas climbed down the chimney.

"Not so much coal, Nanny, it'll burn all night—poor old Father Christmas."

On Christmas Day morning the stockings were discovered, filled with an orange, a rare treat, hard candy and sticks of barley sugar.

"Vi, why don't we ever get regular grown-up chocolates, with soft centres?"

"Oh Bea, they're strictly for grown ups. They say hard candy is better for us!"

"How can they tell? I love soft centres, but not the ones with brandy—I took one once in the dining room when Nanny was upstairs."

They opened their presents—small boxes of odd-smelling Plasticine, black Windsor & Newton painting tins, little rag dolls and a bright turned wooden guardee painted for sentry duty.

Squabbling and showing, trading and enjoying, they took their presents to the breakfast table with them. Nanny blew up the coal fire to warm the room.

"Oh Nanny, please, please hurry. It's time to light the candles!"

The stepladder was needed to reach the upper candles, which burned fast. They were a quarter gone before the lower candles were alight.

Nothing was like a candle-lit tree—it was twenty minutes of delight. Each candle a star, so the girls were told, and they believed. Then the first candle winked out into a little spiral of smoke, then another. In twenty minutes the tree was its old self, with the fancy glass balls and a windrow of presents underneath. A fire burned bright and with the gas lamps turned up, the stack of brown paper presents seemed to have grown overnight.

James, in a smoking jacket that glowed in the gaslight, gave out presents, one at a time.

"Violet!" James avoided showing a preference.

Beatrix could hardly wait for her older sister to open her present. Violet undid the knot, saved the string, undid the tan paper, spread the tailored ends, smoothed and, "don't make a mess," folded the paper. Finally, the end of the suspense - the inner box and the toy, made poignant knowing the name of the sender, perhaps six weeks away by steamer in Bombay, Madras, or even Seringapatam. Addresses had been well checked, and thank you letters were to be sent within the week. Would it be a German or a French doll. What colour would the pinafores be from ancient queer smelling aunts, who, if not sending pinafores would send tiny girl's lawn linen hankies, edges hand rolled, embroidered with a B or V? Linen hankies were for church and parties, cotton for ordinary or colds.

Books! This is what James had been waiting for, adding to the girls' libraries. At age six, *Water Babies, Strawl Peter* with his bleeding thumbs. At eight, with reading well in hand, Vi received *Black Beauty* and *Lorna Doon.*

James preferred to stretch his girls with books slightly beyond their reading level. Walter Scott was a favourite, with his facile romances to fit the Empire, in full swing with the Old Queen reigning "just like Old Queen Bess." The Scott romances gave luster to the Queen and her country.

Christmas holidays concluded with the Lord Mayor's fancy dress ball for children at the Mansion House, where the Lord Mayor and his Lady wore their robes and chains of office.

Mary enjoyed entertaining friends, inviting them to afternoon *At Homes*.

> Mrs. James Innes Minchin will be at home,
> at 8 Westbourne Gardens Park,
> the afternoon of the Eighth May, 1893.

When Beatrix was involved, she was expected to pass cups of tea and the little rolled sandwiches with the mustard and cress, grown on damp cloth by the gardener. Beatrix, with her pleasant diction and memory for poetry, was always asked to recite for the guests. She stood balanced on the ottoman as she declaimed *Horatio at the Bridge*. The heroic stand of Horatio on the enemy side of the bridge into Rome moved her almost to tears, and the defiant plunge into the Tiber after the bridge had been cut, restored her composure. When James was persuaded, he too would declaim favourite pieces—the Latin version of Beatrix's poem: "Oh Tiberini, Pater... Oh Tiber, Father Tiber, to whom the Romans pray..."

Guests occasionally included the beautiful American, Jeannette Churchill, Lord Randolph's long-suffering wife. She had been the toast of the eastern seaboard of the United States before she became the toast of London.

With her came Lady Irving, tall and thin in black, like Lady Macbeth.

They were special guests who gave Beatrix the social sense, the awareness, acted but unspoken, of social level—the *we* and the *them.* Of course, she knew that rights, obligations and advantages went with her social level. Her days were always seamed with disciplines. Life was disciplines, which was to govern all behaviour, especially around James. For Beatrix, the disciplines came naturally, for they were the way of her father and were demonstrated by heroes in the books they read—*Quentin Durwood, Kidnapped, Kim,* and *Water Babies.* Beatrix learned the lessons and rules of deportment from knights and squires, often pictured kneeling at an altar with the crossed hilt of his sword held up before their eyes.

As James read, he could conjure up wonders from the text, even from the banal text of *Water Babies* with Mrs. DoAsYouWouldBeDoneBy. When he read *Toomai of the Elephants,* Beatrix and Vi were transported deep in the Indian jungles, the very jungles James had crept through, with only the company of one gun bearer. The tiger skins grinned on the parlour carpet.

The girls and their father traveled on seemingly endless roads: Grand Trunk, the road Mahbub Ali shared with bullock carts and impatient post chaises, with Livingstone in the African jungle and Blake's unforgettable Little Black Boy: "I am black, but oh! my heart is white!." The girls strode with them all, sharing the colour, the sounds and the discussions.

Once, when she was with her father, Beatrix unexpectedly burst out: "Father, what was Dolly's mother like? She must have been very different from Mother."

He knew this might be difficult, and played for time. "How do you mean, Beatrix?"

"Well, Dolly is so beautiful, and she's so much nicer than Violet and me. Her mother must have been special."

James hesitated: "Of course, you must remember they were very different women. Dolly's mother was Anglo–Indian, born in Madras, in India. Your mother was brought up in Scotland, by Scottish nannies, much more rigid than Indian amahs. And when I met Dolly's mother in Madras, she was eighteen. I was young, too."

"I know that Dolly and I are half sisters, and I understand the consanguinity bit. I looked it up in the Book of Common Prayer, right at the back. It says I can't marry you, your sons, your brothers and their sons, and on and on. But what am I to Dolly's mother? If Dolly is a half sister, then I must be half daughter to her mother. I think I'd like that."

"Beatrix, that's specious logic. Certainly, you are a half sister to Dolly. That does not make her mother your half mother."

"It is puzzling, but I think they just avoided the issue in the prayer book."

"Now I think on it, I'm quite sure. If you and Mary McLeod were alive together, you would be as strangers to each other, just any people of the whole wide world to each other, not related any more than anybody is to just any body else. You and she share no blood, so you share no need to consider mutual rules. If she had married again, you might legitimately marry her sons."

James was glad to leave the question of his wife's unpleasant nature aside. There were other ironies, looked at, mulled over, but never understood by Beatrix and never fully explained by James, which moved Beatrix. Occasionally, when their coachman would take a short cut through

London and pass a railroad bridge, deserted, Beatrix would see that the dry shelter underneath was inhabited by people in ragged poverty, including children in rags with ropes of yellow snot sliding down their chapped, inflamed lips.

"Hurry by, driver!"

On another occasion, when leaving Paddington Station after a holiday in the country, the hampers were piled on the luggage rack behind the coach.

"Home, please."

A ragged man, dressed in an overcoat with little else underneath, trotted behind the carriage to the home address. Sweating, he would beg permission to carry the trunks up to the bedrooms, in return for a tip. His sweating, stinking body reproached Beatrix for decades. Beatrix could neither understand nor explain these unearned inequalities and injustices. She knew riches and privilege, and could not know poverty. The mystery of undeserved injustice continued to puzzle her.

CHAPTER FOUR

Go and catch a falling star,
Get with child a mandrake root.
Tell me where all past years are,
Or who cleft the Devil's foot;
Teach me to hear the mermaid's singing,
And find
What wind
Serves to advance an honest mind

—John Donne, 1573 – 1631

"One for his knobs!" rang through the library. The old tiger hunter modulated his voice to suit his little companion. But, however much Beatrix learned from their games and reading the classics, James knew they were not a real education. His daughter had to start school.

Schooling for children of the gentry was provided in the 1880s by upright, but poor gentlewomen, often widows who dressed in black—shawls with jet black beads, black straw bonnets. Classes, held in the parlour in the homes of these black nuns, taught gentle girls and boys learned to write their first literate strokes with slate pencils on slates. The slates had painted lines for the "pot hooks and hangers," the shapes of sevens and capital Ls on their backs or on their bellies.

James was not keen on these dame schools; he preferred the newfangled kindergarten, described in Charles Dickens' *Household Words* as German kindergartens where children learned through play with special toys, songs and stories. The pasting, weaving, singing and little marching bands with drums and cymbals were unfamiliar to many Londoners. This new kindergarten—continental and exotic—suited James and Mary. Indeed, it would keep Beatrix out of her mother's hair for a year. Beatrix enjoyed this entry to learning. And it was here that she met Kitty Barry, who became a lifelong friend.

Later that year, ill health sent James to the seaside spa, Bournemouth. It was warmer than London, and advertised for its "ozone midst the pines". By good chance, the Barry family also went down to Bournemouth that year.

James found his comfortable, quiet life replaced by the Barry family's anarchy. For anarchy it was. The Barrys were spending the wealth accumulated by Mr. Wright, Kitty's grandfather, who invented inlaid linoleum. Mr. Barry made old Mr. Wright's money grow, and with it his huge family enjoyed a life where naughtiness was well thought of. One November day, it almost divided the families:

"Oh Kitty, are we going to have a Guy Fawkes bonfire?"

"And a party, Bee. Daddy's not here now so we can have a bonfire. He's a Catholic and won't like burning Guy Fawkes."

"Then let's make a Guy Fawkes to burn, and start a fire."

"No, let's get a pope and burn him. It will be worse!"

Mr. Barry came home unexpectedly to discover his

daughter and her friends in the midst of the burning of the effigy, chanting and dancing round the fire. He immediately sent all the children home with requests for "condign punishments."

James laughed uproariously: "Condign, indeed! Why that word's been out of currency for at least a hundred years. You'd think they'd beatified that old traitor, Fawkes, who tried to blow up the Houses of Parliament! Serves Barry right, for being in league with old Gladstone. The children were quite right to burn him in effigy. Too bad for Barry. He wants his rule and that's almost treason, after all!

"Beatrix, tell Mrs. Barry we punished you, but don't specify. I sentence you, Beatrix Mary Minchin, to read the chapter on Fawkes in Carlyle. Condign indeed!"

James thought it all so funny, especially as Mr. Barry was not only a Catholic, but also lacked the saving grace of loyalty to his Queen and country.

"Why, he could join the High Anglican Catholics, hardly change his faith at all, and have the government foot most of the bill for his church."

"But Father, why are you punishing me and laughing at it at the same time?"

"Don't worry. It's not really much punishment to read Carlyle. You'll enjoy it!"

The eldest Barry son, Con, was the love of Beatrix's young life. He was more serious than his brother Louis, "the inventor" who made a parachute. When he jumped off a roof, the chute didn't open.

"La–la!" cried Mademoiselle, "Le pauvre garcon, il est mort!" But he had not died; he escaped with two broken legs.

James, as a member of the Primrose League, a conservative election organization, wore the primrose emblem,

Benjamin Disraeli's favourite flower, at election time. The servants and tenants, knowing which way their bread was buttered, also wore the primrose and the dark blue rosette of the Tories. Mary Dickson and her friends raised funds for the party, putting on shows, getting support from the upper classes and the aristocracy, the theatre and the Royal Academy. Mary loved these efforts and knew many volunteers she could summon for help, including Gilbert and Sullivan, who were at the height of their popularity. With their help, the League successfully staged H.M.S. Pinafore.

Young Beatrix, an unwilling player, appeared with Winston Churchill, a stout youth with red hair and a stutter, dressed in a sailor suit. He escaped at every opportunity. When his mother Jennie Churchill collared him and sat him firmly on the bench with Beatrix, four impenetrable years younger than he, he had no one else to talk to.

"Did you see how m'Mother tore into me just then, just because I missed my b'bloody cue?"

Beatrix was shocked to silence. She had never before heard the word bloody.

"I should have walked out, but I'm getting a pony tomorrow so I'll do it her way."

"What kind of a pony? I have a donkey."

"What can you do with a donkey? Only take the animal to the beach." His stammer was worse because his mother had caught him out.

"My donkey is just as useful as a pony. I harness him up to a little dogcart, and drive my father to his club. I'm going to get a pony when I'm eight."

This little girl was no help to Winston, and he

flounced off.

In the 1890s, the Primrose League staged *Tadema Tableaux,* in which well-swathed men and women stood immobile for fifteen seconds behind a scrim in poses reminiscent of Grecian marble figures in the neoclassical paintings of Sir Alfred Tadema. The audience, Victorian prudes, peered attentively, titillated by the sight of imagined flesh, disguised as classical figures.

Beatrix appeared in another tableaux—dressed as a young boy in an advertisement for Pears Soap. The scene showed a large woman in an apron near a big wooden tub filled with suds, using a cake of Pear's Soap to wash a small boy who was covered with dirt. The scene was called *He Shrinks from Washing.* Between scenes, Beatrix wandered about the stage corridors and happened into a man dressed in a Cockney suit covered with pearl buttons. He noticed Beatrix's tears.

"What's the matter, little girl?"

"Oh! I hate being dressed up as a boy and having a dirty face. The people laugh at me!"

"Why, you look just capital! Look at me in this suit. People laugh at the buttons, but I love it. When you are on stage, being laughed at is capital stuff. You'll be all right."

Though mortified, Beatrix thanked the kind man who was Albert Chevalier, then at the height of his music hall career. He was famous for his performance *My Old Dutch,* a song sung in a Cockney dialect about an old man no longer capable of caring for himself and his wife, Old Dutch. The Poor Laws of London allowed them to live in the work-house, but they were parted, and not allowed to stay as a couple. The song had special significance for Mary and James, who had established the Minchin Habitation hostel. James was the ruling councilor and Mary his aide.

In the autumn of 1891, James told Beatrix, "I've enrolled you at a school in Wantage, Saint Mary's, not far into the country…"

Beatrix broke in: "But Father, I don't want to be sent away. I don't want to leave you."

"Well Beatrix, you have to go to school, and it is not convenient to send you to day school in London. Of course, nobody is sending you away. Your mother and I have agreed on this. Wantage is only a short train trip from London. You will make friends, and the sisters have a wonderful reputation. The nuns are Church of England, and won't deviate from what you know of the Church."

James accompanied his daughter on the two-hour train ride, a tearful eternity for Beatrix, who was losing her companion. James made much of her on the trip—tea and buns in the carriage, and a tuck box of sweets for her new companions.

James knew that, as a newcomer to a school, everyone is your friend if you have tuck. As a special consolation, James also bought the illustrated child's book *Chatterbox*, a treasure of pictures, little stories, and little puzzles. He had to inquire from his club doorman where to buy such a scallywag book.

"Wells, Darton & Gardner is just your ticket, Sir. They carry all that high class sort of thing."

"High class, indeed! What could he be thinking of?"

In her first months at Wantage, Beatrix endured her first homesickness. Although she suffered through arithmetic and fractions, the lessons stuck. She learned how to subtract three figures from five in her head. Mental quickness was important to her. She loved grammar, became familiar with French and made geography and history part of her literary memories. And she read and read, knowing it would please her father.

One of Beatrix's favourite school activities was going out to the country on school walks. On these outings, the girls walked quietly in a crocodile, pair by pair with the littlest six-year-old at the head. The wimpled and veiled grey nuns followed. After they passed along Belmont to Detchworth Road or Ham Gates onto Ickleton Road, they were allowed to talk in quiet, ladylike voices.

They continued on into the English countryside, a tamed wildness with subtle contours, past a gate where a thousand years of passing animals had tempered a dip in the path. The Pilgrims Way to Canterbury Cathedral was a path cut deep into the fields, a legacy of the passing pilgrims' shoes, which carried away bits of dust. These deep paths demonstrated the daily use of these fields since the Iron Age and ancient times. The girls and the nuns took in these features without thought.

On some days, the students were allowed to take a picnic lunch to the countryside. When they sat down for lunch, the girls watched as the nuns who would kneel on the dense grass before sitting, so their habits would continuously cover their ankles. The girls wore the school uniform—blue lisle stockings held up by elastics bands above the knee, bloomers, dark blue sweaters and tunics with square-cut shoulder straps, fit for games and for study.

Beatrix's best friend was Irene, who came from the Yorkshire Dales. They were both homesick and felt far from home.

"Please call me Ireenie; it sounds better than Irene."

Irene asked Beatrix to describe her home.

"It is so big, Ireenie, a tall London house, double-fronted, with wide steps leading to the front door. The kitchens, larder, storeroom, the housekeeper's room and a huge coal cellar are all below stairs. Sometimes when they deliver the coal, a cart stops at the rear steps, the horses stamping and shaking their heads. The men loop the nosebags over the horses' heads so they can munch. But you don't want to hear all this business..."

"Oh yes I do. I've never been to London. Please go on; of course, I love horses..."

"All right, we have a little time before tea. You know horses, don't you? These horses can pull four tons of coal, and when they arrive they are entitled to a breather while the men go to work unloading the coal. The men wear empty coal sacks on their heads, like the monks in *Ivanhoe*. The sacks keep their scalps and jackets from the coal dust, as they carry the sacks down into the cellar where they shoot the coal over their shoulders into the bin."

"Do they spill much?"

"Only a little. Our housemaid watches to make sure they don't. She takes them tea when they have half of it in. I asked one of them how many trips he made to get our coal in, and he told me forty."

" I don't know how they do it, but it is the same at our haying. It takes so many sheaves to make a haystack, and one of the kitchen maids carries out a mug of perry for each worker."

"What's perry?"

"Oh it's a cider made with pears. Our house is old. It has ghost!"

"Did you ever see it?"

"I think it lives in the cellar, with the perry. When the

rat catcher takes his tiny rat terrier down there to catch the rats, he says that as he counts the rats he has heard the ghost behind the perry casks."

"Our housekeeper sleeps in our cellar, guarding our family silver. She is supposed to guard it with her life, but I never heard of a burglar breaking in. Our whole house is gas–lit."

"We just use candles and paraffin lamps."

"London got gas a long time ago. We have flat flares on in the darker places, that is, fire left on with only a spark of light, ready to be turned up. My father can go into a small closet off the library and pull the tassel on the end of a chain to light the closet."

"We have mantles here at school, that are ever so bright—do you have mantles at home?"

"Of course, and they are ever so delicate. Alfred, our coachman, comes in to tie on the mantles when we break one. The housemaid cleans the glass chimneys, ever so pretty, like Venetian glasses. She uses newspaper to polish them every day."

"Tell me about the other rooms, like the nursery."

"We have two. Our nanny sleeps in Night with us; we play and eat meals in Day. It's four stories up, of course, and we have an iron bar across the Day window to keep us from falling into the Area Way. Above us in the roof, are servants' rooms and the box rooms where we are not allowed. Under us are Mother and Father's bedroom and the library."

"Mine too, not so high up as yours, but up just under the thatch. No windows under the thatch, you just have to carry a lantern—no candles because the dry thatch is so easy to set alight!"

"Have you ever burned?"

"No, but the barn did! The horses almost went mad,

before the stable boy got them all out, but it burnt off all his hair. Father was so grateful he bought the stable boy a new cap, an expensive one. He only wears it in church."

"Tell me about your parlour, Irene?"

"We always have a lot of people there, with the piano and singing. The mantle has a stuffed peacock under a glass dome. It has to be dusted every day. We keep our ribbons tacked along the edge of the mantle, the ribbons we won for cattle at the show. Then we have a painting of Grandfather with a champion bull called Grayson, painted by a tinker—they're so clever. He got Grayson right but messed up on Grandfather! But you haven't finished with your house. I must know about it. We're so 'farm'."

"I know I'd love to be on a farm because I love the animals so."

"We all have our own ponies and try to follow the hunt. But the ponies won't jump, so we are left to open and close gates. I suppose as we grow we'll get taller horses and really follow the hunt. I've never been at the kill."

"I wouldn't like that. Father belonged to a Devon stag hunt—imagine chasing a stag. It usually gets away!"

"Not the fox, they feed it to the hounds!"

"They should write a *Black Beauty* for foxes. It's so cruel."

"Tell me about the rest of the rooms."

"On the floor below Day is father's library. He buys many of the newest books even before they were sold bound. We have most of Dickens in the pamphlet edit. Father has rebound most books in colours—green for the classics— Greek, that is—and brown for English. Father stays there most of the time; he's a scholar and reads constantly. That's the room I love best, where I talk with Father about books and his life. He's such a wonderful father."

"What about your Mother?"

"Oh she's quite different. I don't think Mother loves me. She scolds me a lot, and is impatient. We don't get along."

"Tell me about the dining room."

"A big room, with a dark red carpet with black flowers. Gloomy. Family portraits—all those Anglo-Indian officers in red uniforms—with stern faces and beards. There's a piano, of course. Vi and I wind up the music stool far as it will go, climb on and Vi twirls me right down to the bottom. It's out of bounds, except when Mother is away.

"At the top of the kitchen stairs there's the gents' lavatory. It isn't proper for ladies or children to use it. The lavatory for the servants' use is in the cellar. The drawing room is big, with a fireplace at each end. The big mantelpiece has a peacock, tail spread, under glass. The carpet is red with black flowers, covered with the skins of tigers and leopards Father shot. Some days the servants move all the furniture, roll up the carpet and hang it outside and beat it to clean it. Can you imagine?"

"Do you have elephant foot footstools? We have."

"Of course, and bright Indian scarves here and there, cashmeres. My mother cut up some of them to make a fancy dress and Father was furious. He kept on about the shawls being real antiques with their pretty mango pattern, relics of the Moghul emperors. I ended up being very cross with Mother, even though I had originally thought the dress was a good idea."

The school bell interrupted.

"Oh I must hurry to Chapel. I'm Thurifer and doing the incense, Bea, I'll puff a bit towards you."

"I'll sit on the aisle."

Although the nuns seemed loving in their distant way, Beatrix missed her home dreadfully. She only saw her relatives on school half-holidays, when her father or her beloved half sister, Dolly, would visit, bringing a tuck box and special books. After what seemed an eternity, the term ended, and Beatrix was reunited with her father.

"My dear, tonight we'll have supper at home. Everyone is anxious to see you. It is such a treat to have you home. We'll all have supper in the dining room. I ordered turbot, as I know how you love it."

Indeed, she loved being home. At dinner, she particularly watched her father divide the creamy white flesh along the spine of the fish, carefully using the broad silver fish slice to lay the upper fillet aside on the big fishplate. Then, *mirabile dictu*, he lifted the head and all the bones onto a spare dish. There lay the turbot, without the bones, the bane of every small child.

At home she also enjoyed the company of her brother and sister and all the cousins. There always seemed to be visiting cousins, aunts and great-aunts. James kept up with them all, even brothers and brothers-in-law with whom he was crosswise. His brother, the vicar, still refused to pray with James—"A Heathen!"

The adolescent Beatrix and James became closer and closer, their interaction a protracted honeymoon of the minds. But, as James became older, he began to feel the strain of his years in the tropics and, now the life with his wife. As she marched to her own drummer, spreading her social net, James turned inward with his books, reading his beloved Greek Bible each morning and marking his thoughts in his Greek diary. Now at seventy, his active life was over.

"What can I do with it all? How can I make all this useful, or it is wasted? I speak six dialects, and have no one to speak with. I've learned to serve the Queen, to serve India and the Indians, to serve mankind, to be true to my school, my family. When I die, does it all die? How can I deal with it all? I cannot believe in that claptrap about souls in heaven, but where can I put my faith?

"Beatrix, my little Beatrix, must carry it for me, all that I've poured into her. She will learn it. It won't be wasted; I won't be wasted."

The feeling was so private he could not trust it even to the Greek of his diary.

And so as Beatrix's young years passed and his old years piled up, he gave his mind's milk to nourish her. His fine lean body, once so keen it could spear a wild pig, grew flaccid. The robust voice, tuned to cut through the babble and noise of a Bengal caravanserai, softened.

Only once in all those years did Beatrix hear her father's voice raised in anger—the day they visited the battleship, *HMS Victory*. To James this was a shrine. As she followed her father aboard the great wooden battleship to see the place where Nelson died, a nondescript man followed them down into the cockpit. As the three of them stood in silence in the low chamber, James noticed the man wearing his cap. He swung his slender malacca and struck the man's cap from his head.

"How dare you, Sir, desecrate this spot by wearing your cap where the great Nelson died!"

Later Beatrix asked, "Father, why didn't that man know about his cap?"

"My dear, he didn't know any better. The poor man was ignorant. I was momentarily terribly angry, and acted without thinking, or acknowledging that man's humanity. We can't all be equally granted education, position and upbringing. He was wrong without knowing that he was wrong, and I was very wrong to strike him with my cane."

"Father, why are people the way they are, some rich, some poor, and some ignorant?"

"Daughter, I've told you about our ancestor who came across the English Channel at the time of the Norman Conquest. When William the Conqueror took possession of the estates in England, he sold the land to rich people from Normandy to help pay for the Norman Conquest. I understand that our ancestor bought the land near Avening and an estate later called Minchin Hampden, in Gloucestershire. His name was Chambray Minchin, our first English ancestor. He had money, and because of that, he had power. He was the lord of his estates and more. Why he was rich and not poor is a difficult question. Your old aunts who listen to their parson and read holy books would tell you that God decreed "each to his estate," as the hymn says. I'm not so sure they are right.

"There seems to be some sort of a providence that sorts the things of this world somewhat unevenly. Since Chambray's time, our family has had money, the Queen has more, others have a lot less. It's a mystery why circumstance is so uneven, but you must do your best to make life for unfortunates as satisfying as you can. Poor people don't need any more burdens than they have. You must be careful not to add to them."

"But Father, why do we have so much money, much more than the poor legless beggar outside of Whitely's?"

"Well, I was well paid during my forty years in the Madras civil service. India is a rich country and pays a great deal of taxes to the British treasury. And then the Minchin family seems to have kept its hand on money and power for more than nine centuries. The money stayed in the family, perhaps helped by some providence, perhaps it was God, perhaps we are good managers. If your aunts are right it was God. I don't think God pays attention to riches or poverty or He would spread the money around more evenly.

"If you promise never to tell your Uncle Harry, I'm not so certain that the Book of Revelations or the Book of Common Prayer should be read literally. My years in India convinced me that God is in more places and in more ways than the clever churchmen of King James ever thought of."

"But Father, if you don't agree with Aunt Fanny, about who rode round Jerusalem on a donkey like Christ, then why do you read from the Bible every morning?"

"Pish girl. The Bible is worth reading as an interesting book, and now and then I come across a person in it who seems to have a lot to say to me."

"But what about God?"

"When you've been into as many temples as I've seen, you would know that God is everywhere, not just in the Church of England."

"That's not the way that Uncle Harry tells about it in church. He never allows that God might be somewhere else, like an Indian temple."

"Oh I know. You know that they call me a freethinker and they think that is bad – how could thinking be bad? I suppose that they would be uncomfortable in my church even though I'm quite comfortable in theirs. It's really a matter of taste, like a person wanting to be a Presbyterian rather than C of E."

"But Father I want you to go to heaven."

"Never mind, I don't think they know any more than I do where we are going to go to, but I'm sure we are going somewhere, thanks to God."

Beatrix had a general awareness of the religious beliefs of the Minchin servants. Above stairs their beliefs were often characterized dismissively as chapel, meaning non-conformist. The servants' churches were tiny cottage, like chapels.

Beatrix was also taught that to play with an iron hoop was common. In the park she could run her wooden hoop, with a modest wooden baton to strike it along. But she envied the boys from poor homes, running alongside their stiff steel wire hoops, struck with a hooked steel striker. The velocity and ringing sound of their hoops were infinitely attractive, but these wire hoops, considered common, were ineluctably denied to Beatrix and her sister.

To eat a street–side saveloy or fish and chips was considered common, as were enjoying street–side winkles or whelks. The ranks in the military services and the preachers without surplices in the chapels were also considered common.

Beatrix's education continued – by example, observation and injunction. "Don't speak through your nose, that's common," or "Your fork is not a spoon, use your knife to put the food on it," or "Don't be rude, it's so common." Conversely, there were "well bred" habits: eat your dessert with your fork and spoon, wear your hair flat, not roached up, use eau de Cologne on your handkerchief, and stand up when ladies join the group. The oddity of one whole upper class having a speech, tone, manner, fashion, a whole culture, differing from that of 'others', though patent to them both, was not mentioned or debated. It was taken for granted.

Beatrix always enjoyed her time with Miss Clarkson.

"Miss Beatrix, promise not to tell any one, I have an adventure...but you must promise!"

"Oh yes, I promise, I promise!"

"We must wait until we have the house to ourselves. I have tickets to the Hippodrome, a new theatre with Cinderella and the Lancashire Lads, a pantomime. They dress up with clogs, and dance. They're wonderful!"

The pantomime would present the standard characters. Buttons, the essential intelligence behind all the inanities, was a famous French clown, who perched on the edge of a stage waterworks and fished for chorus girls who would take the bait of diamond necklaces.

"Now watch, Mistress Beatrix, watch now. See that little person in the cat costume, he's just killing, so funny, tipping up Buttons, and pretending to be a dog pretending to be a cat!"

"I know, and pretending to be a boy pretending to be a cat pretending to be a dog! Who is he?"

"I've seen him once before, his name is Charlie Chaplin."

CHAPTER FIVE

To promote a woman to bear rule, superiority, dominion, or empire above any realm, nation or city, is repugnant to nature, contumely to God, a thing most contrarious to his revealed will and approved ordinance; and finally, it is the subversion of good order, of all equity and justice.

—John Knox, 1505–1572, *The Regiment of Women*

Mr. Barry, father of Beatrix's friend Kitty, owned the magnificent estate of the Cocoa King, Van Houten, with its stables, kennels and aviary of game birds and acres of pine woods near Bournemouth. To Beatrix the Barry household was an eye–opener. Their household included French and German governesses, a French ladies maid for Mrs. Barry, an Italian butler, as well as a French chef. The house was always in an uproar. At their midday dinner, the children, the newest baby, her nanny, the governesses and visiting children sat on one side of the table, facing Mr. and Mrs. Barry. Mrs. Barry, who carved the big roast, said children needed good beefies in their diet.

It was said, behind a fan, that Mrs. Barry occasionally would ask her chamber maid up to her bedroom to share a cup of tea and talk. Well–off Scots were more egalitarian than their lowland cousins.

In the summer, the Minchin and Barry families often made a trip to a Dorsetshire farm for a special picnic meal cooked by the farm wife. They traveled in the wagonette, harnessed to Sweetest, a fussy mare, which would not drink from a trough but had to have her own bucket.

When they arrived at the farm, all the children crowded into an old boat that was used for cutting thatch reeds. As the children paddled across the pond, using a broken spade for an oar, they discovered the punt was leaking. It suddenly sank into the deep pond. Beatrix was terrified in the water. She sank, gurgling and gasping, as the lily stems half strangled her. Somehow the other children pulled her ashore. Everyone else remembered her terror, but she remembered her embarrassment as the farmer's wife decked out all the children in red flannel petticoats while the wet clothes dried on a clotheshorse in front of the range.

In her adolescence, Beatrix became more and more devoted to animals. On one trip, the family returned home with a baby donkey, which became Molly, Beatrix's special pet. She regaled her friend, Kitty, with the donkey's adventures.

"I groomed her until her pale gray coat was like silk, and polished her little black hooves with shoe blacking. With her dark eyes and cross on her back, she's the loveliest little creature in the world. She follows me like a dog. I taught her to jump over the tennis net, which upsets the gardener. Last week while Mother was receiving, an *at home*, I rode Molly through the garden. When I jumped off, Molly bolted into the house. She grabbed lumps of sugar from the table. Mother's guests screamed!"

"And what did your mother say?"

"She knew it wouldn't do any good to talk to my father. She went to our rector, who's preparing me for confirmation. Mother thought he'd be more critical of my lawless behaviour. I am very fond of the rector. We talked, and he sent for tea. We talked about donkeys—how the Blessed Virgin rode on one and, because they carried Jesus, donkeys have a cross on their backs. The rector called me his little lamb and made me promise to make peace with Mother."

"So it wasn't at all bad, considering."

"No. I'll have to break Molly to harness now I am getting too heavy for her. I'll have to break her in—lead her around so she learns to drag the garden roller, and then teach her to pull the governess cart."

"Don't you think the governess cart will be too big for her?"

"I've been saving my tips from my uncles and other visitors, to have a little dogcart made to fit her, just the right weight. It will have a black patent leather harness with blue cushions and silver plate fittings. I don't have enough money, but Father will help me."

Beatrix loved taking her father for rides in the dogcart. On the days that the two of them rode to his club, the members laughed at the sight of their decorous peer with his long legs folded like scissors. Although Beatrix loved her animals and cared for them, and treated them well, she never personalized them. She considered them inferior to humans and entitled to animal, not human, care.

One rainy morning, the Minchin household acquired another pet. As she did every morning, the kitchen maid was scrubbing the front steps before she whitened them with a brick. Immaculate front steps were standard in the neighbourhood. As the maid turned, she saw a small dog, very dirty, shivering and whining. The girl picked him up and ran inside where she encountered her master on his way to breakfast.

"Oh Sir, Sir! Can we keep him? He'll bring good luck for the election."

The sentimental James responded, "Of course. Please wash him and give him something to eat. Yes, it is the year of a general election. I think, as a lesson to that Liberal Gladstone, we will call the dog Tory."

Tory turned out to be a beautiful white Maltese poodle with a dozen tricks to his name, probably learned as a circus performer. Tory became an important member of the Minchin household, a much-loved pet, despite his habit of howling pitifully at the singing during Mary's musical at homes.

Every day when Beatrix was at home, she read the newspaper to her father and discussed the news.

"Father, what do you think of women's suffrage?"

"You ask the perplexing questions, Beatrix, but then, you are a free thinker, as your Christian uncles would say. Suffrage—it really depends on whether you think women should be equal to men. The Bible is fairly clear that women should be judged differently, by their womanly qualities, even as men are to be judged by their manly qualities. If you believe that, and it is in the Bible, then the suffragettes are mistaken. Personally, I believe that women should be protected from harm because they are usually smaller and weaker. Good breeding tells us that the weaker should always be protected. I think that the vote and equality would expose women terribly."

"But Father, what about widows and women nobody

wants to marry? They have no protectors. They need some rights to protect themselves."

"It's not an easy question..."

"But Father, if it's only size that counts to be equal, what about small men and really strong and big women? I think women should be equal to men."

"In the four decades I was a civil servant in India, I had to deal with many problems, such as suttee, where women were made unequal to men. These problems were dealt with by men, never women. I don't think the advances we made would have been better accomplished by women. At that time, the women themselves would have protected suttee, but that begs the question. Good things were done by good men and bad things were done by bad men."

"I wonder if women have the strength to rule; I know how much it takes."

"Well Father, I hope the suffragettes win and I will get to vote."

"Working class men have the vote, and it's been no royal road for them."

James could see the changes the humanists had achieved in his century—child labour laws, better prisons, an end to the treadmill and transportation to Van Diemen's Land or penal Australia. James felt it was hard for his young daughter, born to luxury, to understand the meaning of the changes happening in England.

Beatrix loved to visit Raasay, Oxshott Heath, Surrey, the country estate of her sister, Dolly, and her husband, Henry Dumas. Henry was the son of a rich immigrant French family. As a child, he was sent to an English prep school where, on his first day, he encountered one of the schoolmasters.

"You pronounce your name Doomaah?" he said. "What nonsense! In England, your name is Doo-mass, the way it is spelled." And Doomass he was all through his school years.

Henry later became a junior partner in Lloyd's of London, Dumas and Wiley, later Willis Faber Dumas and Wiley. The Dumas were wealthy county people of the twentieth century, in contrast to the older, nineteenth century wealthy city people Mary and James cultivated.

Henry was generous and spent money lavishly on his beautiful wife, their sons Raymond and Basil, and their beautiful home, Raasay. Dolly enjoyed her pastimes – photography, gardening with the help of four gardeners, and the care of her pets. In 1898, on one of her early visits, Beatrix and her nephews, Raymond and Basil, were invited to a sailing party in Captain Trinnick's small ketch. Some miles off the rocky heads of Salcombe Bay, a sudden squall laid the ketch over and the boat was half under water. Captain Trinnick, told his young crew that their lives depended on absolute obedience to his orders. They obeyed to the letter—pulled in the mainsail and started to bail while the ketch raced through the churning water past the rock bound point until they were safe. When Henry heard, he made Beatrix promise not to tell James of her narrow escape.

Henry's large yacht, the *Adriadne*, was manned with eight well-trained sailors. When coming to the landing, the oarsmen would sweep to the float, at speed, and *toss oars* to a vertical position, saluting visitors or the skipper, and sideslip in to the landing at the last moment. Beatrix was very impressed by the sailors in spotless white uniforms and their precision drill. But later she questioned the meaning of the drill. What she first saw as an evolution, a simple elegance, performed by men without question or demur, later seemed an operation which sailors might well question, or refuse as inelegant.

When Beatrix was home from Wantage, she and her mother frequently disagreed. Mary expected her daughter to complement the family's social status, particularly at the social events dear to her heart. Beatrix was just as determined to spend her time with the animals, reading and with her father. One day, when a nanny goat was heard bleating for her missing kids, the kids were discovered in Beatrix's bed. Her mother, outraged, complained to James who found little to criticize.

James, now seventy-five years old, was enjoying Bournemouth, where the sea air was kinder to his bronchitis than London fog. He took Beatrix to see the Fleet assembled at Spit Head. As they sailed through the fleets gathered from around the world to honour Queen Victoria's Jubilee, James told Beatrix of his life in the service of the Queen.

"You know, Beatrix, I can hardly remember before her, she was always there. Her favourite minister, Benjamin Disraeli, joined all the territories of India, the countless principalities with endless separate relationships, joined them together into one great parcel to be ruled by the Queen. This made her Queen and Empress. That was a great moment. After I left school in England, I returned to India and served her for the rest of my active life. She was most gracious whenever I was in her presence. It's hard to imagine her as "The Old Queen" now, or that I am an old man, but there it is, and the world is honouring her."

When Queen Victoria died 1901, she was unlamented by the seventeen-year-old Beatrix, who saw Victoria as an agent of repression.

Some time later, after King Edward had shown his new definition of how his court would be handled, Beatrix confided to Kitty, "What a relief it is not to have the old Queen in Buckingham Palace. She quashed pleasure and made everything naughty, I might say, dirty."

"Have you ever read the Shaw reviews?"

"Oh, yes. Shaw said that kings are made by universal hallucination. As Father read Shaw's opinion to me, he almost had a fit laughing. I suppose Shaw meant that the King was really popular. No, it must mean that the King was chosen by people who were potty!"

"Have you heard about Mrs. Keppel? I heard from below stairs that she's a married woman who spends the night with the King and …. I wonder what it's like, when it isn't with your wife, or if it's different with someone else' husband or wife!"

"I wish we could find out what really happens!"

"You can bet we won't. *Anne Veronica* was banned by the Royal Examiner because Shaw committed an unspeakable offense. He suggested that a nineteen–year–old girl had sensations before she was married. I was hoping to find out something from Shaw's play, but the Examiner scotched that."

"We won't get much more information from the stage. There isn't any information in father's books. Nobody will speak about it, not even Dolly! I suppose we'll just have to laugh along with that music hall performer, Stanley Lupino, pretending we understand the jokes. But there must be something; after all, think about our pets. It's hard to think about people doing those things, but what about our pets. Their babies seem to come out of it all right!"

"That's right, but all that fur!"

They collapsed in laughter.

The years of London fog, the rigours of life in India, and a disinterested wife, weakened James. In 1900, influenza swept the country. The Minchin family was without servants, except the faithful coachman, who did the cooking and took care of the family as well as he could. Then James came down with the influenza. Three nurses, one after the other, became sick and left. Pneumonia set in, and though oxygen was used, it was of no avail. There were no antibiotics. Beatrix helped the nurses and read to James. And then, at seventy-seven years of age, her father died.

The day before the funeral when all was quiet and the numerous relatives had gone to their rooms, Beatrix got up, put on a dressing gown, and went down to the library where her father lay. She went in quietly and saw his coffin, with tall candles at head and foot, lighting the room and his beloved books.

Beatrix knelt down and prayed beside him.

"I believe in the Communion of Saints, the Forgiveness of Sins, the Resurrection of the Body, and Life Everlasting."

The next day, everyone including the servants, went to the little church in Branksome Woods to bury James beside his brother, Charles, under a small bunch of primroses. For Beatrix, primroses always meant Father. He who had given so much of himself to her, was gone.

CHAPTER SIX

My new-cut ashlar takes the light
Where crimson-blank the windows flare:
By my own work, before the night,
Great Overseer, I make my prayer.

Take not that vision from my ken;
O, whatsoe'er may spoil or speed,
Help me to need no aid from men,
That I may help such men as need!

— Rudyard Kipling, 1865-1936

After her husband's death, Mary Dickson returned to London, where her social aspirations would be better served. She closed the Minchin mansion, and rented a flat in Kensington. Mary's desire to climb in the world in which James lived so gracefully did not suit Beatrix. They quarreled more and more. To make matters worse, her mother had developed diabetes for which there was no treatment. She became increasingly difficult to live with.

After the funeral, Henry and Dolly suggested Beatrix come to their country home. Her guardian uncles, Harry and James, remonstrated when they heard of the invitation.

"You would best stay with your mother, who can care for you, and lead you to a righteous life."

Harry added, "Indeed, she should be with her mother. All girls should be with their mothers. Beatrix is no exception, regardless of how James brought her up. James had such a destructive attitude towards orthodoxy. He never connected orthodoxy with the immortal soul, so I'm sure he damaged his daughter. We must do our best to get her to stay with her mother, who is, after all, a regular churchgoer and communicant."

Beatrix suspected that it was the control of her money that motivated her uncles. She told Dolly, "You know, Dolly, I just will not live with Mother! We like such different things. I dislike having to dress up and recite to guests at her parties. I would much prefer being with the horses or with Molly."

"Let's see what Henry says, he's so wise and forceful. After all, he managed to get Uncle Harry to take your father's burial service, despite his nonconformity."

Henry Dumas visited the uncles and, using the subterfuge of Beatrix's convalescence from the flu, convinced them that Beatrix would be better off staying with Dolly. The uncles relented and permitted Beatrix to go to Raasay, expecting that it would help James' widow get through her bereavement, and period of mourning.

Mary confided to a friend, "Trix is taking James' death very hard. She sits in the library, crying as she goes through his books. It seems that James left all those dusty books to Beatrix's brother, Hamilton. Meanwhile my plans to get her presented at Court have gone a-glimmering. She can't be presented at Court in black.

She's making much more of James' death than I think reasonable."

"She's nineteen, isn't she? You are responsible for her for two more years."

Beatrix went to stay with Dolly and Henry in Surrey, a visit that was to last for many years, until she was married. Dolly was very pleased to have her younger sister in the household.

"Beatrix dear, you can be my companion and help with the duties of the household and our huge garden, which are taxing me. For a start, would you take on the care of our two Persian cats and my dogs? I know how you love them."

Dolly, an amateur photographer, often drove to Winchester to photograph the cathedral. Dolly and Beatrix would roam the nave and side chapel, waiting for the sun to stream through the rose window. The light caught a marble crypt–cover with the reclining statue of an old crusader lying with his head on a marble pillow, the helmet visor open to show his face, and his dog lying asleep at his feet. Dolly quickly photographed the atmospheric moment and entered the print in the French Salon competition with the caption:

> *"Knights bodye's duste,*
> *His good sword's rust.*
> *His soul is with the Saints,*
> *I trust."*

She won the gold medal.

Dolly and Henry often took the high road, inviting radicals, such as Sidney and Beatrix Webb, the burgeoning labour activists. When Beatrix read their manifestoes and the manifestoes of the red–haired radical critic, Bernard Shaw, she was reminded of her father who had found a resonance in these ideas. She recognized the liberal credo—people were equal in their need for respect and consideration.

Once a week, Dolly and Beatrix visited a workhouse to read the Bible and newspapers to the old ones. The sisters took tea and tobacco, luxuries to the residents. Her experience of the workhouse gave Beatrix further misgivings about undeserved poverty.

Mary remained in London through her year of mourning. When her period of mourning was over, she would have Beatrix presented at the Court of St. James. When a letter arrived from Sir Henry Cotton Minchin, Beatrix's cousin and trustee, mentioning the intended arrangements, Beatrix acquiesced, knowing how important it was for her mother.

She returned to her mother's flat in London to begin the months of preparations—days filled with visits to the court dressmakers and lessons in court deportment. Their calendars filled with fittings, shopping and invitations. Debutantes and, where necessary, their chaperone presenters, had to learn how to curtsey before royalty and how to walk backwards without tripping on a train. They took lessons to rehearse every move, in every detail. A stumble was unthinkable. Mary found it difficult, her years and arthritis made deep curtseys and walking backwards difficult. She was also relieved to no longer be held back by James' disparagement of such ceremony, and pleased that James' prestige guaranteed her welcome.

Mary and Beatrix were invited to tea by other debutante families to review the details and precedence, and memorize communications from the Royal Chamberlain. The list of those invited and those excluded was discussed. Beatrix knew that her dear friend, Catherine, had planned to be presented. Her family was well-to-do, her father, a financier in the stock-broking trade. But, as he handled money, he was not considered to be of the appropriate elevated elite, and his daughter was not included on the list of invitees.

As the day of the presentation approached, Beatrix became more and more excited. She took great delight in describing the details of her presentation gown to her friends, particularly to Kitty:

"I think you will like my dress. It is made of white chiffon, pleated on the bodice, with an overskirt of frilled, embroidered layers. My train—seven feet long—is made of silk and falls from my shoulders. I am still learning how to manage it. And my bouquet will have lilies of the valley. I have asked the coiffeur to put my hair up" (Beatrix couldn't resist a bit of preening,) "with a crown of three white feathers, the Prince of Wales feathers, with a floating veil. I don't really like the veil, but it is part of the whole thing."

"Oh Trix, I'm so envious; it is marvelous. What will your mother wear? She will do her best to look grand without outshining you."

Beatrix was not so certain.

"Mother's dress is old gold satin with a swathed bodice, short sleeves caught up to the shoulders with ostrich plumes, with a train from the shoulders, deep olive green. I am jealous of her train, and she has clusters of old gold ostrich plumes as a bouquet, curled up tight. She looks quite smashing."

"Well, she needs all the help she can get."

"She's not too well, and I think this is the last big do

she will take part in."

A week before the day of the presentation, Mary invited a few special friends to celebrate her daughter's presentation at court. Plans for this event engendered hours of consideration and debate. Mary gave detailed instructions to her staff:

"I plan to have an *ambigu,* a collation for twenty guests. Everything must be elegant, including the table centre flower decorations. In my directions, I have listed the names of the guests and where each will sit so you can prepare place cards.

On the table, there should be a high stand of bonbons at each end of the table. Between every other table setting, I want water decanters, plates of petit fours and fresh fruit. We will start the collation with Dover Sole Marguery, dressed with shrimp and mussels. Keep them in the warming oven and finish them under the grill of a red–hot salamander. You will have to be quick—at the moment you announce the dinner for the guests to come into the dining room, start glazing the sole for serving."

A week later, the day of Beatrix's presentation at court arrived. The professional ladies' maid came to dress Beatrix, and the coiffeur, working round the clock to attend to all his clients, arrived for the final coiffure, adding plumes and the veil. Finally, all was ready.

"Tell the coachman to be ready. Where are the umbrellas?"

The carriage was waiting. It had taken all day to polish the carriage, its leather harness and silver buckles. Even the horse's hooves were gleaming. Everything smelled of polish except the lilies–of–the valley in the little cut glass cruets by each passenger. The rig was perfection.

"Alfred, you are aware of the order of the carriages on the route to the palace."

As the carriage joined the procession, Beatrix and her mother hardly spoke; the weight of the preparations lay on their spirits. Beatrix wondered whether her nose was shiny.

At Buckingham Palace, a uniformed footman opened the carriage door and handed Mary and Beatrix down onto the pavement. Inside, the huge palace anteroom was filled with expectant parents and debutantes, ears cocked as names of those next in line were called.

"Mother, is my nose shining?"

"No dear, but do you have your chamois? I hid it in your bouquet."

"Are we next?" The protocol and the order of appearance had been posted for weeks. However sure they were of their position, they suddenly became uncertain, fearing the white-wigged footman might scramble the order. Then the announcement:

"Mrs. James Innes Minchin and Miss Beatrix Mary Minchin."

Beatrix and her mother walked forward for their formal introduction and presentation to the King and Queen. As Mary and Beatrix made their entrance through a festoon of dresses and uniforms, they were too caught up in the moment to see notice the crowd. They released their trains and, with the silk fabric hissing slightly on the parquet, walked toward King Edward. He was dressed in full regimental uniform of the Coldstream guards.

Again, their names were called.

"Mrs. James Innes Minchin, Miss Beatrix Mary Minchin!" Mary had practiced her delivery for weeks.

"Your Majesty, may I present my daughter, Beatrix Mary?"

"Beatrix, what a lovely name! We miss your dear Papa at the race meets, and our times at Sandown and the Derby."

The beautiful Alexandra murmured to Beatrix as she received her curtsey.

"We are sorry to hear about your dear father. He was so important to us."

At the moment of presentation, the splendour of the Queen's blue eyes and her gracious comment were welded in Beatrix's memory. Then, without turning, Beatrix and her mother moved delicately backward to the other debutantes and their parents. Breathless with excitement, they found their escort, a young officer of the Household Regiment, dressed in regimental evening dress, including a plumed helmet with the feathers long enough to hang below his shoulders. A friend of the family, Colonel Fletcher of the Household Cavalry at the Palace, had arranged for this young escort. He accompanied Beatrix and Mary to their appointed places in the banquet hall as Royal Artillery String Band played dinner music. Their escort placed his helmet on a chair of its own, plumes draped over the side, and the King and Queen took their seats, signaling the banqueters to be seated. Footmen in scarlet livery, with white silk stockings, buckled shoes and white gloves, passed gold trimmed plates.

Beatrix was overwhelmed with a sense of grandeur and ceremony. She was so overcome she later realized she could not remember the details of the meal, except for the champagne. She also tasted a moment of triumph as she saw a debutante friend and her mother alone at a nearby a table. The friend had crowed over Beatrix, extolling her own frilly and gorgeous gown. However she had no princely escort, nor a chair with a helmet.

At the end of the meal, the King and Queen rose as the pomaded waiters pulled back their chairs. After the royal couple left, the guests moved to the doors. The officer escorted Beatrix and Mary to their carriage, where the footman folded the ladies' trains beside them on the seats.

The carriage took Beatrix and Mary through the park to the Bond Street studio of the photographer, Lafayette. He knew how to pose debutantes with the right haughtiness, and to capture the sense of the moment, this ceremony of coming of age in this society. In her photograph, Beatrix is posed regally, her fresh youth exalted by her elegant dress, the fashion showing off her bust and shoulders. The feathers and her upswept hair add to her height, and the lilies–of–the–valley look fresh on her train. Her face is serene, she is in charge of herself without arrogance. Beatrix never looked better.

The twelve–hour moment was over. Later at home, the memory of the night of fantasy, the King and Queen, the champagne, the Band, the plumed helmet, and the society photographer, blended in Beatrix's mind as she unhooked her corset.

CHAPTER SEVEN

*O'er the smooth enameled green
Where no print of step hath been,
Follow me as I sing,
And touch the warbled string.
Under the shady roof
Of the branching Elm Star–proof,
Follow me,
I will bring you where she sits
Clad in splendor as befits
Her deity.
Such a rural queen
All Arcady hath never seen.*

—John Milton, 1608 – 1674 From 'Arcades'

Picnics in England are seldom perfect. The summer weather often presages a thunderstorm and a wet meal even under a tree. In the summer of 1901, Beatrix's enchanted life with her sister at Raasay was suddenly rained out.

In May, Dolly noticed her Yorkshire terrier, Little Jimmie, was not his usual energetic self. The veterinarian suggested leaving the dog in his cage for a while, and when Dolly bent over to pick up Jimmie, the little dog suddenly lunged and bit her. She went to her doctor, who cauterized the bite with lunar caustic. He pointed out his concern over rabies, which was rare in England. In France, the cry, *chien enrage,* cleared a street immediately. To be bitten by a rabid dog meant a lingering suffering with an agonizing demented fear of drinking water, and the prospect of dying.

Louis Pasteur had discovered the cause and cure.

Henry and Dolly went at once to see Sir Richard Douglas Powell, a great physician in London.

"Take your wife on the night boat to Paris. The bite is near the brain and it may be too late. Go directly to the Pasteur Institute, where they know about rabies. Observe her closely for terror of drinking."

The ordeal began. No amount of money could buy any privileges in Paris. Rich and poor alike lined up for the primitive treatment: serial injections of dried and pulverized spine of a rabid dog divided into larger and larger doses. This was the only hope. Dolly's bite, so near the brain, called for the most immediate and stringent application. The doctor in charge, a close associate of the great Pasteur, seemed brutal, treating the patients roughly. For two weeks, twice a day, Dolly was given the injections.

The treatment weakened Dolly's heart and lungs. Although no–one ever knew if Dolly or the dog had been rabid, Little Jimmie was destroyed and Dolly was left a life–long invalid.

When Henry and Dolly returned from Paris, the house at Raasay seemed a hollow shadow of its former self. The home, which had echoed and shaken with convivial hospitality, became quiet. It was an end to tennis and much of the photography. Dolly tried to garden from her wheelchair. Despite her weakness, Dolly tried to help Beatrix by opening social doors for her sister.

Beatrix and Dolly also continued to enjoy books together, as they had with their father. Now Beatrix read to Dolly.

"Read to me, Beatrix, something new, perhaps that new man, St. John. Peculiar name, but he has traveled with Conrad, who can do no wrong."

James had carefully taught the sisters to pronounce St. John, "Sinjen."

"I'd love to hear you read. Sometimes I feel too weak to hold up a book. Would you read that new book, *The Man of Property?*"

Beatrix settled in her chair in the sitting room in the light from a delicate Louis Seize lamp. She took a reading breath, and with her refined diction launched into the book.

"Those privileged to be present at a family festival of the Forsytes have seen that charming sight."

Much care and coaching had gone into the refinement of the sisters' voice and diction. "Don't speak through your nose, it's common," or "Do not speak with a twang." They were taught how to read aloud with the proper style, but not too much dramatics, which was badly thought of.

As her eyes ran down the page, Beatrix was reminded of her own life.

"...A charming and instinctive sight, an upper middle class family in full plumage..."

Could be the Minchins, or better, the Barry family...

"...That mysterious tenacity...so clear a reproduction of society in miniature..."

Beatrix continued the story that reproduced society in miniature. Her musical voice fitted the middle class cadences of Galsworthy.

"...June 15, 1886, at four in the afternoon..."

Why, I was only two then, up in the nursery leaning over the safety bar of the window at Westbourne Gardens Court...

"...Philip Bosiney was known as a young man without a fortune..."

She and Dolly laughed about Philip's shapeless hat, so oddly different from high silk toppers of their girlhood. Bosiney had paid his duty calls on the old aunts, who observed his punctilious behaviour with hawk eyes,

"He was wearing dark blue trousers and a shapeless soft grey felt hat, a dusty, shapeless object that the short-sighted Hester had tried to shoo off the hall chair. Shameless to dress like that!"

Dolly and her sister rocked with laughter over Bosiney's unforgivably *outre* performance.

"Father would have said, 'Imagine Fanny trying to shoo a hat off the hall chair.'"

The sisters' laughter echoed into the halls. They had another cup of tea, and again thought of their father as they read about Old Jolyon, so pitiful and alone, saying good–night to his grown son:

"The old face looked worn and hollow again. 'Good-bye, my boy; take care of yourself!'"

"Father had those hollow cheeks, towards the last. He was also like Old Jolyon in that he could never say to us that he loved us. This is too like us, so circumspect with our feelings!"

Dolly was no help in disentangling these feelings.

Although Dolly was more and more invalided, she and Henry continued to entertain, occasionally inviting people involved in the arts, music, theater and politics. Beatrix enjoyed these encounters because up until her time at Raasay, her chaperoned life had been rather protected.

Dolly made sure that when her acquaintance, Bimba Pain, was giving a singing soiree in her home and Beatrix was invited. Bimba, the younger daughter of Frank and Florence Pain of Frimley, near Guildford, was called Bimba from her "bambina" days in an Italian voice school. She had abandoned her voice training when her health was threatened "by the garlic and oil the Italians cook with!" although she still sang, privately, for her friends.

Bimba was a fine looking woman, with long, almost black hair, affecting the loose, trailing romantic clothes of post–Victorian artistes. Her brother, John Pain, helped host her party.

When Beatrix returned home after the party, Dolly asked about the concert and the soiree, "What was it like, Trix?"

"I met John Pain."

"But how was the concert?"

"I met John Pain, the most handsome man I have ever seen."

CHAPTER EIGHT

So it is, Mistress, said he, that yesterday driving my sheep up the stately hill...I happened up on
the side of it, in little falling of the ground which was a rampier against the Sun's rage, to perceive a young maid, truly of the first stamp ...her apparel was but such as Shepherds' daughters are wont to wear: as for her hair, it hung down at the free liberty of his goodly length...in her lap there lay a Shepherd, so well wrapped up in that well–liked place, that I could not discern no piece of his face...her Angel–like voice strake mine ears with this song:
My true love hath my heart, and I have his,
By just exchange, one for the other giv'n.
I hold his dear, and mine he cannot miss;
There never was a better bargain driv'n.
His heart in me, keeps me and him in one, My heart in him, his thoughts and sense guides:
He loves my heart, for once it was his own:
I cherish his, because in me it bides.

—Sir Phillip Sidney, 1554 – 1586, *Love in Arcady*

Florence Pain's determination was legendary. As a young woman, she had climbed out of the second story window at her prestigious boarding school to elope with John's father, Frank. He was waiting with a gig and fast pony, which raced them to a steam tugboat and then over to France where they married. They lived with little money until the family forgave them and welcomed them back. Frank read for the law, and finally became a judge.

All their ancestry, connections, estate, and social talents made the Pains *county*. They lived quietly, Frank commuting to his duties as a judge in Lincoln's Inn, London.

Beatrix's modest looks did not meet Florence's hopes for her handsome Johnny, the dearest of her sons, who was devoted to his mother. With characteristic resolve, Florence fainted dead away when she learned of her Johnny's engagement to Beatrix. She had no intention of allowing a city socialite to take her special son away from her. Her strength of character was marked by her nickname, Tet.

Beatrix, raised in an upper class family, never needed nor had been permitted to learn the skills of servants who served her. She could neither cook, nor clean nor mend. She had never washed a garment, set a fire, cleaned a window or cooked an egg, but she knew the social graces—how to meet and greet royalty or a shopkeeper.

Florence doubted Beatrix could run a country household, such as Frimley, with its perpetual supplies of both furry and feathered game to be cared for, and water that needed to be hand pumped from half a mile away. Florence wondered if Beatrix could even manage to walk the four miles to church.

Florence was already separated from her oldest son, Henning, who, when he ran away to sea in 1892, had not written to his parents. Only once they had news—a newspaper from Sidney, Australia told of Henning, a young seaman who, for a prize of five pounds, climbed the town flagpole to replace the rotting halyard.

John envied his older brother's exploits, later as a Royal Canadian Mounted Police officer in the Klondike gold rush, or adventurously running the Grand Canyon in a rowboat. Henning later became the second mate of the Lindisfarne, a steel clad full clipper in the grain trade. Rounding the Horn in a full gale, bringing wheat to England from Australia, the crew of the Lindisfarne manned the yards to take in sail. Second mate, Henning, climbed to help the short handed gang, and was blown off the yard, plummeting down onto the backstay, which broke his fall and his jaw. Beatrix and Johnny were able to visit Henning in hospital before he died of injuries and tuberculosis. Johnny was now the only son of Frank and Florence Pain.

While Johnny was courting Beatrix in London, Frank and Florence fell ill with influenza. When their only servant went home sick, John and Beatrix came to help and the Pains found that Beatrix was not the worthless girl they had imagined. Tet and Beatrix became firm friends and to show her trust, Tet gave her a family miniature of her father General Holland as a personal memento of Beatrix's care during her sickness.

John Pain became "Johnny" to Beatrix, who became "Trix" or "Doight" to him. They were married, January 21, 1909, at a quiet wedding in the Church of the Good Shepherd, Lee, London, near Johnny's London home, 75 Burnt Ash Road, Lee. The wedding party included John's father, Frank, Beatrix's oldest half brother, J.G. Cotton Minchin, Henry Dumas and his son Basil, and Gladys Flumnes. Johnny wore tweeds and a cloth cap, Beatrix wore a light grey traveling suit with a matching hat.

On their honeymoon in Christchurch, the newlyweds bucketed about the English Channel in their little ketch

Princess, rowing ashore to the Isle of Wight, in the tiny skiff, to visit seaside teashops built under upturned boats, enjoying high tea of fresh lobster, newly baked brown bread and strong brown tea. They visited pubs in the New Forest, John driving the trap with a part Arabian pony, his engagement present to Beatrix. They met tribes of gypsies navigating their decorated caravans and fashionable coaches-and-four, tooling round the forest.

Halcyon high tea days, days with no goal but pleasure, when Beatrix measured the depths of John's country personality, heard his description of the hedgehog's life, how to set a favourite hound's broken leg, or tell why "If a wood cock had a partridge thigh, he be the finest bird that e'er did fly."

And she, in turn, told him of her pet dogs, of days in the British Museum, of Indians and Anglo Indians and their tales of the Khyber Pass, of her visits to France, of her father and his lore, of her love for him and her love for her sister Dolly.

At the wedding there was no premonition that the age-old contract could be so demanding, "Wilt thou, Beatrix, have this man... to have and to hold, from this day forward, for better for worse, for richer for poorer, in sickness and in health, to love, honour and obey, till death do you part...for thou shalt eat the labour of thine hands...shall be as the fruitful vine, Thy children like the olive branches round about thy table..."

Easy promises, hard destinies. Those days, the perfect halcyon days, were not to return. But Trix had the seal of those days deep below her waist. A special seal from John.

They set up house in Bournemouth, where they had honeymooned. They had decided to spend her dowry on a lively business.

"Tell me, Johnny, more about the business we are going into, tell me how you came to it. It is so completely out of my experience."

"Doight, my father was born a gardener. We lived deep in the country in the house built by my grandmother, Elizabeth Cave, after she moved from her old house near London. My father learned to garden from Uncle Henning, Father's brother, who could graft and bud fruit trees like a Kew gardener. He imported two Wellingtonia trees, which are now so tall they are used as a government survey registry point. When my mother inherited a lot of money from Elizabeth Cave, her mother-in-law, they used it to build four thousand feet of greenhouse, the Frimley Nurseries. Uncle Henning had no experience with glass greenhouses...

"It doesn't sound much like Kew, to me."

"It gets more like Kew later on. Father got advice and hired John Bennett, who was the top gardener in England and president of the Royal Horticultural Society. He taught us everything he knew, including how to test the strength of manure tea; you sip it! After two and a half years, he thought Father and I could run the nursery. But I was only fifteen then and my sister Pooge's husband, Arthur Mayne, an engineer, talked me into going to Siemens Brothers as an apprentice. Now I wish I had stayed with the nursery. I'm a plant man.

"When Father was offered a good price for the nursery he sold it. Now Father and I want to develop a nursery again. The time seems right. The Christchurch site is good—you remember it—I understand that King Edward is for the idea, for what that's worth. He has invested in a French Intensive garden himself, somewhere over near Hythe. Valois, our French gardener, visited the site and didn't think much of it; the irrigation wasn't right. The government has passed the Smallholdings Act, and is helping the agricultural side a lot. The city people are demanding fresh vegetables year round, even in winter, and are willing to pay for them. As you know, they expect lettuce every month, at a price, mostly greenhouse stuff. Labour is cheap; one can get a labourer for fifteen shillings a week. Agriculture is picking up. The plantation of lavender at Mitcham, not far from here, is completely competitive with the French farms. You should see the carts piled high with the bales, smelling so wonderful."

"Well, you and your father know how to go about it. Will you get some help to set it up?"

"We've already hired the expert, Jules Valois. Valois will soon be getting the cloche bells to go over the freshly planted seeds. By the way, it takes a thousand glass cloches to protect an acre of plants. With these cloches, the produce will be ready for market earlier than the regular field crops and command higher prices. We could make daily deliveries of greens and melons to the City, and a return on your—our—investment.

"When will we make our first deliveries of lettuce?'

"Last week we took some lettuce to the Voules, your cousins. Did I tell you they told my friend and partner Gordon-Craig to go to the back door with the pony trap. They couldn't stand the tradesman's cart with a relative's name on it at the front door. What side!"

"What side indeed! Obviously they didn't know Gordon-Craig was a peer. What would they have said had they known?"

"Goodness only knows. It'd be fun to let it slip and see how they'd squirm."

"By the way, how do you like our Barracks Road cottage?"

"To be honest Johnny, it seems small. I know I've been coddled all my life. I have to learn the housekeeping things and I suppose I'd better I start with a small place. Fewer things to take care of."

"Doight, I'm not going to be hard to care for. Though Frimley was big, we lived a rather simple life, not the Mayfair life you had."

"Yes, when you have never boiled an egg, or washed or swept, you have a lot to learn. Mrs. Beaton's has pages and pages on how to run a household with one servant and even passages on how to do it alone. I'm getting the hang of a few thing, although I wouldn't dream of inviting anybody in the family to supper yet."

"Whenever you feel up to it, Doight. I'm sure you could carry it off. Maybe we can get someone in for a few hours a day to help, and you can pick up hints from her."

"I'll try to get an older woman, who has raised a family."

Beatrix and Johnny's first child, Jacqueline, was born in Christchurch on September 5, 1910, with the help of a nurse and a local doctor. Beatrix breast-fed her daughter and, when she regained her figure, resumed her corsets. She took to motherhood and soon learned how to keep the house. As soon as Jacky could walk, she wandered about the garden, chatting with the gardeners among the acres of cloches

John began painting again. He did watercolours of Christchurch scenery - riverbanks with elms and a white houseboat drifting to the marshes. He was at peace with the world, pleased to be caring for his family. The garden was flourishing and Doight had the household well in hand.

England was in the long transition to modern times, applying the new ideas of science and technology: steam and electrical power, the discoveries of chemistry, and scientific agriculture. The French Intensive Method of gardening was on this cusp of change. The expert would use a thermometer to test the soil temperature, instead of dropping his clout and sitting bare-arsed on the ploughed field to test the warmth of their fields, as had farmers for hundreds of years.

Taking up this new Method, Johnny and his father co-opered together hundreds of boxes, stuffed them with fresh horse manure topped with River Stour silt, and capped the lot with glass bells, the cloches of the French method. The fermenting manure would warm the soil, the seeds would germinate, and the cold would be held off with protective mats. In January, the Christchurch French Gardens, Ltd. had over a hundred boxes with thirty-six lettuce plants to the box. Each lettuce would be worth over a shilling each. The crop could fetch one hundred and eighty pounds for less than three months' work.

When it was dry, they watered by hand, using the water from the Stour River. The lazy river rounded the promontory of the garden, dropping silt from the hills. It was flat country with alluvial soil—mellow and sweet, fine, open to watering, and easy to wash off. No Sussex clay here.

Here, the Stour River was in its last looping turn before flowing into the wide estuary flanked by the Grimbury Marsh and the Stanpit marshes, encompassing the mouth of the Avon, and the old city moat. The estuary was shaped like a trumpet, easily discharging the flow of both the Stour and the Avon. The land of the estuary was shaped like a funnel, which in turn received the full rush of the Solent tide. Upstream, the Gardens lay on the toe of low land protecting the southwest flank of the town castle.

The last downstream bridge, Tuckton Bridge, with its tollgate, crossed the Stour, carrying Stour Street. The tollhouse had flood markers painted on its foundations. Johnny had never noted them.

That year, rains and storms covered the south of England. When Johnny went home, he paused at the toll house to watch the ripples climbing, salt water with marsh wrack breasting upstream at the bridge, Stour flood trash reversing as the fresh and salt water contended. When the ebb tide emptied the river, he knew the ripples would go down.

But a new tide came in the night, a spring tide, with an on shore wind. Floods from the headwaters of the Avon and the Stour crested at Christchurch. The wrack from the marshes came up from the sea, the flotsam came down the rivers and contended at Tuckton Bridge as they had for hundreds of years. But this time, the combined crests rapidly climbed over Christchurch Gardens. The four crests had united, the wind, the tide, the Avon and the Stour crests, and the marsh trash from Grimby Island surged up the funnel gaining height and momentum as the funnel narrowed.

When Mr. Broomfield, the head gardener, rowed to work the next morning he rowed right over the garden, and tied up to the toll booth. Though he had worked at Tuckton House since he was a boy and had a long memory, he had never seen the likes of this flood. Johnny and Beatrix were there with Jules Valois on the bridge, watching the flotsam and jetsam of the river eddy with the salt marsh water.

Beatrix

The Stour and the Avon had struck their blow, and the whole spit of Christchurch Gardens, Ltd. was swept clean. The flood had reached above the highest of the witness marks on the tollbooth foundation. As the tide ebbed and the rivers emptied, they could see where the hundreds of manure boxes had been, where the office had been, where the hundreds of glass cloches, melons, lettuces and carrots had been, where their work and investment had been. The outgoing tide carried off everything. Now all they could see was mud, laced with the shrubs and trees, snatched from the riverbanks.

Beatrix wept, Johnny watched, stony–faced. Their future, and family and friends' money, five thousand pounds, floated off. Johnny's dream of returning profits, his dream of caring for his family, washed away.

His plaint sagged through his words:

"Oh Doight—what shall we tell our friends, their money—our money—it looked so good. It isn't fair. I loved it so, and Father loved it so! We are swept clean. What will we say to the people, what shall we do?"

Beatrix thought of Kipling's 'brace up', 'worn out tools.' "Now I know why I'm here. I'm here to share." After a pause, Beatrix spoke.

"They took their chances, Johnny, as we did. We did our level best and the rivers rose. They'll understand. Maybe we'll just have to make a new start. You could be a gardener again, you could follow your dream again."

"But the money—it was all we had! And much of what friends and family had. They had confidence in us, they trusted us."

"Johnny, we can borrow a bit for tickets from the life insurance and go to Florida where you said you had friends from the cable steamer days. Your friend, the railroad builder, needs a landscaper, and he said that Florida is having a boom. We could go to Florida and earn it all back."

Before she went to bed that night, Beatrix picked up the little volume of verses that reminded her of her father. To ease her pain, she looked for Wordsworth's poem, *Stepping Westward.*

> *What, are you stepping westward? Yea.*
> *'Twould be a wildish destiny*
> *If we, who thus together roam...*

"And Johnny, we are about to roam..."

> *In a strange land, and far from home*
> *Were in this place the guests of Chance*
> *Yet who would stop, or fear to advance*
> *Though home or shelter he had none,*
> *With such a sky to lead him on?*

> *"We are being driven, not led?"*
> *The dewy ground was dark and cold;*
> *Behind, all gloomy to behold;*
> *And stepping westward seemed to be*
> *A kind of heavenly destiny;*
> *I like the greeting;'was the sound*
> *Of something without place or bound?*
> *And seemed to give me spiritual right*
> *To travel through that region bright*

"It would seem brighter, if I knew more about it."

> *The voice was soft, and she who spake*
> *Was walking by her native lake:*
> *The salutation had to me,*
> *The very sound of courtesy*
> *Its power was felt; and when my eye*

Beatrix

> *Was fixed upon the glowing sky,*
> *The echo of the voice enwrought*
> *The human sweetness of the thought*
> *Of traveling through the world that lay*
> *Before me in my endless way.*

"I hope it is a heavenly destiny."
And they went to Florida.

CHAPTER NINE

*Although our ordinary air be good
by nature or art, yet it is not amiss,
as I have said, still to alter it;
no better Physic for a melancholy man,
than change of air, and variety of
places, to travel abroad and see fashions.
Leo Afer speaks of many of his
countrymen so cured, without all
other Physic: amongst the Negroes
there is such an excellent air,
that if any...and brought thither,
he be instantly recovered...Many
other things helped, but change of
air was that which wrought the cure,
and did most good.*

—Robert Burton, 1577 – 1640, *The Anatomy of Melancholy*

In 1922, Tampa was a burgeoning town, known for its American bonhomie and easygoing friendliness. But for Beatrix, everything felt topsy–turvy—the heat, strange southern food and the people. She longed for the green of English country, Dolly's soirees and Yorkshire pudding. When she shopped in Tampa, she was affronted by drug-store cowboys who sat by the boardwalk, commenting on the passing women, while spitting gobs of tobacco juice onto the planked sidewalks. She knew the men meant to be overheard. She was offended by Florida's social snakiness—people expected her to sleep with a revolver under her pillow "in case a Negro should break in." Despite Reconstruction, there were constant reminders of slavery; Beatrix could see the profound effect it had on the Negro population and, conversely, on the whites. It was a hard adjustment.

"Johnny, we had brown people in our home as guests of father's. The British outlawed slavery in 1833. But here the legacy of slavery still has people at odds. The whites are terrified of the Negroes, who are terrified of the whites."

"Yes, Doight, it's a problem. I use black men for my commissions. They certainly work well."

In 1911, the United States, only fifty years away from the Civil War and emancipation, was a short generation into reconstruction. Nearly half the Negroes in Florida had been slaves. Beatrix was shocked when riding on a streetcar through a rural area to see the conductor draw a pistol and shoot at the feet of an elderly black farmhand "just to see him dance." People talked about lynchings.

Without the prop of family investments, Beatrix and Johnny's life in the thriving city of Tampa was modest. Johnny worked hard at his new landscape gardening. His contracts varied from grassing the town baseball diamond to landscaping a series of railroad stations. The custom of having Negroes doing all the manual labour with whites supervising did not prevent Johnny from helping on the jobs, and his reputation as a hard worker and an artistic planner soon grew. He used the evenings to make presentation sketches for his landscape designs, presentations tricked out in watercolours. He had a genius for growing things, and threw himself into designing flower-beds and furniture.

"What news today from the work front, Johnny?"

Beatrix kept up a facade of interest for his self-esteem, which she knew, was badly crushed by the Christchurch flood.

"Pretty good, Doight. This tropical climate is a challenge—the four seasons mean nothing here. The heat makes things leggy, but I'm getting the hang of it. It's pretty good, I'd say."

There were few enjoyments for Beatrix. She did not appreciate landscape gardening—her life in London had no gardening and with Dolly there were always gardeners to help you play at gardening. Why Dolly even gardened from a wheelchair! When the smell of the Florida orange blossoms washed through their garden she would have happily exchanged it for the scent of violets.

When Johnny was away at work, Beatrix dipped into poetry, trying to limit the hurt and take her mind somewhere else. She turned to *A Boy's Song*, wanting to contain her feelings with the poetry and to protect John's self-confidence.

> Where the pools are bright and deep,
> Where the grey trout lies asleep,
> Up the river and over the lea,
> That's the way for Billy and me.
>
> Where the blackbird sings the latest,
> When the hawthorn blooms the sweetest,
> Where the nestlings chirp and flee,
> That's the way for Billy and me.
>
> Where the hazel bank is steepest,

> *Where the shadow falls the deepest,*
> *Where the...*

She couldn't read on, and looked out at the dusty palms.

"Johnny, Johnny! Be quick! Jacky's got a snake by her.

A copperhead!"

Beatrix stood transfixed, her hands cupped to her cheeks and her breath stopped in her throat, seeing the snake by Jacky's leg. She watched in horror as Johnny hacked at it with a hoe, diverting it from the unwary Jacky. The snake coiled and lashed at the hoe. He finally wounded it and drove it into the stream.

"Oh Johnny, what are we doing in this horrible place?"

Johnny had no quick answer, and Beatrix had no more questions. He had bested the snake and it was out of his mind. Beatrix continued to monitor her garden, the "yard" as her neighbours called it. She quartered it every hour, inventorying every bush and clod where Jacky played. No further rattler or copperhead ever threatened, but the memory stayed.

John's first partner was G.F. Young, a Southern Baptist and a fundamentalist. One Sunday, Beatrix and John joined him in a visit to his church, a novelty for Beatrix and Johnny, who had never before been to "chapel." It was a word they used as a term of not so subtle opprobrium for anything but the Church of England. To Beatrix' horror, Mr. Young used the church visit as an opportunity to advertise their business.

On another occasion, Johnny and Beatrix, who both smoked, visited a cigar factory. In one room they saw forty people at benches, rolling tobacco leaves into characteristic shapes and pressed them into wooden moulds. There was enough space between the benches for carts to pass and collect the finished cigars and distribute piles of the large, sticky tobacco leaves. The air was thick with the familiar odour of tobacco. As they entered, they were surprised that the employees were from Cuba and spoke in Spanish . To Beatrix's astonishment, a man sitting on a raised dais was reading aloud from Dickens' *Pickwick Papers*. The familiar English cadences rolled out: "Mr. Snodgrass, Mr. Tupman, Mr. Pickwick." The reading droned on. In the frequent amusing scenes, not one person laughed, not even a titter. The Cubans heard but had not understood a syllable.

"Why is he reading an English novel, in English, to these Spanish–speaking people, Mr. Lopez?"

"Oh Senora, we read to the workers to keep them happy, and we ran out of Spanish authors, so we take English ones."

Beatrix felt a thrill of comradeship with the workers, hearing Dickens. To her, a book was a special route to conversations, exchanges, perhaps challenges, but to the Cubans, the book was only noise.

CHAPTER TEN

Bunyan, Blake, Hogarth and Turner.
Goethe, Shelley, Schopenhauer,
Wagner, Ibsen, Morris, Tolstoy and
Nietszche are among the writers
whose peculiar sense of the world
I recognize...akin to my own...
I read Dickens and Shakespeare without
shame or stint. Both have the
specific genius of the fictionist
and the common sympathies of human
feeling and thought in pre–eminent degree.

—George Bernard Shaw, 1856 – 1950, *Man and Superman*

For Beatrix, half the charm of books was exchanging and discussing them, and identifying the social declension, the distinctions of the characters. She discovered the Carnegie Library in Tampa, a legacy of the hard–headed Scottish-American industrialist who decided that, having spent half his life making money, he would spend the second half distributing it for the betterment of mankind, especially English-speaking communities. The handsome stone Carnegie Library stood like a bank near the main street, brown and austere, and enticing.

Until now Beatrix had relied on books sent by Dolly, annotated with her comments. In Tampa, there was no one to discuss them with. In the one bookshop Beatrix had found, all the books were arranged by height so interior decorators could buy a neat shelf of eight or ten books, all the same size or colour to make a den look well-read. She felt more and more alone in this grits prison where people drank either corn liquor or bad coffee.

Beatrix was heartened when she was invited to the Tampa Swimming Club, scene of the local elite.

"Johnny—I've been invited into the Swimming Club, I think it's a bit posh. I'll wear my club suit with the emblem on the pocket."

"Good for you, Doight. I hope you meet some literary types."

Beatrix was proud of her svelte swimsuit, cut to lines appropriate for Bournemouth and Biarritz, and the jaunty shield of the club could do no harm.

But in the locker room, the ladies of the Club informed Beatrix that the skirt of her suit was too short. They listened solicitously as she explained that the costume was pleasing to the best in England and France, but they turned up their eyes in dismay. "Oh, Mrs. Pain, they'll arrest you for *showing*, and it is against the law to be in public with no stockings."

And in friendly guise, with a not too hidden antagonism for things British, they tacked a little skirt of printed cotton onto Beatrix's suit to meet the local mores and uphold their modesty. This tarnished swimming for Beatrix.

Tampa, with its garish three-million-dollar hotel with its thirteen Moorish minarets, lacked lustre. The grotesque red brick five-story facade on the Hillsborough could not compete with Claridges or Carleton.

At last, when Beatrix met the music schoolteacher, she felt she had found a friend. When invited for tea, she was relieved to find that her hostess did not serve tea, but sherry and cigarettes. The music schoolteacher lived a life of secret rebellion and Beatrix reveled in clandestine meetings.

"Did you see plays and concerts in London?"

"Of course, we had them at least once a week. Covent Garden for much of the music, and all the other theatres for drama. Of course there was continuous Gilbert and Sullivan by the D'Oyly Carte, and always a Shakespeare."

"How I envy you, hearing all that music. We get very little here, sometimes the touring minstrels, and the odd second-rate concert. My teaching has to make do with what I remember from New York."

"Is Jacksonville a bit more cosmopolitan?"

"Yes, but Beatrix—have another sherry—You know that in this busy-body town I have to lock the doors and pull the shades when I have a sherry or smoke. I would lose my job if it were even talked about. So please be discreet."

Gradually things looked up. There was the pleasure of caring for Jacky, who was so graceful, pretty and dark like Johnny. The huge silk bows Beatrix tied to the temple lock on the side of Jacky's Dutch bob were much admired. The bows were like huge butterflies, a full four inches of the most exotic colours and finishes, bought at the kaleidoscope ribbon room in Liberty's, on Regent Street.

Things also brightened with a visit from John's sister Bimba, bringing newspapers, new seeds from Sutton's, news and snapshots of John's parents.

"How are they doing, Bim? Does Onslow Village

please them?"

"Johnny, it's a deep sea change for them. Frimley was a park and in Onslow they're in a newly-made village. There will be years of bare soil before the little trees grow; no giant sequoias such as we had at Frimley. And they don't have a feeling for close neighbours. But there it is, short commons for short people. We can't afford much else. You know they lost most of their money when the Australian banks failed."

For Johnny, there was little to enjoy about the news of his parents, and Bimba was able to stay for just two weeks because her parents needed her back in England.

Johnny's work prospered, his commissions filling his days and evenings. The only satisfaction for Beatrix was that she saw they were getting out of debt. Johnny included her in the social circle of his work but often to Beatrix's regret. She was introduced to Mr. Nails, a prominent salesman who came for supper and, after the meal, he insisted on displaying all the wares in his series of suitcases while sitting out on the porch. Despite the mosquitoes, she not only had to endure his several display cases and all the nails, but also the sight of Mr. Nails as he let a thin thread of brown tobacco juice seep down the crease in the corner of his mouth before he mopped it with a red bandana. And, when he spat, he occasionally missed the brass spittoon. He boasted that he had ground down three sets of gold teeth as he chewed tobacco. Beatrix felt ground down when he left.

"Doight, today I heard I've a commission from a prominent family, a congressman and his wife, whatever a congressman is!"

"A congressman is like our member of parliament at home. What is his name?"

"Potter-Palmer. He has an office in the Houses of

Parliament."

"I think they call it Congress."

"Congress? Still the Houses of Parliament to me. They try so hard to differentiate themselves from the English. But this couple is just as snobby as the British, you'll see. I'm not much higher than a black, because I use a shovel."

"Well, Johnny,
Where the bee sucks, there suck I:
In a cowslip's bell I lie;
There I couch when owls do cry.

But I'm crying for England. I'm really sick of this paradise."

"Oh Doight, we are beginning to pull out of it. Please give it a bit more—we won't be here forever. I know it is hard—there are so few of the things we used to enjoy, but we'll do it and go to somewhere else where it isn't so like Blackpool on a hot bank holiday."

But it wasn't the Potter–Palmers who would make the change Beatrix longed for. It was the Kaiser.

CHAPTER ELEVEN

...in a gigantic cage was a light-brown bird...just at noon...
the little feathered exile began as it were to tune his pipes...uttered some uncertain chirps...then the same sun that had warmed his heart at home...came down on him...out burst in that distant land his English song...these shaggy men, full of oaths and strife...had strolled the English fields and seen the lark rise, and heard him sing this very song.

—Charles Reade, 1814 – 1884, *It is Never too Late to Mend*

War with Germany! War was like a knife to Beatrix's throat. Did this mean Johnny would enlist? Beatrix hesitated, caught between love, family and loyalty. Johnny hesitated too.

"What do you think we should do, Johnny?"

"Let's wait a little while, Doight. It may blow over. I can't see the Germans doing this. After all, the Kaiser and the King are relatives, they gamble together. They probably went to race meets with your father and Lord Bentink. Let's wait. We are just getting started here, and England has little for us."

"Yes. We're here, not there. England rejected us,

America has allowed us get ahead."

For Beatrix the dilemma was acute—keep Johnny safe in the America she hated, or risk his life by going back to Britain, for which she pined. She found her solace in Watts–Dunton in her poetry book.

> *I cannot brook thy gaze, beloved bird*
> *That sorrow is more than human in thine eye*
> *Too deeply, brother, is my spirit stirred;*
> *To see you here, beneath the landsman's eye*
> *Cooped in a cage with food thou can'st not eat.*

"Food thou can'st not eat!! I'd give a dollar for Devonshire cream, or a Cox's Orange Pippin, or fresh herring. But there's the irony, the wonderful oranges here, so different from the stringy things at home, which were so sour we had to hollow a small hole to sweeten them with a lump of sugar! The oranges here—well—the juice runs down your elbow!"

She felt as though she had "fallen among thieves." Americans had stolen her integrity, her sense of self, her balance. But then, they were not at war. Would Johnny enlist and she become a war widow? Here, or in England?

> *What will ye more of your guest and some time friend?*
> *Blood for our blood they said*
> *You shall die at dawn*
> *He flung his empty revolver down the slope*
> *He climbed alone to the eastward edge of the trees,*
> *He brooded, clasping his knees.*
> *He saw the April noon on his books aglow,*
> *He heard his father's voice below*
> *He saw the school close sunny and green*
> *He saw the dark wainscote and the timbered roof*
> *He watched the liner's stem plough the foam*

And now it was dawn,
He turned and saw the golden circle at last...
A sword swept,
The voices faded, and the hill slept.

"If I take Johnny back to England, and he is killed fighting, will the voices fade, will just the hill sleep, sleep with me?"

England had been so much for Beatrix. The privileges of her family, privileges of position, wealth, respect, devoted servants, and idealized relatives—her sister, her aunts, the Egans, and the Barry family and the Roses. She missed the places—Raasay, Bournemouth, Christchurch, the New Forest. One ancient beech tree was worth more to her than the whole everglades. The smell of drying hay, the breath of cows! So much of that had gone, swept to sea with the market garden.

Jacky tugged at her apron. "Mudderkees, tell me a poem!"

Jacky called her Mudderkees for 'Motherkins' and her father 'Nacko' for Jack or Daddy.

But the mood was on Beatrix. Melancholy quatrains were all she could summon up:

"Under the wide and starry sky
Dig the grave and let me lie:
Glad did I live and gladly die,
And I laid me down with a will."

And she told the last four lines more feelingly, to last long in Jacky's mind,

"This be the verse you grave for me:
Here he lies where he long'd to be;
Home is the sailor, home from the sea,

And the hunter home from the hill."

Johnny also was torn. Should he continue in his successful new business with the friends he had made, or go back to England where his failures were chronicled, back to his parents and sister, and the war?

"Will these immigrant thoughts and doubts never stop, Doight? We change our language, our clothes and our skills, and change our child so we hardly recognize her. Do we stay against our heritage, or do we, must we reverse all this?"

The recruiting poster in an English newspaper made up his mind. It pictured a little girl on her father's lap, asking, "What did you do in the Great War, Daddy?" Staying in America was an increasing dishonour. He decided to return to England and join up.

Johnny, Beatrix and Jacky left on a packet boat from Jacksonville, as there were no rail connections from Tampa to New York. The heat was unendurable, but their deck cabins were open to sea breezes. They enjoyed their last Southern cooking and Southern courtesies from the Negro crew—hot biscuits from the oven. What an irony, that it was these recent slaves who offered the niceties!

In New York, John was recruited with a King's shilling, to be shipped to Britain. Beatrix and Jacky would run the gauntlet of the Atlantic submarines on the White Star liner, *Baltic*. The New York newspapers trumpeted "White Star Liner Loaded With Troops and Ammunition Dares German U Boats."

Beatrix dropped notes onto the dock to John who was to sail later on his ship for England. Her companions, other wives returning to Great Britain, were dropping notes to their husbands.

The liner sailed, loaded with Royal Northwest Mounted Police, cases of high explosives, returning children and wives. The ship was blacked out and sailed alone without a convoy. The women were each assigned a man to help with emergency drills. Beatrix locked her cabin door and slept with her clothes on. The *Baltic* bolted across the Atlantic, greeted by British mine sweepers clearing the approaches, clearing the soundings, the shallows where the Germans moored floating mines.

"Jacky, see our mine sweepers!"

"What do they do, Mudderkees?"

"The fishermen gave up their livelihood to protect us from the German mines planted to sink our ships near to home. Usually the fisherman "fish for the herring fish", you know, as in *Wynken, Blynken and Nod*. Now they fish for mines, so we won't hit one and sink."

"Tell me Wynken, Blynken, Mudderkees."

"Just the first and the last verses, it's cold out here.

"Wynken, Blynken, and Nod, one night
Sailed off in a wooden shoe
Sailed on a river of crystal light,
Into a sea of dew.
"Where are you going, and what do you wish?"
The old moon asked the three.
"We have come to fish for the herring fish
That live in this beautiful sea;
Nets of silver and gold have we,"
Said Wynken
Blynken,
and Nod.

All night long their nets they threw
To the stars in the twinkling foam—

Then down from the skies came the wooden shoe,
Bringing the fishermen home;
'Twas all so pretty a sail, it seemed
As if it could not be,
And some folks thought was a dream they'd dreamed
Of sailing that beautiful sea—
But I shall name the fisherman three
Wynken,
Blynken,
And Nod.

"Now that's all. It's too cold and windy here to tell poetry. Let's go to our cabin."

The minesweepers bobbed in the wake of the *Baltic*, and the liner berthed in Southampton. Beatrix wanted to kiss the littered and muddy quay—it was England!

CHAPTER TWELVE

We are all bowmen in this place.
The pattern of the birds against the sky
Our arrows overprint, and then they die.
But is also common to our race
That when the birds fall down we weep.
Reason's a thing we dimly see in sleep.

—Conway Power, *Guide to a Disturbed Planet*

At Raasay, all was on a war footing. Most of the servants were gone and flowerbeds dug up for vegetables. The National Service women did the horticulture; the luxuries of the table became tiny rations of tea, milk, butter, and meat. Clothes and petrol were rationed and cars put to the use of the military.

If Beatrix thought that a return to Britain from Florida would set all back as it had been before, she had misjudged the effects of the war. With their money mostly gone, Johnny and Beatrix were now decayed gentry - they could enter the best bar in England, but they had no money to buy a drink.

Johnny had no care for money and Beatrix, as she grew up, had enjoyed almost complete independence from money. She had learned to take for granted the services that money afforded her and her family. She had been accustomed, for instance, to putting her shoes outside the hotel suite before going to bed so the "Boots" would pick them up, shine them and return them in time for early breakfast. The minor tip repaid Boots for his secret service and for his anonymity. Money undergirt the luxuries they had known.

When Beatrix first returned to her sister, Dolly's home, the place was responding to the wartime state. There were still many of the luxuries of the rich life - house servants, gardeners, and the chauffeur.

Each day newspapers brought highlights of the war—the fate of the first 10,000, the optimistic warriors who were sent to destroy the Germans, but instead met the belly of the German war machine. Almost a million men would be sent. The papers frequently listed official casualties and "missing and presumed dead." On some days, 30,000 died.

Letters arrived too; a telegram was so dangerous that even strangers were asked to open and read them for you.

Beatrix had so much to learn and accommodate to - to be a mother, to be strapped for money, to not have a home, to be without Johnny while her England was twisted and wrung. One morning, the quiet of Raasay was suddenly torn.

"News from Johnny! News from Johnny!"

Beatrix called out as she tore open the envelope with the familiar handwriting. Johnny had sketched a tiny ship with three little figures at the rail. Beatrix fumbled, the paper shook and she couldn't see the writing. Collecting herself, she started to read.

Johnny had survived the Atlantic crossing, landed in Scotland, and called on his friendship with Gibson–Craig, whose father commanded the Highland Light Infantry. Johnny was now a private soldier in the HLI. He would write again soon. Beatrix knew that writing for him was like pulling hair, he had little experience of separation to train him.

At Raasay, Beatrix prepared to go to Scotland to join him, when Hilda Dumas, Dolly's daughter-in-law proposed, "Trix, I have this wonderful Scottish nanny for my baby. Why don't you leave Jacky with her until you make arrangements to be with Johnny?"

"How wonderful of you—but I couldn't—she'd be a trouble."

"Oh no trouble, Nanny's not overburdened with one baby. We have to help each other."

Beatrix and Johnny were reunited, but not for long. Beatrix had volunteered to run a YMCA canteen in Stirling, brimming with Cameron and Seaforth Highlanders.

CHAPTER THIRTEEN

> ...Mr. Burchell sat with his face to the fire, and at the conclusion of every sentence would cry out FUDGE, an expression which displeased us all and damped the spirit of the conversation.
> "That I know," cried Miss Skeggs. "One refused to do plain–work an hour a day, another thought twenty–five guineas a year too small...I was obliged to send away the third because I suspected an intrigue with the chaplain...virtue is worth any price; but where is it to be found? FUDGE!"
> —Oliver Goldsmith, 1728 – 1774, *The Vicar of Wakefield*

The canteen was open eight hours in the evening for the Cameron and Seaforth Highlanders. Twenty-four volunteers dispensed floods of tea, coffee and cocoa from urns, and sandwiches—small comfort for the nonce.

The unbloodied, pristine soldiers confronted their fate every two weeks, when they might be posted to step into the shoes of comrades, dead and maimed in France. These young men were in their teens, many from the Hebrides, and Gaelic speaking, never before far from mothers and fathers. They waited, lonely, for their names to be posted on the bulletin board. Their colonel, the Laird, comforted them and watched them dance their strathspeys, singing the mouth–music of their shielings as two weeks shortened to the dangerous days.

"Name's up, get ready. Muster at two this morning. Look sharp!"

In the afternoon, the canteen was busy with a concert party, everyone singing and dancing to keep spirits up with good–byes to new friends. Beatrix's kitchen was the scene of private good–byes between sons and mothers down from the Highlands, the Orkneys or the Hebrides.

"Mither, Mither, dinna greet, air we no' the bonnie fechters?"

Scant comfort to a mother, who cared not that her son was a fine fighter, or that she might cry.

The soldiers mustered at two in the morning outside in the snow, as the flakes crowned the sixty-pound packs, kilts shrouded in khaki. The pipers blew and held a high note.

"Shun!"

"By the right, columnoffours, quick –

"Harch!"

At the "harch" the pipers broke seamlessly into *Scotland the Brave* and the young soldiers marched off to the transport. They were fighting within the week. "For a' that and a' that", and for all that they had cried "Guid, ichn Reich", for God and the Right, they were dropped in the pit of the Battle of the Somme, eaten by the war. Few came back, even fewer intact. Beatrix put the mothers up while they waited for a train back to the Highlands.

Beatrix had not known that wars were like this. She had heard parlour tales of the Khyber Pass, Gunga Dhin, officers in red with blazing white helmets, officers mounted in their kilties, swinging into view to relieve the siege—a discrete number dying. Her uncles and cousins had returned as heroes, with medals for resounding victories at Seringapatam, Afghanistan. Stories of their victories were all so neat and tidy. Now it was different—her Johnny was in battle.

When he was unexpectedly sent to the front, Beatrix volunteered as chef for a Salvation Army hospital for twenty men wounded in action. She had the primitive feeling that, if she did something for the war effort, this might bribe fate to get it over a little faster, or even, God forbid, she might make a contract with God to spare him if she did her bit. So she volunteered, although untrained as a cook. Only her Christchurch housemaid, a black servant in Tampa, some colloquies with Dolly's cook, and a dear old Highland woman who taught her how to make Scotch broth, gave her some clues for this awesome responsibility.

Her guide was *Mrs. Beeton's Cookery Book, A Household Guide, instructions in Cookery, Household Work, Trussing, Serving, Carving, Menus, Etc., with Illustrations.*

In the kitchen, two volunteers prepared vegetables, usually potatoes, turnips, carrots and cabbage. Rationed food was supplemented by local gentry, who brought river–run salmon and stags from the heath. Beatrix found the work of butchering venison carcasses daunting. The rank, almost rancid smell of the fur and fat of the venison, hung long enough to make it tender and tasty, penetrated her hands and would not wash off. Beatrix used jam tarts to bribe patients into plucking and drawing the game birds and grinding the rationed mutton.

Nursing duties were handled by a one–legged Boer war nurse, the matron, and two nursing volunteers. With each step the matron swung her wooden leg, which had no knee joint, to clear the floor. Pranksters followed her, mimicking her swinging gait, convulsing Beatrix and the staff. When the matron complained, one of the men carried an axe over his shoulder, "Ready to chop off her leg!"

Every second Saturday, Beatrix managed a visit to six-year-old Jacky in an Edinburgh convent, where the steadfast nuns cared for her and a dozen other children separated from their parents. Beatrix and Jacky made firm friends with the nuns who became like family. The bows in Jacky's hair were effulgent, and Beatrix enjoyed the reflected admiration. Marmalade tarts were tuck again.

Although Jacky had no heart for memorizing verse, Beatrix taught her:
> The Queen of Hearts she made some tarts
> All of a summer day;
> The Knave of hearts he stole those tarts
> And took them quite away.

At Jacky's age, Beatrix used to stand on a hassock to recite long ballads. But no hassock for Jacky; she preferred to dance, and pirouetted prettily at every opportunity.

"Perhaps this will be her talent," Beatrix thought.

Beatrix's apprenticeship in the little cottage hospital led to another posting in an old, run-down hotel in Edinburgh, the Craiglochart. The previous chef had run away and left the place in chaos and raddled with dirt, cockroaches, rats and mice. Two hundred shell-shocked officers, "neurasthenic" war victims, were billeted here, along with nurses, orderlies, doctors and servants. The opening battles of the war had jumbled the officers' psyches.

Every day she dealt with the cruel grind at Craiglochart Hospital, where the kitchen had to be scraped clean and disinfected. The smell of Lysol joined the aroma of Brussels sprouts. The army orderlies scraped the ranges and shelves and whitewashed walls.

Beatrix had a kitchen staff of seven, the "brigade"—a kitchen maid, who was studying opera, her assistant chef, a vegetable maid fresh from Ireland, and two dishwashers, one a cook from the Duke of Argyle's home who had drunk herself out of her ducal job. She was a saviour for Beatrix, teaching her how to make 'pottie heed,' brawn, Scottish broth and, of course, when the butcher sent her the wherewithal, haggis.

One day, the wherewithal included the unopened sheep stomach, a mystery to Beatrix.

"Carlin! I've heard about haggis, but never seen or tasted it."

"Och Misthress. 'Tis a bonnie pudd'n, a bonnie pudd'n! You make it with a sheep, no, just the pluck."

"The pluck?"

"Aye, Misthress, the pluck. You take the pluck, that is, the stomach wi' the pipes on it, an' the rest of the pluck when a sheep is skinned and hung up and you cut the belly and the offal falls off..."

"Falls off?"

"Why yes, Misthress, that's why it's offal, it falls off!"

"Go on."

"That's the pluck, if you put your hand in, grip it, and pluck it, that's the pluck!"

"Oh my goodness."

"Well y'take the pluck, the lungs, stomach, liver, the melt, kidneys and boil it all except the stomach, gently, and wi' an onion, and chop it up, an' I put in a drappit o' whisky, though some don't."

"A drappit?"

"Oh, less than a quaich an' more than a dribble. Chop

it sort of coarse-ish, brown an equal part of oatmeal, mix with the pluck an' a pound or so of suet, and wet it with some stock, slit the stomach and stuff the mixture in, sew it up an' set it to simmer, wi' the pipes hanging over the pot to let out the steam. That's it."

"Well thank you, Carlin. I hear they pipe in the haggis."

"Och aye, the Haggis is King for the day! Some cooks, the dainty ones, just use the liver—and oh yes, salt and pepper. And they serve you a slice and a quaich of whiskey!"

"I'd need a couple of quaiches!"

Beatrix wrote the Haggis and other recipes on her letter paper:

>GAMMON
>*Boil from cold a fresh shoulder or leg of pork, skimming, with onions, bayleaf and celery, 2—3 hours, s/p*
>*Drain, wipe, grease with butter or lard*
>*Roll in oatmeal to cover*
>*Bake and baste for ¾ to 1 hour*

One day when they were treated to a side of fresh pork, Beatrix hummed to herself, tunelessly, "With a roly poly gammon and spinach, Heigh Ho! said Anthony Rowley."

The demands of the kitchen left scant time for humming or reminiscing about past meals with *Le Saumon, Sauce homard et Persil.* Now any salmon they had was 'poached' by local anglers from the laird's stream, and served poached in onion water, without a sauce.

The kitchen had no slicing machines, and no butcher to seam, break down and cut the half carcasses from the flat top of the butcher's cart. The orderlies and the vegetable girl peeled a sack of potatoes and five pounds of turnips every day, scraped ten pounds of carrots, and often cut fifteen pounds of kidney fat into tiny cubes, the size of dried peas, for steak and kidney puddings. Boiled suet puddings, made with few raisins, were called Spotted Dick.

Mrs. Beeton was explicit:

> *Suet Crust, for pies or puddings.*
> *Ingredients.—To every lb. of flour allow 5 or 6 oz. of beef suet, ½ pint water.*
> *Free the suet from skin and shred, chop it extremely fine, and rub it well into the flour; work the whole into a smooth paste and the above proportion of water, and roll it out. This crust is rich enough for ordinary purposes, but when a better one is desired, use from ½ to ¾ lb. of suet to every lb. of flour.*

Beatrix' recipes, kept in an old shoebox, had to be multiplied by fifty to feed the sitting. If she needed help, she called on the Duke of Argyle's refugee. The only books she had time for now were *Showell's Tradesman's Calculator* and Mrs. Beeton's. Mrs. Beeton did rise to the occasion, offering breakfasts, luncheons and dinners for twelve, with spring, summer, autumn and winter menus.

She was taken aback one day when a helper staggered into the kitchen with a carcass.

"Goodness, Jock, what d'you have there?"

"It's a full stag, Misthrrress, they kept the head."

"They kept back very little else, I see—do you—do you know how to skin and dress a stag?"

"Not rrreally, people like us don't eat that kind of meat, mum."

"Please find someone who does, and find out if someone wants the hide. And please, would you carry the carcass out of the kitchen into the scullery? It's dripping, and smells awful, so gamy."

The Duke of Argyle's wayward dishwasher came in from the scullery. "What are you to do with the venison, Mistress Pain?"

"What do you suggest, Carlin?"

"When I was at the Dukes," she began, with the *side* appropriate to a Duke's follower, "we had venison, but neverr auld venison like this one. It will be tough, and strrong. If we must use it, then soaking in vinegar water will help, in the big wooden washtub for a couple of days. In joints."

"Thank you Carlin. When the men get it cleaned up, we can cut it into joints. Please ask the orderly to sharpen the knives on the brick in the pantry."

"Aye, Mistress, if I can find an orderly. Ye ken they'rr flighty, and into their beer. But they might be intrrestid in the venison."

There were times when Beatrix longed for a good laugh. She was up at six taking care to make the porridge, which was easily scorched. After breakfast and clean up, it was time to prepare mid-day dinner for the staff - soup, main meal and dessert. After a quarter hour lie-down, then clean up the kitchen and prepare dinner for the officer patients, supper for the staff and then check next day's preparation on the range. Both the Scotch broth and pea soup needed stock, so the bones were put on to simmer through the night. As the day was almost over, Beatrix had to finish the accounts. Finally to sleep.

"We're doing our bit! Doing whose bit? I hear people are beginning to take advantage of the shortages of the war. They talk about that profiteer McConachie, for example, who makes such distasteful canned mutton, even my best efforts have not been able to disguise it. I can't even use the mutton in stew, it's so rank, and I hear he's making millions. No wonder the troops hurl his swill out as soon as they see *McConachie's Lamb*.

"Some days I wonder what I am doing here. I have been working for two weeks straight and haven't been to see Jacky. And dear Johnny... What is that stirring? Why do I feel peculiar at odd times? I wonder why I felt sick when Jock broke an egg and it was not fresh?"

So that was it, she was with child and Johnny so far away!

Dear Johnny,

Please sit down and take a deep breath. Remember that leave two months ago in early July? Remember the deer in the heather and the old woman who made us mutton pie? You had two helpings. Well, the pie must have been an aphrodisiac, or the old woman put a spell in it. We will have to think up more names and get Godparents again. I'm at least two months pregnant.

On the days when Beatrix went to visit Jacky in the Catholic school, the nuns' rule seemed familiar to Beatrix, who remembered the ways of the Anglican nuns at Wantage School. The nuns had their archaic ways, keeping a pepper pot of hot sand on the hob to sprinkle on letters to dry the ink, and sealing their envelopes with hot wax. Beatrix did that too, licking the signet ring so the wax wouldn't stick. Whenever Beatrix had to work for more than a week at a stretch, the nuns would write, sending encouraging news of Jacky. They were very thoughtful of the wives of soldiers.

Whenever nights were moonlit and clear, Zeppelins now floated over Edinburgh. The maroons, the ululating sirens sounded to warn people who rushed to bomb shelters in the ancient cellars, crypts and buried galleries of Edinburgh. Many in the shelters had the dismal feeling of being buried alive in a crypt; the dead outnumbered those who were alive.

One night when Zeppelins threatened, the nuns grabbed the children in their care, wrapped them in bed–clothes, and rushed to safety in the chapel crypt.

"Where is Jacky, did anyone bring Jacky?" cried the Mother Superior.

One nun ran back, fearfully looking overhead to see if bombs were dropping from the otherworldly evil shapes in the sky, to collect the sleeping Jacky and carry her to the crypt.

CHAPTER FOURTEEN

Come live with me and be my Love,
And we will all the pleasures prove
That hills and valleys, dales and fields,
Or woods or steepy mountain yields.
—*Christopher Marlowe, 1564–1593*

But could youth last, and love still breed,
Had joys no date, nor age no need,
Then these delights my mind might move
To live with thee and be thy Love.
—*Sir Walter Raleigh 1552-1618*

Beatrix felt her work getting harder, the stone floors worse on her feet, and the food smells almost sick–making. She had to vomit when she smelled steak and kidney pie, which she usually relished.

"Well, the staff can sit deeper in the saddle for a little while. This appointment needs me for a while longer, but it will be easier to leave all these good people knowing I have broken the ground. I'll stick it out until I'm three months off."

And then a letter came from Johnny. His letter writing

was spotty—sometimes two weeks between, and then a deluge. She loved the little figures he drew—they spoke the words he could not render. Although Johnny, a straightforward country boy, was not a letter writer, his love letters drew an unexpected sweetness from him. She longed for them, and wrote long replies almost every day. She could recall almost every minute they had spent together, and remembered these times in her letters. And he told her stories of the trenches.

Doight, I have tragic news for you. You remember little Alfie, the Cockney batman assigned to me. I saw Alf coming down the trench to me, on the run. He said, "Sir– take–this" all in a run, and handed me a gas mask and ran down the trench out of sight. A cloud of phosgene gas came over just then as I put on the mask. I was safe, but the mask had been Alfie's own. He had gone without for me. I cried, but what could one do. The dear chap had said he would die for me, and he did.

Johnny never ever talked about it again. Beatrix felt awful, and ultimately grateful. In some way, Alfie guaranteed the life she and Johnny had pledged together, and she couldn't get it out of her mind that Alfie had, in some way, made possible the child who was kicking below her belt. She never told her children that Alfie had saved their father.

When Beatrix was seven months' pregnant, the work was too much for her. Her aunt, Emily Begbie, found her a place to live in an old servant's house. When the baby was born, Beatrix planned to stay a month in a small maternity hospital, where most of the eight patients were wives of overseas officers without much money.

Emily Begbie again rescued her niece, getting Beatrix into the practice of a famous physician, Haig Ferguson, who very kindly returned her proffered cheque.

"I would not take a fee from the wife of one of our boys in the trenches!"

On the day of the birth, April 14, 1917, Doctor Ferguson arrived, snow thick on the cape of his greatcoat. Beatrix gave birth to a 14-pound boy, a difficult delivery, leaving her with a scarred cervix.

Beatrix's friends, staff from Craiglochart Hospital visited.

"Mistress Pain, we knew you could do it. Anyone who could clean up that filthy old hotel could pull through and no mistake."

"You should call him The Pilot, he has such a voice!"

"And his face is red, just like a pilot's!"

In St. Mary's Cathedral, Cousin Emily, with whom Beatrix and her infant had stayed before the christening, stood up with Beatrix, representing family and friends who would have been there in peacetime. Rodney Hamish Hope Pain roared when Bishop Walpole anointed him with holy oil and the holy water, and roared through the ritual and the psalms and roared for the next few months. The Pilot.

CHAPTER FIFTEEN

Johnny was in France in the spring of 1918, and Beatrix was a war widow with two children, no home of her own, and limited income. Every day she hoped and prayed for a change, for good fortune. Then the telegram came, delivered by a messenger on bicycle. Telegrams from the War Office felt like enemies inside your walls—bad or devastating news. One could not open them, but one had to, expecting the worst.

Beatrix sat down and began to open the envelope slowly. Jacky asked:

"What's the matter, Mudderkees, you're shaking."

"Oh—I'm afraid of bad news, afraid…"

But it was wonderful news! Johnny was ill and in hospital. When he improved, he would be invalided back to England. Beatrix danced around, holding hands with Jacky, crying out "He's coming home, he's coming home, Johnny's ill, Nacko's ill! Your father's coming home soon!"

She picked up the telegram and re-read it. It was true. He was in a French hospital in Rouen, suffering from trench rheumatism, having stood long hours in knee-deep mud, protected only by issue boots and puttees, the woolen bandages wrapped around soldiers' ankles and calves for "protection." Thousands of British soldiers were dressed in these clothes, originally designed to protect feet and ankles from the thorns and snakes of India. But in the trenches of France there was mud, often freezing mud, soaking the legs and joints to rheumatism or worse.

Beatrix and the children waited for Johnny in Exeter, straining to see the first glimpse of him as troops poured off the train, the wounded passed down in litters. The crutch men clumped along the platform, swinging injured legs between their wooden limbs. But, no Johnny. One, an emaciated cripple shambling between two walking sticks, came towards them wearing the narrow Highland Light Infantry tartan trousers, the trews. Could it be? Yes, Beatrix saw it was Johnny! It was Johnny himself—whole, but damaged, hardly able to walk. Beatrix got him into Exeter Hospital to recuperate, while she and the family stayed with a cousin who had agreed to take them, even though the children were sick with whooping cough.

The sick and convalescent in England suffered privations. The German submarine blockades were sinking much of the British merchant fleet, and what food was available was diverted to the men at the front. So, even in hospital, Johnny continued to be desperately emaciated. Beatrix made up little potties of food, little extras to bulk out his hospital rations. Cousin Emily Begbie sent her butter ration, half an ounce a week, for the one-year-old Roddy, and Emily's sister, Carrie sent hers to Jacky. Tiny amounts of meat, cheese, margarine, tea, cocoa, and sugar were brought in, at such sacrifice. Nearly half the convoy ships had been sunk by the Germans.

Bournemouth winds were harsh for those who stood in

line for rations. When Johnny's health improved, he often stood in the queue because soldiers received a slightly larger helping.

"Good luck to you, soldier."

The butcher sometimes gave Beatrix a knucklebone of beef with a shred of meat on it and she would make the good soups of Scotland. A bit of suet made dumplings or Spotted Dick, that ominous dessert like Hangman's Pie. When Beatrix asked for ingredients of Hangman's Pie, she was told, "a bit of rope."

She sometimes thought back to dear old Mrs. Biggs, the family cook, who had provided so much to make her and Vi happy.

"When will I stop struggling? When will the good days come back? When will a Mrs. Biggs ever get me a cup of tea, a haddock or a chop? Maybe I'm Mrs. Biggs now."

Days were filled with household chores. When clothes needed ironing, Beatrix dampened them, scattering warm water in drops, and rolled the clothes into little bales. She left the irons to heat on the range, their soles to the fire. Nellie had shown her how to take the hottest in line and hold it near her cheek to estimate the heat by the glow on her skin. Sometimes she took a chance and judged by the hiss of spit on the hot iron. She started with dishtowels—better scorch a towel than a shirt. Johnny's shirts were a trial; the cuffs and collars had to be dipped in liquid starch so the ironing would glaze them into cardboard stiffness. Fortunately there weren't many shirts, just for the occasional evening when he went out wearing civvies.

Sir Gordon Gibson–Craig, who had been Johnny's gardening partner, helped arrange for him to serve with the Fourth Battalion, Highland Light Infantry. In its early battle, this respected regiment had fallen on a camp of General John Copes' English troops asleep in their tents.

The Infantry, who cut the troops to ribbons as they ran out of the tents, were disgraced for this cowardly action. As punishment, kilts were banned for their officers, who were ordered to wear the hated Sassenach trews, trousers cut from the same tartan cloth as the kilts. As a protest, the HLI sang "Hey Johnny Cope, are ye wau'kin yet?" as their wakeup tune.

"I'll be on light duty while I convalesce, Doight. I'm to recuperate in the Tank Corps."

"Oh Johnny, I hope you won't go to the front again. It is so hard to wait for you while you are the front."

The Tank Corps was demanding—Johnny had to supervise the experimental construction of the "tanks", so named as a cover to hide their construction and experimental field operation from spies.

In his spare time Johnny made a set of bellows with wooden cheeks decorated with copper panels that Beatrix could use to start fires.

"Where on earth did you get the copper, Johnny? It must be like gold these days."

"I was able to scrounge it from some of the wrecked tanks which had copper radiators on the engines. The teak is from 'un–en–ditching beams,' rather like railroad sleepers that they bolt to the caterpillar tracks and rotate to dig the tank out when it is trapped in a muddy hole or ditch. They are worth a fortune, but I've scrounged a split beam. With the help of the shop artificer, I'm also making a box of 'bricks', building blocks for the children to use to build houses. I'll make them so they'll fit into a box we can store under a bed."

"I'm glad you can make things. Money will be scarce for Christmas. Have you given any thought to what we'll do after the war, to make a living?"

"I can't look forward that far. Anyone at the front has his work cut out for him."

"Oh, I know how frightening it must be for you."

"Doight, think how lucky we've been so far. Think of the Somme, tens of thousands lost in a day."

"Did you ever see the Times after the Somme. That day they printed only lists of casualties, eighteen pages of them. Women fainted on the street as they read the paper."

"Try not to think about it."

Almost every evening Johnny would roar home from his barracks on his BSA motor bike, sometimes with a little something—a bone or some rice from the cookhouse.

Beatrix enjoyed walks around Bovington, pushing the pram. She held to her conviction that children should be walked for at least two miles a day, rain or shine, to benefit from fresh air. with their marmalade cat stalking along. The striped marmalade cat, which accompanied her, was named Sastrugi, after the wind ripples on the South Polar snow described by Robert Falcon Scott in his accounts of his Antarctic expedition.

Their little cottage in Grantham had a stone flag floor, one bedroom, and a chimney with no smoke shelf or damper; it let the fire look at the stars. Tradition told that this cottage had been an early, illegal non-conformist chapel built to accommodate a secret congregation during the religious schism between Queen Elizabeth and Mary Queen of Scots. Beatrix felt the cottage had more romance than amenities. Drinking water came in a salvaged five-gallon gas can, carried by the old gardener. Washing water came from a well in the garden. The stove was primitive and a hard rain would flood the place from the back door out through the front. But it was home for a while.

"Oh Johnny, I guess it had to come. How long before you leave?"

"Very soon, two or three days—they don't like to leave families on tenterhooks. Let's make the best of our short time and visit our families."

The prospect of another separation was cruel hard on Johnny's parents, Florence and Frank, and his sister Bimba, who could barely contain her grief.

"You will write, Johnny, you must. We live for your letters. We'll send packages and pray for you. We kneel and pray for you every night. Don't forget, Johnny dear."

Johnny was churned by this goodbye. His parents were aging and increasingly dependent, and already grieving over Henning. The time fleeted by, every moment poignant with presence. And then it was a last sharing with Beatrix, his staunch Beatrix and the little ones, his darling Jacky and Rod. It was heartrending moment when he took them in his arms, smelling them, and trying not to curdle them with the terrors in his heart. They had just minutes, torn with the sorrowful, sobbing bagpipes, unrelenting in their clotted sobs and cries for courage.

"I have to go, Doight. Got to go now. Be strong, be strong for me, and the children!"

She pushed him away for him to go, clutched him back for one more sob, and pushed him away and turned to the wall to hold together. He, at least, had his men to rally. He would array the poor men in the night, the ranks of raw young Scots, with the peat smoke in their clothes, tears stinging their eyes as they dressed their lines, steadying to the cruel separation with the route packs heavy on their shoulders, the snow piling on the sixty pound kits.

"By the right, column offours. Quick—HARCH!"

And the ranks obediently stamped, the pipers struck their bags, sounding *Kenmure's Up and Awa'* and the troops stepped out with a gradually lengthening stride swinging away to the transport. The pipers and the side-drummers alone marked a quick time, all else sensed doom, walking in the dark to a bad end.

"Let's have a treat. What would you like?"

"Oh! A cake, a cake!"

"A Nice Plain Cake for Children, or Common Cake, suitable for children, or Lardy Cake?"

The names rolled out of Mrs. Beeton's Cookery Book.

"Lardy cake, lardy cake! Lardy, lardy, good old lardy cake!"

No mistaking their choice. Mrs. Beeton's was pushed aside, she took out the hand written recipe from the Duke of Argyle's kitchen, from the bibulous Carlin, "Heather in Bloom", the washing up maid.

The Duke's Recipe for Lardy Cake
Take, for the dough:
eight ounces of flour
¾ gill of milk
½ ounce of yeast
1 teaspoon sugar
1 egg
and for the filling:
a pinch of salt
2 ounces of lard
2 ounces of sugar
2 ounces of currants
2 ounces raisins, or peel, or both
½ teaspoon of cinnamon and nutmeg.

The Method
Sift together flour and salt and leave in a warm place.

Beatrix

> *Cream the yeast with sugar, add the egg and warmed milk and mix with the flour to make a soft dough.*
> *"Leave in a warm place and when doubled in bulk roll out on a floured board. Now, divide the filling into two portions and spread one half on to two thirds of the dough then fold in three as for flaky pastry and roll out again. Spread the remainder of the filling, refold and roll out twice, finally shape to fit in an eight-inch cake tin. Allow to rise and bake in a hot oven for thirty to thirty five minutes.*

"Turn it over, Mudderkees, so the lard will seep through!" What could be a better way to liven the good-bye feeling?

The lardy cake recipe was mysterious and involved with its mixture of Scottish primitive and French patisserie. Beatrix enjoyed seeing her hands specked with lard, flour and pastry. She enjoyed the richness of the lard, its sensuous aroma and the way it softened her skin.

Jacky and Beatrix stuffed themselves with the lardy cake, little Rod looking on, sucking the coral and silver teether, a family heirloom. Was that the name and the fame of the family, a silver teether and a humble little cottage? What would it be if Johnny didn't return?

Beatrix felt alone and vulnerable. Now her mother and uncles had died, Vi and her husband, Wilson Nesbitt, were off to Australia and there seemed no chance of recouping the family fortunes, lost at gambling.

CHAPTER SIXTEEN

*Should auld acquaintance be forgot,
And never brought to min'?
Should auld acquaintance be forgot,
And days o' lang syne?
  We twa hae rin about the braes,
And pu'd the gowans fine;
But we've wander'd monie a weary fit
Sin' auld lang syne.
  We twa hae paidl't i' the burn,
Frae mornin' sun till dine;
But seas between us braid hae roar'd
Sin' auld lang syne.
  And here' a hand, my trusty fiere,
And gie's a hand o' thine;
And we'll tak a right guid-willie waught
For auld lang syne.
  And surely ye'll be your pint-stowp,
And surely I'll be mine;
And we'll tak a cup o' kindness yet
For auld lang syne!
  For auld lang syne, my dear,
For auld lang syne,
We'll tak a cup o' kindness yet
For auld lang syne.*

—Robert Burns, 1759 – 1796

Johnny survived the machine gun war despite the steady rain of slicing bullets, which dismembered any living thing in their path. He survived the thunking heavies, the big machine guns with half inch bullets which were marshaled to tear down the revetments, the temporary masonry built up to protect the lighter machine guns. He survived the pinpoints, six-pounders crossing their aiming points on his position, ready to blow the country to bits. He survived snipers and the trench warfare, creeping up and over after the barrage shells had chewed and churned the no man's land between English and German, driving the enemy underground.

Johnny wondered if there were any grenades left. He crept up onto the German ramparts, lobbing hand grenades into the trench, looked over the top to see what was left and found the opening into a dugout. The dugout was probably crawling with the rotters, ready to ambush from behind. They could be waiting around the corner of a passage, ready to cut them down as they came. Some one had to clean it out. Which soldier of the First Squad could he tell to go in, to risk being shot to pieces? Whose mother would he have to tell - her son was a dead hero on his orders?

Well here I go, terrified, the entry—clean, the next corner, now all at once, surprise them. Thank God—they are all dead, dead from our barrage. Thank God for the barrage!

For three years Johnny worked hard to keep himself alive, to keep his feet dry, to get deloused. Occasionally he had to send news to a widow, or talk to a dying soldier, duties that were well laid out. "This is your duty today!" The rules were clear. And then suddenly, when he had reached the rank of an Acting Major, he found he was to be demobbed in England. They did not give him back his King's Shilling, just his discharge. Beatrix and Jacky did not complain. Two-year-old Rod looked at his mother's strange companion with wondering eyes, and soon was happy with him.

As he grew up, Rod overheard others repeating tales of his father's war, but from his father he heard only the slogans: "Be sure to look neater and smarter than your troops, shave more often, keep your head down. Never light three cigarettes on a match. Learn to enjoy tea made with condensed milk."

Once out of the service, there was little routine for the demobbed Johnny. He thought of going into business and remembered spending nights in a dugout with Ollington talking cars and business. They pretended they had an agency and garage, called it *Carolus*. It was all talk, but it might solve a problem. He knew Ollington had a little money, to which he could add the bit saved from the sale of the market garden property. It might be possible to get a Woolsey agency.

It wouldn't be hard to look up Ollington through the Regiment.

"Doight, I'm going into business with Ollington, a friend from the trenches. A Tank Corps friend."

"You hadn't told me about it. What do you mean 'going into business'?

"You'll meet him soon. As I said, a man I've known for quite a while. I used to call him Reg in my letters."

"Reg, yes I remember, you talked about him. Reg sounds a bit...well, you know!"

"He has a bit of money to put in, and we have that bit from the property sale, and..."

"Oh Johnny, are you sure? There's so little money left. That's all we have."

"Ollington has lots of experience. He had a successful agency before the war."

"Well the family is in your hands, Johnny If it doesn't go, we're dished. The family can't advance any more money; they've had their reverses. Please be careful."

"The country seems to be on a bit of a rise. I think it's the right time. The returning troops need cars"

Carolus was born in 1920, two years after the armistice. The agency combined a garage work and coach building, the bespoke tailoring of individual car bodies on new frames from the manufacturers.

Johnny was enthralled by the business, asking customers which bodies and styles they wanted, sketching the ideas, watching the locksmith setting the locks, catches and hinges, and hanging the doors. He spent hours watching the body men beat out the curved body panels to mount on the ash framework, the painter laying on coat after coat by hand, flowing on the coatings with a fine brush, and smoothing them with glass paper, pumice and rottenstone for the French Polish finish. He knew their every gesture. Each trade had its gestures - paint men flowed their varnishes so smoothly, body men peened the panels, gradually perfecting the curve, laying a string on a bias to compare the curves. The stripers laid their fairing lines with the long striping brush, every long hair in place. The electro-plating crew polished the silver liners in the headlights to the peak of brilliance, not outdone by the polish on the nickel-plated fittings. He filed their gestures, their craft and their talk in his memory—it might come in handy some time.

The family moved to Anerly, a working class area of London near the Crystal Palace. They felt fortunate to find a place to lay their heads because beds were at premium in post-war London. They lived in an upstairs flat in the home of Mr. and Mrs. Jack Coulsen.

Beatrix now had full charge of the butter and eggs side of the family, or more accurately, the potato and margarine side of things. Johnny was fully involved with *Carolus*, which barely prospered. Johnny took sketches home and with his graceful thick celluloid French curves, created the fashion of the day for cars and caravans, supplying the new rage in the British Isles—camping. The children watched Johnny's drawings on paper, fascinated at how the lines grew, curved and finally joined into a refined picture. Rod wondered that his father's fingers had a genius of their own.

Carolus sold few cars. The workshop was only half occupied. Ollington took care of the books.

In the evenings after supper, Beatrix read to the children. She was teaching the three-year-old Rod to read simple words from the newspaper. When Beatrix took Rod to Johnny's office over the workshop, Rod loved to sit at the typewriter near the window where he could see the sign *Carolus*. He mimicked the letters onto a sheet of paper in the typewriter. The old upright clanked out *Carolus Woolsey, Custom Coach-building and Repairs.*

"Do you think it's a portent, Doight? He's never seen a typewriter before, and you've only just started him on easy reading."

"Don't be silly Johnny, he's just playing. He can't spell. I had to laugh the other day when he asked what 'fat –ti gueu' meant, meaning fatigue."

"I can understand that. I was a bad speller."

131

At home Rod played with the toys Johnny made and with the small Meccano set, which he felt never was big enough. He played with whatever was available—a blanket thrown over the laundry horse became a castle, a boat, or a steam engine.

On one long railroad trip Beatrix, against her better judgement, succumbed to Rod's entreaties and bought him an "Annual." Rod delighted in the comic strip, *Marzi Pan and his Friends*, which bulged with escapades of urchins who exploded fire–crackers in the Station Master's pockets and hid from the hue and cry in empty milk churns. Beatrix laboured through repeated requests to read from the Annual and had, nightly, to do an incantation called *Marzi–ing*, a ritual waving of hands over Rod's body, to magic him to sleep.

Johnny's voice echoed up the staircase, "Doight, come down and see what I've borrowed! I have a little sports model to give you a ride in, perhaps over to the Crystal Palace and back. Hop in!"

The nameplates were not yet fixed on, but Beatrix scrambled in, as there were no doors, just deep dips in the side panel to climb over. The smart green paint with a very narrow stripe read *British Racing Green* to the world. The engine hood panels were held in place by leather straps with luggage buckles.

Johnny took a handle from the tonneau, swung the little engine, and got in. Beatrix hung on as he swept in a tight curve across the road. This was a rare treat for Beatrix, and soon afterwards Johnny had to return the little racer to the owner. It was a last gasp for *Carolus*, which had diminished and diminished, with nothing remaining. Reg joined the shadows, and the money was gone.

Now Beatrix walked to the shops, Rod by her side, holding her hand, the other holding the wicker shopping basket. One day they came home to find that their peculiar landlord, Mr. Coulsen, had cut the staircase leading to the Pain flat free from the wall and dragged it into the hall.

"Mrs. Coulsen, what's happened to the stairs?"

"Oh, Mr. Coulsen is repairing them. You can use the back stairs."

"I don't like the back stairs. They are narrow, steep and dangerous for Roddy. Please get the front stairs back in use!"

"Oh, don't come the high and mighty over me, Mrs. Pain. You know how hard it is to get lodgings, especially as nice as mine."

"Well, do try to get them repaired. I don't know just what Mr. Pain will say when he comes home."

"What can he say, Mrs. Pain?"

Beatrix was no match for a Cockney landlady on her own ground. When Roddy scratched the thick brown varnish on a wardrobe, testing out a hatpin, Beatrix hid the damage from the fearsome Mrs. Coulsen until Johnny repaired the scratch with brown shoe polish.

Beatrix had her hands full - setting up house for Johnny, learning to be a mother, first with Jacky and then, in wartime, with Roddy who was the bane of landladies. She took strength from Bairnsfather's famous war cartoon of two filthy, whiskered, lousy British foot-soldiers crouched in a shell hole, half filled with water.

"If you know a better hole, move to it."

The Coulsens were Beatrix's shell hole, and it was a poor makeshift of a home. In the back garden, walled around with brick, planted with grass and bushes, Beatrix had gathered a small bonfire of refuse. Rod often played there, and found a curved bit of brass pipe broken from a brass bedstead. It tasted nasty, but a wood screw from the ground fitted nicely in the inner channel of the tube, and by blowing and sucking on the pipe he made it slide back and forth, making a lovely slipping noise, back and forth.

"Oh Mother! I've swallowed a screw!"

"What do you mean you've swallowed a screw, show it to me! Where is it?"

"I swallowed it. Can't you see? I swallowed it, by accident, from my brass tube! What'll I do?"

"Are you sure you're not making this up?"

"Oh Mother, what'll I do? Will I die?"

Beatrix rushed Rod to the nearest hospital, where after a long wait sitting on wooden pew-benches, they were called into the X-ray room, dark as a cloak room, with electric power wires hanging from strings to the ceiling, connecting the naked X-ray tube. Their early encounter with Roentgen equipment seemed medieval.

"Go home, it will be all right — and eat lots of potatoes!"

All went well. Beatrix disposed of the brass tube.

Without *Carolus*, Anerly had no meaning. Housing was desperately hard to find because during the war years few houses had been built, and the young returning soldiers, rather than going home to their parents, looked for homes for their postponed families.

CHAPTER SEVENTEEN

When I consider how my light is spent,
E're half my days, in this dark world and wide,
And that one Talent which is death to hide,
Lodged with me useless, though my Soul more bent
To serve therewith my Maker, and present
My true account, least he returning chide,
Doth God exact day–labour, light deny'd,
I fondly ask; but patience to prevent
That murmur, soon replies, God doth not need
Either man's work or his own gifts, who best
Bear his milde yoak, they serve him best, his State
Is Kingly. Thousands at his bidding speed
And post o'er Land and Ocean without rest:
They also serve who only stand and waite.

—John Milton, 1608 – 1674, *On His Blindness*

When Kitty Barry heard that the Pain family could not find affordable housing, she introduced Beatrix to Alice Russin, a dressmaker to Queen Mary, who owned a row of cottages built in the late eighteen hundreds for railway men working on the Great Western Railway near Maidenhead, Surrey. The workmen, or navvys as they were called, were labourers working on the early construction. The six attached cottages were on a short lane called Ye Meads.

"Beggars can't be choosers, Doight. This cottage is better than Anerly and Bovington, neither of those have been good. Now we have children we can't share with relatives."

"Johnny, it's two up and two down—thousands of miners and mill workers have this for life, however many children, sometimes with an old granny!"

"How many will we be, Doight? Not any room for any more, not enough room for what we have."

"Don't be silly, Johnny. Our youth was spent in mansions, when there was money to do it. Now we have precious little money and these small digs will fit the budget. We'll be better off than in Anerly."

'Number 4 Ye Meads' was to be home for the family for eight years, and Beatrix and Johnny determined to make the best of it.

Soon the pantechnicon, a huge van pulled by two dray horses, arrived, the rear ramp was let down and their furniture carried out. The big round rosewood dining room table that Johnny had sat at for as long as he could remember became the centre, in the kitchen. The wooden settle welcomed another generation to a hard seat in the living room The Oar, a treasure from some ancient Henley regatta, was cut short to fit on a wall. General Brazil's sword, gift of Aunt Fannie, hung next to the print of the General. The cottage was soon full. The parlour was only sixteen feet wide, as was the kitchen, the one upstairs bedroom and both the gardens. The second bedroom was narrower, with access through the front bedroom. The W.C. was in the house but the door was on an outside path and wall. On a stormy night it was an adventure to just slip out of the kitchen and walk down the garden path to the toilet. The bathtub was stored under the hinged kitchen table. When it was time for a bath, the tabletop was pushed aside. To save on hot water, the family used a hip bath set in front of the big black iron range filled with water heated in three saucepans. It was one bath a week, winter and summer, with minor washings in between in a tin basin.

Beatrix's life was now the life of a country wife. She was up at six to cook breakfast for Johnny, who then left for Taplow Station and London, bowler hat and tightly rolled umbrella. At the station, the slip coach waited on the siding until the commuters were aboard, and then it started with a jolt, caught by the London express and whisked away to London in thirty minutes. On foggy days, the engine driver leaned out of his side window, listening to the fog signals popping under his bogie wheels, signaling a clear line; two pops, slow down for Esher Station, three pops and a single, brakes on, ready to hook on the next slip coach, and off, full speed.

Johnny, who still had cars in his blood, hired on as a salesman in another Woolsey showroom. A quiet man, easy for gentle companionship as Beatrix had early discovered, he was friendly but not keen for busy city associations. His approach was to present a case or sale on its merits, without reliance on personal charm or cleverness.

At home Beatrix was feeling the pressure.

"I really need a bicycle, Johnny. The little shop round the corner is not adequate—they have no vegetables, fish, meat or butter. I can get tea, sugar and flour at a price, but I need to go the four miles into Maidenhead to shop properly. It's too far to walk."

"Really a pity I don't have the motor–bike any more, you'd do fine on it!"

"Really Johnny, I'm serious. I need a push bike to get

137

to Maidenhead."

"I'll get you one, soon, Doight, and fit a nice basket to the handle–bars and a seat on the back for Rod."

"I think I'll get a neighbour to take care of Rod at first, until I get my cycling skills up. After all, there is a great deal of traffic on the Bath Road."

In a county laced with saffron coloured gravel lanes, often rutted and puddled, the London to Bath Road was considered special—McAdam topped, tarred and crowned, drained and trafficked. Where it crossed the Thames into Maidenhead, traffic was carried by a magnificent masonry bridge, a bridge that had carried generations of foot traffic, riders, iron–tyred vehicles, and latterly motor vehicles along the route of an ancient Roman road.

"Oh, there are lots of spots I want to ride, or walk to—Bray, Taplow Village, Coockham. With a bike we can get around nicely."

"I am happy that you're getting to like it here—I was worried that we might be repeating the War thing, satisfied as best we could be, getting just what we could, and lumping it."

"For me, this countryside makes all the difference. One couldn't ask for a prettier place. Even the little station is pretty, and the old brick arch for the railway over the Bath Road is picturesque. The village is what it should be, with the old cottages. And Ye Meads is regular Turner, or Gainsborough.

"You'd have enjoyed the walk I took yesterday, to Bray Lock with the children. We turned left at the Ye Meads notice board and walked for ten minutes down an avenue of hollow elms. Then across some fields, no stiles, just a lane, and into the trees, and there you are. The lock keeper's cottage is on an island holding the lock and weir, just half an hour's walk."

"How about a cup of tea? I'm thirsty with this digging. With a little garden like this I'll have it cultivated in a day!"

Beatrix brought out the tea and a bowl of marmalade tarts to the minuscule patch of grass in the back garden. She could make pastry with sweet flakes that crumbled into joy in your mouth, but she could never teach her skill to anyone else.

~~~~~~

Fate, with its feet in history and its hands in the future, again grasped Johnny.

"I hate to think of it, labour is going to strike, you'll see, and it will be horrible. If there is a general strike, what will I do? They probably will put out the call for the Officer Corps, all of us who were commissioned before we were demobbed, and ask us to scab. I don't like it."

"I don't like the idea, either. It assumes that all the officers are willing to support the establishment against the labourers. Since father died, my life has been involved with socialism and labour, the Webbs and Shaw, and Kier Hardy and Lloyd George. It won't go down well with me if you have to scab. But I'm sure that the government will put it to you as a patriotic necessity to ensure essential amenities, such as newspapers, railroads, and dairies. It would be difficult to deny milk to babies."

"I couldn't deny milk to babies, if they put that to me."

So fate called Johnny to *substitute duty on essential service*. He was called to fuel one of the locomotives on the Great Western lines, and admitted to himself, he did enjoy being a stoker on the engine for a few days, feeling almost like an engine driver.

The equipment in Beatrix' kitchen made cooking a challenge. The kitchen had an old coal range, with a side oven, built into the sidewall. When quick heat was needed, Beatrix lit the paraffin-cooking lamp with four blue chimneys with oblong lamp wicks, which needed frequent trimming. Each chimney had a grid on top, used to heat a small kettle quickly, the oil from the reservoir burning hot up the chimney. Beatrix used that oil lamp to cook meals, mostly stews and braised dishes, so dear to the English. Beef, pork, lamb and fowl were as likely to be stewed as not, and fish too. The country folk of Britain had used their native iron to make cauldrons and had cooked over open fires since before the Romans, a cuisine that made tender and seasoned boiled table meat standard. Roasting was for the upper classes, and rarely for less fortunate, who had to take a roast or bird to be roasted in the baker's oven.

"Johnny, turbot for supper!"

"What a treat—you told me how your father served it. I'll try to do it like him."

Johnny's family admired fancy carvers.

"I made a simple parsley sauce to go with it, with flowery potatoes and some peas. You know with this little kitchen it is hard to make fancy things. But then, we only have oil lamps, so nobody can really be critical. I've become used to the oil lamps for lighting too. The gas lamps were brighter, but they smelt and were a bit of trouble to keep clean. I can keep these lamp chimneys polished clean with newspaper.

"Johnny, I'm happier here than I've been anywhere for

years. Though the house is crowded and barebones, we can stay here. Nobody cares if the children make a bit of noise, they can play out of doors, and we are in the country. I can get all the books I want from the Boots Lending. You seem happier, too."

"It would be better if I could find a success, you know, Doight. I want to have better for you all, but I feel dogged. Yes, dogged."

"Oh don't despair. I'm proud of what you've done with so little. I wouldn't have it differently though things are touchy. We'll manage together. This place has few expenses, the children are happy, Jacky is doing well, Rod loves the place, he's explored it already."

Beatrix began to find skills and strengths she didn't realize she had. She felt that if they stayed in Maidenhead, they would be able, with the support of their families, to gradually get ahead. Beatrix took hold of her life with both hands, the debutante hands with nails once polished with a silver handled chamois were now hands roughened and reddened, needing a rub with the rare used lemon rind, to bleach them.

Rod watched, and could not understand why she wanted to whiten her hands. He was reading *Kim* and asked his mother to explain parts he didn't understand.

"Mudderkees, what does 'pukka' mean?"

"That was a word your grandfather used. It meant being correct, certain, reliable and looking it. In India, especially among troops, a certain air helped keep things going well. Anybody in charge was expected to look the part, his clothing was supposed to be neat, his boots polished. If you didn't look the part you might not be reliable."

"Is that why 'pukka' is so important in Kim?"

"You'll understand as it comes up!"

Word came that Arthur and Pooge, Johnny's sister and

her husband, planned to visit. The visit involved an unprecedented forty-mile journey in Arthur's Singer. Letters came and went, and Beatrix planned the day.

"This is the first visit from your family, Johnny. None of them has been to Number Four. How did your sister get that name "Pooge?"

"The same place we got Mudderkees and Nacko, I suppose."

"Pooge and Frank sided with your mother in the beginning, saying I was a silly spoiled sprat from city life who couldn't run a house—only good for balls and the peerage—couldn't raise a child. Now I realize that Pooge and Arthur are fairly without side. They've been fair, a nice couple. They said they would leave their Peter and Marjorie at home to make it easier for us.

"I must check in *Mrs. Beeton's* for clues. Here it is, Johnny,

The lower classes lunch between 10 and 11, the upper, three or four hours later, but in one thing both rich and poor alike agree, that it should be the most informal of all meals. Luncheon dishes vary according to means, station and family.

"Well, that makes it easy—I could buy a tongue and boil it the day before."

Pooge carried good cheer wherever she went. Arthur was an innovator, senior engineer for the Southern Command of the army. He had put little lights on bandsmen's music for the nighttime tattoos, and invented other innovations. He had a special spot for his nephew, Rod, who was fascinated by his archaeological knowledge.

"See that hump over there, Rod, the one with the four trees on the top? That's a tumulus, and when this country was all wooded and impenetrable, one walked from tumulus to tumulus, using the trees as a direction marker."

Rod in turn showed his uncle the unusual boulder by the lane. Boulders were rare in the clay plain of the Thames Valley.

"See this mark, Uncle, just stay and I'll get a kettle of water to pour on it and you will see that somebody cut it!"

"Sorry, Rod, that's not a Paleolithic. It's as old as the world, but the Picts and Scots, or Stone Age men didn't mark it. Let's go in for lunch!"

Beatrix started tentatively, "Pooge, how are Marjorie and Peter?"

"Peter is still at home with us, Marjorie is taking a course in the new style of pianism. In the old school they train you by balancing a tumbler of water on your wrist while you play. Now it's very fluid, they have stopped the tumblers, and the sound is better."

"Tumblers sound like the water cure to me, Pooge."

Lunch was watercress sandwiches, boiled tongue, hard-boiled eggs and a berry pie. Later, they sat on the little patch of grass behind the house.

"How does the little Singer go, Arthur?"

"Very well, Johnny, even on all those hills."

"I understand some of them are a pig to start. Sometimes a little squirt of petrol into the carburetor helps."

"Oh, I know! I installed a wire through the radiator coil so I can tweak it a bit when I'm swinging it."

When they were ready to return home, Pooge tied a heavy white veil over her head to secure her hat in the open car, and Arthur put on his leather motoring coat. He poised himself at the front of the Singer, crank in hand, and reached for the wire loop he had installed through the radiator coils to choke the carburetor. He swung the motor over and it caught. Hurrying back, red faced, carrying the starting crank, he climbed in and they set off with dust from the gravel road swirling round them.

"Johnny, I like the Maynes. They are interesting, friendly, and they like plain cooking."

"Yes, though Arthur is a prominent electrical engineer they have no side. I think he regrets that I left Siemens. Sometimes I do, too. Nice people. Pooge helped Bimba raise me. They know me inside and out, all my exploits and peccadilloes. Arthur is wonderful for advice. I remember riding my bike carrying a red flag in front of him as he tried out some new car."

"I hope we see a lot more of them—they seem to like Rod and Jacky, and it's close enough—almost near enough to make the journey on a bicycle."

"I've done it, and there are lots of hills. It would be a two-day stint, without the children. We'd have to take the train."

"Did you think we did all right with them? It was the first time any of your family visited us."

"Of course, Doight. Your lunch was very nice."

It was faint praise, but Johnny was no orator.

After two more trips to Taplow, Beatrix got her bicycle, and visits to the little shop around the corner were only for immediate shortages. There sugar was served from a barrel, doled out from a tin scoop onto a square of brown paper, weighed in place, and wrapped into a cone, the pointy tip only needing someone to screw it tight. That went into the shopping basket, or the string bag, a convenience, which was becoming popular with the gentry, although still considered by many to be common.

Not long after their visit, the Maynes wrote to Beatrix thanking her for the lovely day and saying how happy they were that she had joined the family. In thinking about the Maynes, Beatrix realized that she was gradually taking on a role in the family, which she had not expected to have to do. Her generation of women did not ordinarily choose roles, but the war, travel, and experiences had toughened her, and the vows she pledged in her marriage with John she now saw from a different perspective. There was the conventional companionship expected of a post-Victorian wife for her husband, of pleasure, of passion, satisfying the conventions, but not of being a partner in what were considered to be men's affairs - the job, the address, and children's schooling. But hard realities, unexpected difficulties, great differences from the world of her growing up, were defining the words of her marriage ceremony in unexpected ways. She felt Johnny should not be forced to bear alone the planning of family affairs. They would share the planning now, the successes and the failures.

Beatrix felt a new message under her belt.

"I recognize the symptoms, Johnny. I know I'm with child again."

The Anglo Saxon mode suited her in these country days in a country life.

"High Apron! Doight, I've been suspecting it!"

There were soon to be five Pains facing the unpredictable world.

The months slipped by for Rod, who had a new playmate, Pamela Weatherstone-Smith. She was the daughter of Doris, Beatrix's nursing friend from the War, who wanted a little respite and left her with Beatrix. Pamela became Rod's bosom friend, almost sister. Their world was the two miles that circled Number Four, up and down the fields and roads and into the hollow elms. The little marsh at the end of Ye Meads was their Eden, with fairy grottoes. Here they chanted to each other *Midsummer Night's Dream*, living out tags of Rackham's pictures, "Fairies away, we shall chide downright, if I longer stay!" or, "Let me play the Lion, too."

In July 1922, as Beatrix approached her confinement, Rodney and Pamela went to stay with Doris at Llewingrwl, a hamlet on the west coast of Wales.

On July 31, the local doctor ushered David Holland Rose Pain to the world of Ye Meads, Taplow. Johnny bought a bundle of nice "deals", and shaped a low chair the right height for breast–feeding, painted it Russian Leather green, with many coats rubbed to unbelievable smoothness. The chair was decorated with details of the cartouches from the newly discovered King Tut's tomb.

As Beatrix expected, Rodney didn't have a passive reaction to David, who contended for her daytime attention, *his* time.

Johnny enjoyed the new child in the family, and made another bed in the little annex room off the bedroom.

The day Jacky came home from school, the house was tighter yet. She was full of tales from school.

"The games we play! Our gymnasium is an old tithe barn mentioned in the Domesday Book. On wet days we play basketball there. We have a lovely meadow for a hockey ground, and I'm the best at hockey."

As she volleyed on, scattering her joys as she wound her way through high tea, her mother wondered at her daughter. She was so free, so physically free. Beatrix herself had always been hindered by social mores, the restraints of birth, convention, money and its results, and now the restraints of poverty. Beatrix envied Jacky's Peter

Pan vision of herself.

"Calm down Ja. You've got weeks to tell it all to us."

"You see, Mudderkees, Miss Clark knows so much, she qualified for the tripos, what ever that is. She tells us how math and geometry really work. We hardly need to use the math book. Clarkie teaches us right from memory."

Jacky told stories of her hardships and triumphs at Fernhill Manor School on the edge of the New Forest. Her stories of gypsies in the New Forest gave new life to *Children of the New Forest*, a favourite book Beatrix had read to the children.

"We made friends with a family, the Mackenzies, who were going by in their caravan. They called themselves 'travellers' and told us never to call them 'gypsies' or 'tinkers'. They showed us how to make baskets from twigs, and how to eat eggs without breaking or cooking them. They knew so much, and seemed happy, but they couldn't read or write, or do arithmetic. But they did make change, counting 'Lethera, Pethera' and then using other numbers that they used to count sheep with, in sixes and twelves. I wanted to run off with them, but they had gone by morning. They had buried all their bits and pieces, and left nothing to show where they had been!

"They spoke in something called cant, which we could not understand. And when they made tea, they used a can over a fire, hanging from a hook on a branch. If they didn't have regular tea, they gathered leaves and made tea from local plants. If we had any clothes that were torn or too tight, they wanted to have them. They had a nice horse and took good care of it. I liked them a lot."

"What was the caravan like?"

"It was all wood with four wheels and shafts, and a little door in the back, with let–down. It had a roof somewhat like a cottage, which kept the windows on the sides dry. And most splendid of all, it was painted bright green all over and decorated to look like the circus. Oh! It was splendid, except for the chickens. They were tied by a cord around their feet and hung upside down under the caravan, swinging with buckets and bundles of twigs."

Jacky rushed on, "And Clarkie and Miss MacNamara, they both stay together in their wing. They're great friends. One of the girls, who had to take a message to them on a Sunday morning, saw them sleeping together in a double bed."

This rather peculiar information did not evoke any response from Beatrix, innocent of seeing any impropriety. She remembered the nuns at Wantage slept alone.

"Clarky leads us at games, most of the times. Macky, that's Miss MacNamara, does the grammar and literature. We see them both everyday, and at meals.

"You've grown and put on weight, so there must be something going well at meal times. Your clothes must be tight—I hope you didn't give them all to the gypsies, or travellers."

"Oh! I'm not so fat—I play games and get very hungry, particularly after the rhythm dancing class that I like. Do you think dancing is something people can do for a living?"

"Oh yes, of course they do. Tomorrow let's go for a walk with Rod, and we can talk then. We can have a nice walk up to Taplow, or better, over towards the Thames. The King's there at Windsor castle. I could see his standard flying on the Round Tower."

The clicking of the front garden iron gate set Jacky off in a rush to meet her father, wreathing him with hugs, kisses, and a breathless: "Oh Nacko! It's so wonderful to have you. I've missed you so. Nothing is quite right without you, Nacko."

She finally let him pick up his umbrella and attaché case. Beatrix greeted him and served tea on the diminutive front lawn, the one that she clipped regularly with hand shears.

"Well Ja, how is it at Fernhill Manor?"

Jacky repeated her news, and Nacko nodded silently, sucking on his pipe, knocking it out against his heel before putting it in his side pocket.

"Those gypsy fellows, I mean travellers, I saw a lot of them at Frimley as a boy. We had a special place where they could light fires, get firewood and graze their horses. Henning and I spent time with them. They loved eating game, so we always had rabbits for them, and the occasional bird when we could spare it. They weren't strong on guns the way we were; they just collected their food."

"Do you think they were too peaceable for guns, Nacko?"

"Well, I never knew one of them to go hunting, even in pheasant country like ours. A fellow with a gun stands out like a bar of soap in a coalscuttle if he's on private land. They would rather put a secret snare and perhaps send a woman to get the rabbit, and tuck it into her pocket. Their women wear long colourful gypsy skirts, with a big apron over it. They have a big pouch, like a cow's udder, but bigger, deeper, that they hang on a belt round their waist, very colourful and bright design, worn under the apron and outside their long skirt. They could slip a goose into it and it would blend with their shape."

"Has that to do with the way people say they steal?"

"Yes, but I've never known one to steal. They sell things they make, such as clothes pegs and baskets, and mend holes in pots and pans."

"I saw a traveller with something of a push cart in Christchurch, an odd cart that he pushed around one way and then set up on its hind legs another way. The traveller sat on it and turned a wheel and ground knives."

"I know, Doight, most of those men are gypsies, and they go on a round of households about twice a year and sharpen all the knives and scissors. It looks like a nice way to make a living, except in cold and rainy weather. I always loved the slithery noise of the grinding wheel as they sharpened knives."

"They called their horse Garron, but they call all horses by the same name, Garron. It's as if everybody called their cats, Fluffy."

"Garron means horse to them. They probably had a special name for it like Jumper or Brownie that they kept a secret. Their animals are trained to be biddable; that is, they'll either come on command or hide when ordered. They are funny people, keep themselves secret but live in public. They need a secret language."

Rod interrupted. "Mudderkees is going to read a *Just So* story to Ja and me. Let's go in and listen."

Beatrix picked up the thin volume bound in soft, embossed leather and turned the pages, scanning the poems between the stories. She had naturally rhythmic speech and loved to read poetry. Rod craned his head to see the pictures.

"I've changed my mind and picked a story that Rod hasn't heard yet, not a jungle story, but a *Northern Ice* story, about the Esquimeau..."

"What's the Esquimeau, Mudderkees?"

"That's the name of the people that live near the North Pole. The story is called *Quiquern* and this is the

poem about them.
> The People of the Eastern Ice, they are melting like the snow.
> They beg for coffee and sugar; they go where the white men go.
> The People of the Western Ice, they learn to steal and fight;
> They sell their furs to the trading-post: they sell their souls to the white.
> The people of the Southern Ice, they trade with the whaler's crew;
> Their women have many ribbons, but their tents are torn and few.
> But the People of the Elder Ice, beyond the white man's ken—
> Their spears are made of narwhal horn, and they are the last of the Men!"

"What are they talking about, Mudderkees, the different directions of Eastern Ice and Elder Ice?"

"I suppose Kipling was writing about different tribes of Esquimeau, who lived in northern Canada, and had made poor arrangements with the white men when they first met. The oldest tribe was true to its traditions and had not made troubles for itself. They did things the Esquimeau way and made their tools the old way, and did not get spoiled with the white men's ways."

"Why was the white man's way no good?"

"It wasn't bad, but it was often bad for the Esquimeau, because it didn't fit their way of living. For example, the sweets the white man brought north made the children's teeth decay, and their clothing was not adequate in the cold weather."

"Go on Mudderkees, I want to hear about Quiquern."

Jacky was impatient with Rod's questions.

"All right Ja, I need to know what the poem means,

and I don't think you understood it either."
Beatrix held up her hand and started.

"He has opened his eyes. Look!
Put him in the skin again. He will be a strong dog.
On the Fourth Month we will name him..."

The children were entranced, living the story as it reeled out, one picture at a time, episode by episode. Johnny sat quietly, drawing on his pipe, watching with pleasure. His Ja was back. His Beatrix was doing what he loved, sitting in front of the fire reading to the children. Beatrix kept on, enjoying the Kipling imagery, and somehow felt James Innes was there, near to her, nodding and stroking his beard. She came to the end of the long story, closed the book gently, and said, "Bed time," There was no argument.

Saturday, Johnny was home. The weather was nice and after lunch Beatrix made up a picnic. She had written to Lord Desborough for permission to picnic on his land.

Your Lordship,

We are downstream neighbours who live in Taplow. Last month in passing along the Thames in our punt we noticed a lovely lea among the riverbank trees at the foot of your estate, and wondered if we might picnic there this next July seventeenth.

My sister, Mrs. Henry Dumas, was your guest and took an award–winning photograph on that spot, and I would like to revisit it. I appreciate your consideration.

Yours most sincerely,

Beatrix Pain

Lord Desborough's social secretary replied, and carrying the note and a picnic, the family rode the two miles to Maidenhead and Skindles, crossing Brunel's bridge, two soaring spans of flat-arched bricks. They debated which was the most famous, Brunell or Skindles. Brunel's bridge had lasted longer, but the Skindles gave more joy.

Johnny chose one of the punts, and the waterman wiped down the varnish, capturing the small pool of water in the flat floor with a short-handled mop that he spun dry over the gunwale. As the mop spun between his palms, the water made a dazzling wheel in the sunlight.

With his family settled in the punt, Johnny punted the light craft upstream, throwing the pole forward, rhythmically pushing on the hard bottom. At a small island, they found the lea and, hidden behind the island, they put the picnic ashore and left to tie the punt.

"Punting is fun, better than canoeing," said Rod who had been reading *The Wind in the Willows* and was given to sententiousness, not missed by Jacky who said,

"Stop being such an ass, Rod, we all know you are just quoting *The Wind in the Willows*. We know you are either Toad or Ratty, take your pick, I choose Toad."

Beatrix had Rod unpack the picnic to keep him from his favourite occupation, finding a target in Jacky's personality that he could prick, or otherwise divert himself with. Jacky did the same.

"Bath Olivers! Oh Mudderkees, did you know how much I've missed them? Mustard and cress sandwiches and hard-boiled eggs. What a wonderful treat!"

Meanwhile, Rod was checking a slender book Beatrix had brought.

"Mudderkees, will you read to us? I'd like a long story,

about India and animals."

"We haven't read the *Miracle of Purun Bhagat*, for a long time. It's about the India of Indias and about animals and Purun Bhagat. Bhagat who was a very educated man who spent his young and middle life providing for people in his care, a very high official with duties and great responsibilities. Although he could have continued being a father to his people, he gave up quit all the gold and silver, the parades, the fancy food and gorgeous clothes and took up the life of being a simple holy man. He always reminds me of your grandfather. My father didn't become a holy man, but he did do most of the other things Purun Bhagat did. Father also liked horses, but he killed birds, pigs and tigers. He became a friend of books."

"But you are a friend of animals and of books too."

"They both please me. There's a swan with her cygnets, and here comes a man."

"How do you do, Sir. Did you know this was private land? Nobody is to tie up here."

"Oh Keeper, of course, and we have permission from Lord Desborough's secretary. Here is the letter."

"Oh yes, I was expecting you. Everything is fine. Good day."

He disappeared with his dog and shotgun, his leather gaiters shining in the sun, whistling as he climbed the bank.

"What was he whistling, Johnny?"

"Oh—Cherry Ripe or some such country tune. I forget; I used to know them all."

"Whistle me a tune Johnny."

Beatrix knew that Johnny did not move easily into self-expression on demand, but the request was so ingenuous that he tried. He was privately proud of his whistling.

"What was that tune? I've not heard it before."

"It was *The Whistler and His Dog* by some popular orchestra leader, I think."

"You are a very special whistler, Johnny."

"Double whistle, for us Nacko. Double whistle—please."

Johnny double whistled *Pop goes the Weasel*. When the sandwiches were eaten and the children tired of trying to whistle, they went skirmishing into Lord Astor's woods and Johnny and Beatrix could talk between themselves.

"The way things are going, your father and mother must be quite upset, Johnny. They are really rooted in the old way of things. And this is no time for backward looking conservatism."

"You're quite right, it's no time for old thinking. The war put an end to that—now women are in factories, driving lorries, tram-cars, motorcycles. This was all a mystery for my parents. They are unable to understand the changes."

"I think the Webbs saw a little farther into a stone wall than others. They defined poverty and what poverty is when you yourself are on the verge of it. Times are ruthless when you are short of money or opportunities."

"You're right, but you know that all that political skirmishing, what with the liberals not getting in, despite their big vote, we just haven't done well! There seems to be nobody speaking for us."

A call floated down from the woods.

Beatrix and Johnny scrambled up the bank and found the children high in the branches of a beech tree.

"Come down and we'll hunt around to see what we can see on Lord Desborough's land. Old Lord Desborough won't mind. We do have a letter in case a keeper stops us."

They turned up the riverbank, and Nacko noticed that the trees were much larger.

"Before the Navy was made of steel, the government encouraged beech and oak growing to provide wood for shipbuilding. Some of these oaks and beeches are hundreds of years old—naval trees. Men would come and cut off crooked branches and take them back to Portsmouth to make ship's ribs, and leave the trunk the way it was to grow more branches. Then they'd come and take the trunk as well, if they were building a lot of ships."

"Wars were not fun for most people. Of course, it depended on which side you were. You children remember that in *Kidnapped*, David Balfour was on the same side as Alan Breck Stuart and the both of them only just scratched by, running through the heather, and generally in danger of being killed. That gives you an idea, that wars of religion are usually terrible. The idea that you should have the right religion or be killed is terrible."

Johnny broke in. "All right all of you. Let's get on board and punt upriver a bit, and see if we can get to Staines before we go back to Skindles."

"If we get to Staines in time could we have tea in a teashop, and a bun?" Rod reliably could be heard speaking for food.

"I think so. Let's try."

The little teashop in Staines was a rare treat.

That night, after the children were in bed, Beatrix and Johnny resumed their talk of politics and national affairs.

"There is a disconcerting thing that I have only just begun to recognize," began Beatrix, "The whole change in the world has meant a startling change to me. When I was a girl in my father's house I looked on him, and myself, in a special way—what we thought of ourselves, who we were, and what we thought about others, what we thought they were."

Johnny broke in. "I've had some of those thoughts myself, Doight, the war, and the changes, and our failures, are not very encouraging influences."

"We seem to be different people now, Johnny, with different views and different possibilities. And we see others differently now. For instance, we are a lot closer to being poor than our parents at our age.

"Of course, there is always the option of going to the colonies, the last chance for what our parents might have called failures."

"Well one might argue over failures, but we certainly have not been lucky—in those days there seemed to be almost unlimited luck for well off people to get ahead."

Beatrix was thinking of how she had stretched Rod's best clothes for almost two years, to outfit him for family gatherings – an Eton collar on a white shirt and an Eton jacket were expected.

"Being well to do can be a problem, when one has to bring up children to live up to expected standards—but with very limited means, given the shortage of money and family influence. Dolly and Henry have been such bricks but we can't go on just taking from them, with no way to repay."

"England was different before the war, Doight. The working class was in our pocket. They voted like us, and had little to say. In fact, I never had heard of them for most of my childhood. Our family didn't follow the plays in London and had not heard of Shaw. We were very protected. But, like you, we had an attitude about ourselves, a sort of 1890 attitude, which gradually changed.

And the attitude towards the 'lower orders', that changed faster because of the war, and now here we are, considering becoming lower orders ourselves."

Beatrix's experiences at Dolly and Henry's had opened mind her to radical ideas not discussed at her father's table.

"Fabian policy was a huge check on the Socialists, who were split between the revolutionary and the peaceful branches." Beatrix continued.

"Amazing how docile the working man has been."

"Yes, and the Liberal Party was a bit of a spoiler."

"The power shilly-shallied between the unions, the radical Socialists and the Liberals. This was the real union to make up the Labour Party."

"But then it would make no sense for you and me to look for a solution with Labour—Labour would never recognize me as a working man, and frankly, at their wage scale, we'd have a hard time to make a go of it. We just don't know how to survive as working people, quite aside from matters of class. We are dropping down, without a safety line." Johnny's attempt to get a job as a labourer at a nearby building site had surprised Beatrix.

"What was that you told me the other day? That you had asked for work at a house under construction and the superintendent told you, 'We don't 're no toffs 're!' What did they mean *toffs?*"

"Toffs, that's an old class term, short for *toffeeheads*, not nice. I certainly didn't like being called a toff when all I was doing was asking for work."

"I suppose the workers were protecting their prerogative, to do the manual work. It would not seem right to labourer to have to share your job with a toff. At the same time, I can see how it must have upset you. What can we do?"

Johnny chewed on the inner skin of his cheek, a sign of his concentrating.

"What about the colonies? The old family solution where there's the opportunity to become a workingman and there are lots of opportunities. England is dead, or almost dead. The well–off few are keeping it to themselves, making the working class work as they haven't worked before but with less respect. Maybe the colonies show a better present and a better future."

"Get the candle, Johnny, let's go upstairs."

CHAPTER EIGHTEEN

How dear to my heart are the scenes of my childhood
When fond recollection presents them to view!
The orchard, the meadow, the deep–tangled wild–wood,
And every loved spot which my fancy knew!
The wide–spreading pond, and the mill that stood by it,
The bridge, and the rock where the cataract fell,
The cot of my father, the dairy–house nigh it,
And e'en the rude bucket, the iron–bound bucket,
The mossed–covered bucket which hung in the well.

—Samuel Woodworth, 1815 – 1842

Luxury was no longer available to Johnny and Beatrix. The "lowly others" were not so distant from them now. Horse, carriage, coachman and cook were not there any more to insulate Beatrix from the reality of daily chores. The Grange in Frimley with its twenty bedrooms and hand–pumped water was not there to insulate Johnny from realizing the sacrifice of the young serving man who saved his life in the trenches. Beatrix and Johnny were developing a different sense of themselves and of others, they were closer to the soil, and nearer to being labourers of the soil.

Johnny realized he wanted to work with his hands; he liked to see physical results, and Beatrix saw her challenge as holding the heart of the family together, keeping Johnny healthy and happy. There seemed no way out, except that they take care of themselves. The system would not do much for them.

Britain could not or would not do for them, so they considered going abroad. America was so far away. It promised adventure and, for many who had not made a go of it, a haven the promise of a new start. Canada loomed large as a land of opportunity for the adventurous, for those who were in danger of prosecution, for the disinherited, and for the Pains, whose work world had shrunk around them. It shouldn't be too much of a change because England had made Canada, and after all, Canadians were much the same as English – with the same King, the same language, and English customs. It wouldn't be too bad.

The first change was to prepare to be immigrants. They conferred with Henry and Alice Dumas.

"Of course you can rely on us, Johnny, we back you and your family."

"We know that, Henry, but we cannot go on just accepting your generosity with no end in sight. We have decided to go to Canada, and make a start there. Things are better there and there is more opportunity and fewer hurdles. Dumas and Wiley have been so good for Jacky, I'm sure she will stay to work with you. But we're for Canada."

"You'll need a hand up, Johnny, to start—it won't be as easy or cheap as you might imagine."

Dolly broke in. "Henry, you know Bonchurch. It's vacant now, and Beatrix and the children can stay there until Johnny gets established. It's a nice house in Kingston, just by the police barracks."

"Could we have it for a while, until we're settled?"

"Of course, and rent free."

"Oh no. We wouldn't think of that! We'll pay rent."

"We can work that out later. Just keep us up to date on what happens."

Dolly had been through this before, and now faced separation, perhaps forever, from her beloved Beatrix, her last remaining link to her childhood with James. That whole life was gone: the horses, the carriages, the uncles and aunts and cousins, all dead. Trix was her confidante, who had nursed her through rabies, who had taken over the management of the household, who had shared the Webbs, Shaw, the music, the photography, and her books. Dolly could not bear the thought of losing her Beatrix.

Johnny embarked for Canada in 1928, the old life insurance policy milked for the ticket. Rod was sent off, protesting, to a boarding school in Calais, and David stayed with Beatrix. Jacky was well established in Henry's firm, as the French Secretary, thanks to Henry who had supported her education in French at school in Blois. Before he left, he spent time with his father, mother and sisters, Bimba and Pooge, perhaps for the last time.

Johnny concentrated on the prospect of Canada to make it easier to leave. It was easier when you looked ahead, to the ship, the arrival, getting a job and sending money home.

I can do it. I will do it and Doight is well up to it. Strong Doight, willing Doight, wonderful Doight!

Johnny's lonely journey to Canada began in a cabin with three other steerage passengers bound for Quebec. A third–class train ticket took him to Sarnia, Ontario, where

James Innes Minchin, Madras Civil Service, circa 1870.
Photographer: Nicholas and Curths, Madras & Ootagamund.

James Innes Minchin, 1900.

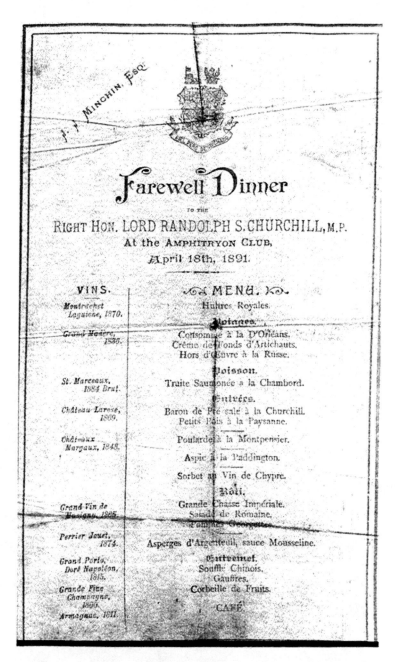

Menu for J.I. Minchin, Esq. Farewell Dinner to the Right Hon. Lord Randolph S. Churchill, MP, at the Amphitryon Club, April 18, 1891.

Alice and Henry Dumas, a newly married couple, 1890.
Photographer: E. Davey Lavender, Bromley, Kent.

Raasay, Oakshott Heath, Home of Henry and Alice Dumas, Surrey.

Violet Minchin, 1890. Photographer: J Russel and Sons.

Beatrix Minchin on the day of her presentation to King Edward VII, 1905.

Mary Dixon Minchin in presentation gown, 1905.
Photographer: Thomas Fall, R. Mason and Co.

Mary Dixon Minchin, portrait by Wilson Nesbitt.
Photographer: Debenham & Gould, Bournemouth.

Left to right: Violet Nesbitt, unknown, Jacky Pain, Beatrix Pain holding Violet's daughter, Oriel, circa 1912.

Jacky Pain and bell cloches, Christchurch French Gardens, Ltd, 1912. Photographer: Geo. Moss, Christchurch.

John Pain in Tank Corps, Bovington, during World War I.

John H. Pain during World War I.

Beatrix Pain and orderlies at YMCA hut, near Stirling, Scotland, 1914.

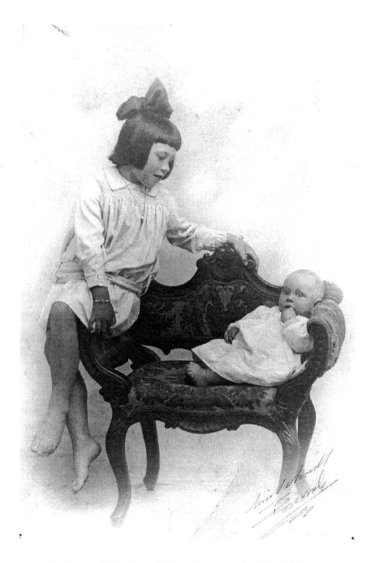

Jacky and Rodney Pain, Bournemouth, 1917.

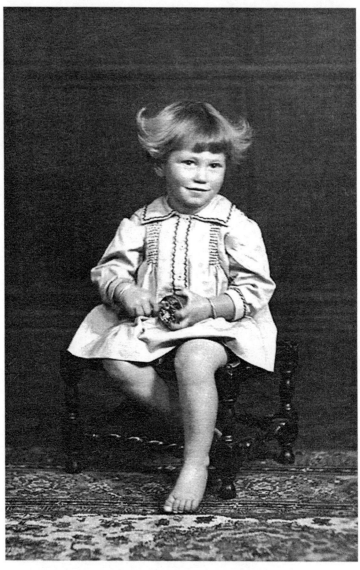

Rodney Pain, wearing dress smocked by Doris Weatherstone-Smith, 1919.
Photographer: Cecilia Fisher, Bournemouth.

Left to right: Jacky Pain, David Pain, "Mac", Rodney Pain, John Pain on automobile trip across United States, 1932.

Left to right: David Pain, Rodney Pain, Billie Seidel, Jacky Pain, 1933.

Beatrix and John Pain, 50th wedding anniversary, San Diego, February 1, 1959.

—San Diego Union Staff Photo

Mr. and Mrs. John H. Pain, who will celebrate their golden wedding anniversary today.

Photo portion of newspaper article on Beatrix and John Pain's 50th wedding anniversary.
The San Diego Union, February 1, 1959.

Pains To Receive On Anniversary

Mr. and Mrs. John H. Pain of 1766 Missouri St., will celebrate their 50th wedding anniversary today at a champagne-tea in the home of their son and daughter-in-law, Mr. and Mrs. David H. R. Pain, 3665 Fenelon, Point Loma.

Receiving with Mr. and Mrs. Pain at the 1 to 5 p.m. party will be their son, Dr. Rodney H. H. Pain of San Francisco, his wife and Mrs. Jackqueline Chilcutt of Fallbrook, daughter of the honorees.

Four of the Pains' 11 grandchildren, Lincoln, Duncan, Helen and Robin Pain, will assist during the afternoon. Presiding at the tea tables will be Mmes. Robert Walterstorff, Robert B. Watts, H. W. Howe, Grace Cutler, Kenneth Glazebrook, Emil W. Ballwanz and John Watson as well as Miss Grace Marner.

Mr. and Mrs. Pain were married in London and made their first trip to the United States in 1912. Returning to England prior to World War I, Mr. Pain became a major in the Highland Light Infantry while his wife did volunteer war work in hospitals throughout the British Isles.

In 1928 the Pain family returned to this country, via Canada, and have resided in California for the past 24 years.

Out of town guests attending today's anniversary event will include Mmes. Wilson Nesbitt, Marjorie Mayne, Doris Weatherstone Smith and Sir Humphery Cotton Minchin, from England; William R. Mesland of Iran; Mr. and Mrs. John Watson of San Francisco; Messrs. and Mmes. Robert Butt, R. D. Roberts, Joseph Perry, Charles E. and E. W. Ballwanz, and Maj. and Mrs. C. E. Collings of Los Angeles, and Mr. and Mrs. George Evans of Hemet.

Left to right: (seated) Jacky Pain Chilcutt, Beatrix, her granddaughter, Robin Pain, (standing) Rogers Chilcutt, David Pain, and John Pain

Beatrix and John Pain with their grandchildren.

Beatrix Pain with her dog, Susie, in the garden, San Diego, 1960.

Doris Weatherstone–Smith had connections. Johnny got in touch with a man who told stories of many jobs for willing backs. Johnny was not only willing, but anxious to earn passage tickets for the family now waiting under Henry and Dolly's roof.

Johnny wrote that he had made the rounds of refineries and factories, and of the rejections—the Canadians were aloof with Brits. He made the round of industrial firms, and bought Canadian working clothes to look the part. With each refusal, his little nest egg diminished - he cut back on meals to make his money stretch for a few more days of searching. Johnny was down to his last seven dollars.

Beatrix was spinning her own dolorous web. Bonchurch was large enough and "nice enough" to accommodate distant cousins, the Storeys, recently returned from India. It was an uneasy mix. Beatrix spread her skills with curries, trying to please their educated palates, attempted to provide what fresh fruit was available and have a good fire burning in their grate, however warm it might be for her. Rod had returned from France and, though Beatrix tried her best to keep the family quiet, his noise irritated the cousins.

The cousins wore on her. Their "side" was intolerable. Mr. Storey had been athletic advisor to a Maharajah, Ranjit Sinji, and rubbed it in. Although Beatrix was in no mood for it, she bit her tongue; their board was a few more shillings towards the steamship tickets.

Johnny wrote from the boarding house:

"I went today to a druggist friend who told me about a job with Ford's in River Rouge. They asked me what I could do and I said "everything." They said "hanging doors and setting locks?" and I said yes. I had watched a tradesman do that at Carolus. The wages are good and,

after I have paid up my boarding house, I'll send the first money. Thank God. It was close. love Johnny."

Johnny was able to fit in and do the work of door-hanger, lock–fitter, and "ding man," despite never having been apprenticed. The two incomes were accumulating. Beatrix was subsisting and steeled herself through a year and a half with the Storeys. Her efforts to provide fresh fruit, Indian meals and extra bedding for the Storeys were as nothing. The cousins, unappreciative, returned to India not long after Johnny found his job. Keeping Rodney quiet had been hard on Beatrix, and on Rod.

Pamela, Doris' daughter, came to stay and Beatrix would send Rod and Pamela outside, to spend hours in the countryside. Though not as prettily romantic as Taplow, there was much farm–land about, English farm–land larded with bosky country for children, hedgerows with hollow centres, ditches covered with shrub and vine, hollow trees, pollarded willows with crowns to climb in, hay and straw stacks to shelter from rain in, barns, dairies, blacksmith shops. The two children could and did get away for hours at a time, accumulating a huge variety of country lore. They loved playing together.

Beatrix was glad she had Polly, the beloved bull terrier, to protect the children and shoulder any encountered passerby off the path. Polly seemed like a member of the family—her pups had supplied two neighbourhoods, and her playfulness spiced dozens of picnics. Beatrix dreaded the thought, but she knew the family would have to part with Polly before going to Canada. She placed an advertisement and the applicants disqualified themselves one by one, until a retired army officer with a home abroad in the wilds, a man whose terrible sincerity and promise of good care, convinced the family. Polly went to a good home, substantiated by letters about her life for years to come.

"*Oh Johnny,*" Beatrix wrote him. "*I have this feeling that the children are being uprooted from their native heath, and all we are giving them is a big question mark. David and Roddy are so young, and we have not really been able to educate them as I'd have liked. This week I took Rod to see What Price Glory, as a sort of introduction and farewell to English stage. David, I took to London. We went to the British Museum and had tea at The Corner House, so he'd have a memory of the Museum and London life, with a cup of tea at Lyon's Tea Shop. It seems so paltry. Next month we'll go to Westminster Abbey, and see the Poet's Corner, and I'll take David to visit my father's grave.*"

She fretted, in between packing and getting passports, visiting Tom Worley for a last goodbye and Godspeed from the lawyer who had cared for her for as long as she could remember.

"What can one say? How can one deal with the terrible tearing that one is doing to oneself, and to them? Our adventure pales to less than nothing, to a tearing hurt that one is imposing on all these loved ones and oneself."

She would discard or sell much of what they had, except the silver. It was rooted so far back in the family history. It winked and glanced from the table, the monograms tying the present to some old past, smoothed from the food and mouths of ancestors. She also packed the mahogany furniture, the rose–wood dining room table Johnny could remember for forty five years, and the rusty tin–plate cylinder containing dozens of steel engraved racing prints. Perhaps they would be worth money in the New World.

Will we ever catch up with the life we're dismantling? It was terrible with Pooge and Arthur last week. We cried, Pooge and I. We cried—and I just had to leave. Then I went to Raasay.

Raasay was the wounding, the killing. Her Dolly, now seventy years old, had little strength to give Beatrix. They sat, as close as could be. Potter brought in the tea, said goodbye and sobbed her way out of the room. Beatrix and Dolly tried to talk about the future, but it was the past they were wearing and tearing. They felt the presence of James Innes. Beatrix kissed her sister and fled in Dolly's car to the station. They never saw each other again; their life together slimmed to the dimension of a trans–Atlantic letter.

Things were packed in the old leather trunk, a hundred pounds of winter clothing, woolens, socks, school caps for David and Rod, the old grey checked school cap of James Innes and Johnny's Greenheart fly–fishing rod. Beatrix also filled another trunk, with the bentwood runners and all the stickers - *P&O, GWR, LSW, CALAIS, Edin* - the medals, the proof of a veteran traveller.

Beatrix despaired and persevered. She hired a char to clean the empty house and then she and the children took a taxi to the station. Kingston to London, measured in tens of minutes, soon to Paddington, the Boat Train, and Southampton.

As they boarded the *Empress of India*, Beatrix, Jacky, Rod and David were treated to one last gesture from Henry, whose firm insured the ship. The purser greeted Beatrix and her brood at the gangway, promising courtesies.

Now she was on her own. Memories of James, his visions, his gentle lessons, her sister's helping hand, Tom Worley's support were slipping away. She felt bereft. She was losing her grip, her hold and balance.

CHAPTER NINETEEN

The second of July we found shoal water, which smelt so sweetly, as if we had been in the midst of some delicate garden, abounding with all kinds of odoriferous flowers; by which we were assured that the land could not be far distant...we arrived upon the coast...and after thanks given to God for our safe arrival...we went to view the land and take possession of the same in the name of the Queen's most excellent Majesty...we viewed the land about us...so full of grapes as the very beating and surge of the sea overflowed them.

—Richard Hakluyt, 1552 – 1616, *The First Voyage Made to the Coasts of America*

Beatrix stood with her three children at the rail and waved good–bye to all the people standing there, good–bye to the flagstones of the quay, to the dear old land, to the sheds on the dock, to the smoke, to—what? There was no–one to wave her good–bye as the ship left the pier, no band, no streamers, no piper.

Beatrix's tears filled her handkerchief. She knew that the widening water was separating her from Dolly, from James' grave, from Johnny's parents, from the Maynes and from everything that meant England. Memories of primroses, meadowsweet, the milk man with the cheery "milk-oh!" Bray, and the Royal Standard across the meadow at Windsor Castle jumbled in her mind.

England had let her down, and now the New World seemed worthless, it held no promise. She was torn, seeing England and her life fade at the horizon, all wrench and tears. With the last sight of the Isle of Wight and the Needle, she turned and hurried to the cabin.

Beatrix settled into their cabin. Each child had a narrow but adequate bunk. Although it was a third class cabin, it had two portholes that were dogged tight. It was almost below the water line. Beatrix hadn't wasted a penny.

Rod and David went off to find the dining room, where they saw passengers from Poland at their early supper sitting.

"Mudderkees! We found people who smelled terrible!"

"What are you saying?"

"In the dining room. We went to see it, and it was full of Poles eating their supper."

"I doubt that they smelled. You must have smelled their food and, of course, you don't know the smell of cooked garlic. It's very strong. I don't like the taste of it myself.

"The steward left us a schedule of the sittings. We'll go in at our turn with English people, who won't smell, I promise you."

That sitting was the last meal Beatrix ate aboard ship. She suffered silently in her cabin.

Since my honeymoon I've never been able to soak in bed for more than a half an hour. I was never seasick on the Channel, but who is there here to know? I was never seasick with Johnny in the Cosmos, but who cares?

I had better rest. The Captain will look out for Jacky

and David.

Rod, also a poor sailor, kept her company. They sucked on ice cubes and ate water biscuits, while Jacky and David rollicked through their week at sea.

"Icebergs off the starboard bow!"

The *Empress of India* was vectored north of Newfoundland, to the Strait of Belle Isle, a channel supposedly free of ice. Despite the re-routing, a scatter of icebergs were in their path. Beatrix and Rod crowded to the two portholes to see the icebergs, floating messengers from the new continent. When she drank the therapeutic tot of brandy from the ship's doctor, she saw the icebergs double.

As the ship approached the immigration wharf in Quebec City, Beatrix gathered her children, each with a burden of migration goods in suitcases, and steamer trunks nearby. The four stood uneasily, clutching their passports.

As they walked down the gangplank to Canada, all was in bright sunlight. Jacky went first, happy to be on the same continent as her Nacko. She'd not do anything foolish. David went next, with the smallest suitcase, happy in the adventure and ready for anything. Then darkly thoughtful Rod, blinking in the sun and banging his bared knees on two heavy suitcases as he descended the cleated ramp into a dark and clamorous landing shed. They joined a queue, waiting their turn to be checked off by those dry-eyed officials in uniforms, with hard brimmed caps and metal badges. This was a new reality, on soil foreign to their feet. The hopeful bright sun of the gangway contrasted with the dank landing shed with its slight but unmistakable odor from the press of immigrants, of unchanged underwear, and the taste of anxiety in their mouths. Beatrix kept the three children serried to her, sensing their need to be protected and her feeling of inadequacy in the face of the unknown.

"David, do you have your passport ready? Don't drop it! Rod, yours? Ja?"

She didn't realize the authorities were just as anxious to avoid losing children and passports. Her anxieties were her first immigrant experience.

What if we're not on their lists? What will I do if it isn't all right? What if the doctor refuses any of us? What if they separate us? If they decide to let us go, where will we go?

They stepped up with the queues, pushing forward their passports like weapons, hearts pounding.

"Voila, Madame. There you are, Ma'am, your children are all right. Good luck, bonne chance!"

A taxi delivered them with their luggage to the pension of Madame Chouinard, who served them all coffee. Beatrix, in her distraction and relief to be there, did not even notice it was coffee. It was another lesson of an immigrant.

That evening, Jacky and Rod toured the neighbourhood and wondered at "the castle", Chateau Frontenac, which overlooked Quebec City. The young immigrants thought of themselves at home with neighbours, but the people of Quebec found the Pains' Continental French hard to understand. The youngsters did not understand not being understood.

The pension breakfast was a challenge quickly disposed of.

"Where is the railway station?"

In French and fractured English, Mme. Chouinard told her. Beatrix's very British response she could not change.

"Thank you, thank you very much!"

There seemed to be no end of decisions to be made over unforeseen problems.

"For goodness' sake, children, stay close to me and don't scatter. Let's just sit here for a minute. The train isn't here yet. We have twenty minutes 'till it leaves. It goes through Buffalo...no, there aren't any buffaloes here David. They are all *out west*, wherever that is! Ask Rod."

Their train was called, and the children weren't going to scatter if she could prevent it.

"All right, up into the train all of you, David first. Thank goodness the nice porter has put a step to reach the stair—what a stretch!" and to the porter, "Can you help me with this big bag?"

"You sho' put a lot in that lil' grip, Ma'am."

"Oh! It's got most of our clothes, shoes, Burberrys, and a few things too delicate to pack. That's why it's so heavy, thank you, thank you very much!"

The only familiar thing about the train or the station was the friendly, warm, oily smell of steam.

"We're moving, at last!"

Beatrix gave a sigh "Well, that's done. I wonder what's next?" She finally had a moment to look around her. The boys had found a vacant seat to swing back and forth, having heard that the seat backs were swung over to change direction with the train.

"We're reversing the train, Mudderkees!"

"Well stop it, stop that monsing around! Just stop playing with the seat."

She composed herself and enjoyed a moment with no decisions to make. The countryside was unfamiliar—huge fields with patterns of disciplined ploughing, right up to barbed wire fences. There were no headlands at the end of the furrows. Where would rabbits live? Where were the deep hedgerows, the ditches, steadied with elm and beech? Where were the little villages clustered round a Norman church? Here she saw strict divisions—lanes without ditches, hedges or trees on either side. She missed the softness and wonderful unevenness of the English countryside.

She sighed and again realized what she had forsaken. Immigration was more than giving up. It meant accommodating oneself to wonderful and repugnant realities.

"I wish had Johnny here to share it with. It's been a long while, and he's such a meagre letter writer. I treasure that sketch he did of himself, slouched in a chair smoking his pipe, the swirling tobacco smoke with "Trix" in the little cloud! Here we are both forty–five years old, with a hive of children. It's no honeymoon."

The family made it way to the dining car, clutching the seat handles to steady themselves. As they passed, they glimpsed the galley slaves throwing hardwood sticks into the range to flare up oven heat for hot biscuits.

"Of course, you can have tea, Ma'am, what kind?"

"What do you have, India?"

"Oh no, Ma'am. Iced or hot?"

He had saved her from noticing that the rest of the passengers were eating lunch. How did they manage to eat such big plates full with those generous helpings of meat? Beatrix noted they spooned food up on the inside of their forks.

"Did you say milk in your tea, not lemon?"

"Please, and could we have a pot of tea, please?"

"I'll fix it up. Is there anything else?"

"Yes, some bread and butter, please. Thank you very much."

"Think nothing of it, Ma'am."

"There it is again—think nothing? I want to think of it a little, enough for a piece of bread and butter. But not 'nothing'. I certainly look forward to a slice of bread and butter, and tea."

If only there was one familiar face—Dolly or Johnny who would say, 'There, there, it's all right' but we're miles away in the middle of these ugly fields. There are no open woods with grass growing between the trees.. Don't harrow yourself, Beatrix. Keep your calm, keep your strength to show. They need you.

The train for Windsor, unaccountably routed through New York State, wound its slow way through raw countryside of the East Coast farmlands, wire fences and steel gates.

"Mudderkees have you ever seen such big barns?"

"Everything seems bigger here, Rod. During the war, the Americans had a way of saying, "It's bigger at home" that became wearisome. They were bigger men, too. We found the Canadians more modest. They did as much for us as the Yanks, but never boasted or blustered. We were happy to see them on our side – we couldn't have won the war without either of them.

"But then we couldn't have won the war without the Ghurkas, the Australians, the New Zealanders – all of the Empire. You will hear some things about England you may be surprised at, but pass it off without comment. We have plenty of more important stuff to take care of, like getting back to Nacko..."

"Good old Nacko! Hello Nacko, hurry up Nacko!"

They danced in the wide aisle, so much wider than the narrow carriages of the Great Western.

"Why are the workmen on the train black, Mudderkees? Are they slaves?"

"Of course they are not slaves! They don't have slaves here. Careful how you speak!"

"Why do they wear hats with basket round the top?"

"I have no idea—keeps them cool! For heaven's sake, stop nattering at me. I'm thinking of what we have to do when we get off the train."

A pleasant gentleman stopped.

"Are you from the Old Country?"

Beatrix had not thought of Britain as the old country

"Why yes, just a long week from Southampton. Everything is so strange!"

"Not as strange as you will find it, I'm sure. I have to join my wife. I wish you a pleasant journey."

"Thank you, thank you. It is so nice to hear a familiar voice."

"Well, I hope you will be able to meet others like us to gentle the shock."

"Thank you so much."

The train began to make its way into the sooty suburbs of Windsor and through tenements as black and trashy as anything London had to offer.

Beatrix's head buzzed, full of impressions and anticipations tied to imaginations that failed to connect with what she saw. Everything was peaking – the months of yearning and anticipation, the cold necessities of doing it alone, all for the promise of new freedoms.

Windsor station was the end of the track, and the train wound slowly along the low platform.

"I think this is the station. Watch for Nacko!"

"How will we ever get down the steps? The train is just inching along, clanging like a fire engine. And those brakes, how they moan. A jolt! We're here!"

Everybody crowded to the end of the carriage. The bags got mislaid and found.

"There's Johnny! Pushing through the crowd and the baggage wagons. Here's Nacko!"

CHAPTER TWENTY

In ancient times bread was a very different kind of food to what it is now.
The Assyrians, Egyptians and Greeks used to make it with oil and spices, more like a cake than a loaf, for leavened bread was then a thing unknown...The slave of an Archon at Athens (had forgotten his dough) till he found it days later and mixed it with some fresh dough...yeast bread.
—Mrs. Beaton's Shilling Useful Book

"Oh, Johnny! I've waited so long for this moment!"

"You've no idea, Doight, how often I've imagined your being here, being together again! How I've missed you and the children!"

"And you're well! But you look thin."

"I haven't had your good food."

The children gradually peeled themselves off Johnny, hugging his legs, his body. Everyone was talking at once. They crowded the baggage into the borrowed car, Beatrix in front, on the right.

"Johnny, what're you doing on this side? You mean everyone drives on the wrong side of the street? Why?"

Windsor looked strange with its ugly houses, painted long ago, and wide square streets, every corner the same.

Street names on corner poles were Frenchified, like Pellissier. People in the streets were dressed in unfamiliar ways—small boys wore long trousers, "bags" or britches, with wool socks. There were no horses, and so many cars. On the way to their house, Johnny stopped by a funny yellow cart with a ringing bell where he bought ice cream cones. The ice cream was amazingly yellow and unforgettably rich and creamy.

Then they arrived at a big gray house, their new home.

"Mudderkees, make some tea, make some real tea. It's been weeks since we've had a good cup of tea!"

The family was together, around the table with a proper tablecloth to enjoying the familiar—tea with bread and butter.

Beatrix changed her clothes and cooked a special supper—potatoes, Brussels' sprouts and sausages.

Roddy thought, "It's so good to have a proper Mudderkees meal."

And Nacko was there, smiling while the two boys and Jacky kissed him. "Good old Nacko." Beatrix too looked glad, happy after so many months of frowns.

Hours later, when the children were in bed, dead to the world, Beatrix and Johnny sat quietly together.

"How do we do it?"

All the years, the war, hospitals, business failures, leaving their families in England – it made no difference. It was as if they were in Christchurch again, in that funny old inn. Just Johnny and Beatrix. They were honeymooners again, not forty-five year old immigrants.

The next morning, Beatrix asked, "Where's the fireplace to toast the bread Nacko?"

"No fireplace. Toast your bread in the oven—this is a

gas and electricity country."

"Nacko, we've never had electric lights before!"

"Oh, we're near Niagara Falls where they make electricity. It's so cheap that some people don't have switches on their lights, just leave them on all the time."

"What a waste, Johnny."

"There's not the cruel poverty here that we left in England. Here they think the electricity is less wasteful than buying electric switches. I don't know…"

Beatrix was learning that immigrants weren't choosers. The immigrant rule was that even if you didn't like it, you were stuck with it. Immigrants were supposed to listen and learn. Things from the old country were thought out of fashion, unsuitable, and often wrong. You grieved as you wished for the old, and put up with the new. The rest of the family took their time, adapting to the New World as they could. For Rod, at age twelve, it was hard, for Jacky impossible. David was not dismayed. As a seven–year–old, he seemed ready for North America.

Rod looked around, wanting to earn some money selling newspapers. He fell among young newsies, who directed him to a dark corner in the factory district, where few tramcars and cars passed. He lasted one evening as a newsboy. He then tried a bowling alley, setting pins and quickly learned the rules—be nippy, be careful, be accurate, be out of the way. He had to step on the pedal, spring the pegs up in the floor, set the pins quicker than snap, and then hop onto the divider to escape the flying pins rocketing from the cannon balls flung down the alley. These missives would bruise a slow pin–boy.

Beatrix faced a barrage of changes. She first learned not to stare at Johnny's fingernails, which even after scrubbing had a dark mechanics' line around and under the nails. When she was at the butcher shop, she asked for a joint, to discover it was called a roast. The grocer had not heard of self-rising flour. When she was asked by a neighbour to play bridge, she stunned the ladies by calling Johnny's paycheck his "screw."

After school, one hot afternoon, Rod was sitting on a lawn talking with a friend about this and that, spitting to the rhythm of their sentences.

Beatrix passed, unobserved. Later she asked, "Rod, who was that boy with you on the lawn this afternoon?"

"That was Charley, from school. I like him because he shows me things. He knows an awful lot, like where to smoke, where to be away from girls."

"Why were you both spitting?"

"It's the way fellows are, they spit when they talk. Different from at home."

"Well, I don't like it. That's one thing I won't have. I realize that here in Canada we may not pay as much attention to making friends within one's own class, which I respect. But that doesn't mean that one takes up bad habits."

"I like Charley. He seems so natural."

"Natural or not, I won't have spitting!"

"I'll try."

"How's school?"

"We sing *God Save the King* sometimes, and mustn't speak to each other in class. History is the same as at home. I like it."

"Have you had trouble talking in class?"

"What do you mean, Mother?"

"You know what I mean. You've always had trouble with keeping quiet in class."

"Well, Charley and I sit side by side. We were caught

whispering and exchanging notes, and got strapped, once on each hand. I had an extra. Charley is used to it – he does not pull back his hands."

"Back in England you might have had the cane. I don't want you to use bad language, or spitting"

"Yes, Mother."

Not long after, Beatrix was discussing Rod's job in the bowling alley with a neighbour.

"A bowling alley! My dear, that's no place for your children. Bowling alleys, bars, and pool halls all have terrible reputations. You never know what kind of people he'll meet, or the language he'll pick up!"

Here was talk Beatrix understood and, whatever the stresses, Beatrix hewed to the line with Rod and David's behaviour.

"Of course, you must go and tell your boss that you have to quit your job. You can't just leave him in the lurch. Even though he may run a disreputable place, he is entitled to the courtesy of a call."

Rod soon found work with Tony, a cobbler, who took him in and showed a friendly stripe.

"You wanna fix your family shoes, and decorate the front window? Why sure, just take da things off da shelf. Go ahead, you can use the machinery, too, but not da stitcher! It will sew your arm to y'r elbow."

Tony taught Rod enough about cobbling to keep his family dry shod. Rod kept his iron cobbler's last for years and repaired their shoes with cards of rubber soles from Woolworth's, cement and tacks until the family could afford bespoke cobbling.

Johnny had come to Canada to work, and North America offered Nacko the opportunity to earn a living with his hands. His hands learned to earn a day's wage and became hardened in the work. But the family was unlucky in their timing. Canada was faltering in 1929 and the Pains staggered with it. Ford Motor Company Model A was not selling and the men struck for wages. Ford closed, and armed their rooftops. New words entered Johnny's vocabulary: *scab, on the bricks, strike pay,* and *Pinkertons.*

Every day Beatrix watched for Johnny's return from the picket line, to comfort him and share his disappointment. The New World was becoming like the Old World, except that they were now looking up from the cheap seats, not down from the balcony. *Out of work* was the same here as in Surrey; there was no cure in sight or reasonable response. And there was no family to back them up.

"Johnny. How was the picket duty today?"

"Doight, you wouldn't believe it! The management of Ford had machine guns trained on us today! Machine guns!"

"I can't believe it! Man against man, Canadians shooting Canadians! The irony of it, you, Johnny, a striker on the street, menaced by machine guns, the same Johnny, Acting Major in the Machine Gun Corps, that scabbed on the steam engines during the General Strike."

"You can be sure I'll not tell them that! I've learned a thing or two since Siemens. It's really no better here than in England—deep depression, no work again."

Beatrix softened the blow with a good pot of tea.

"Doight, I think Canada is in the same soup as the old country, with the same politicians trying to work it out. Did you see that picture of Prime Minister Bennett? He looked just like one of our fellows; same hat, same coat, same ideas. We just changed countries—the same old poverty is dogging us."

"Did you see that advertisement I cut out asking for a wood carver to work for Elbert Hubbard at Roycrofters?"

"I thought he was dead, drowned on the Titanic. It seems Roycrofters is still alive though. I'll write for the job."

"It's about time we were lucky, Johnny. A job at a William Morris place should be more in your line of work than car body work."

"Let's hope for Roycrofters, although I know very little about woodcarving. I'll look up that carving book Dolly sent me. It has good examples, and I have most of the tools. And, I know I can do it."

Again he resolved to meet fate, though it seemed never to give him an equal footing.

CHAPTER TWENTY-ONE

*I celebrate myself, and sing myself,
And what I assume you shall assume,
For every atom belonging to me as
good belongs to you,
I loaf and invite my soul,
I lean and loaf at my ease
observing a leaf of grass...*

—Walt Whitman, 1819 – 1899

Jacky soon went to work with the American Consul, making use of her French language skills. After Johnny sent his application to Roycrofters, Jacky quietly put the Pains to the head of a list of immigrants permitted into the United States, and the family moved to East Aurora, New York State in 1930. The town was wooded and gracious, notable for being the home of Roycrofters, a firm modeled on the teachings of William Morris. They manufactured Mission style furniture and needed a wood-carver.

Beatrix felt uneasy and degraded by the rate her family was sliding into the working class. Occasionally, she could see the optimistic side, and imagined Johnny in a flowing artiste's shirt, with an artiste's mobcap, smoking his pipe as he carved the end boards of pews for an Episcopal Church. Though she would have denied it, she was relieved that Johnny's hands and nails would no longer be grimy.

Although Beatrix and Johnny both agonized over the symbolic and real changes that were encroaching them, they could not discuss their situation together. Beatrix knew Johnny was hurting and she would not risk undercutting him. They never reviled at their fate in front of the youngsters. They were learning to wear the stripes of humility.

In East Aurora, the Pains boarded with the Knieblichs. Mudderkees and Nacko had not been near anyone German since the war and had reservations about a close association with people having a German name. But they knew "when you're hungry you swallow hard."

The first meal with the Knieblichs was a revelation, beans served as a main course. In England, the only dry beans that upper class people ate were Windsor, or marrowfats, usually served with boiled pork, and watery gravy. The Knieblichs who were the first vegetarians the Pains had encountered, introduced them to the tiny white navy beans, cooked with a fragrant dark brown sauce and pungent flavour.

"What have you flavoured these beans with, they are wonderful!"

"Mostly with molasses, and ketchup, Mrs. Pain."

"Molasses? Would you tell me what that is?"

"It comes from pressing sugar cane for the juice."

Beatrix's ancestor, a governor of Jamaica, must have smiled on her—her beans ever after were as fragrant as the Kneiblich's.

Before Elbert's death, Roycrofters was run by managers

who were devoted to William Morris' principles of old-fashioned craftsmanship. The firm's major products were wooden wall hangings with burned-on messages. "God Bless Our Happy Home," was a best seller. But now the curio business was slumping and there were no pious platitudes for the unemployed on Elbert's plaques. In his short term with the firm, it taught Johnny to be a carver. He also learned that his British experience was of little account. He was let go after a short while.

Beatrix was finding life in America a challenge, She salvaged what she could, but her perspective was limited. In England, the fire straights of a family on this kind of an economic slide could often be camouflaged. A gentleman might not have soles on his shoes, but his shoes were polished. Here, there were no fallback mechanisms for toffeehead poverty, no poverty culture for English gentry to fit to. The lower classes had countless generations of depressed situations forced on them by those who used poverty to control them, and had established the official poverty line, the dole. The stratification was so ancient it was difficult to question. But for Beatrix and Johnny there was no experience to explain the blow or offer understanding. For them, poverty and the dole were unthinkable as they were unfamiliar. Of course, Beatrix and Johnny had no idea that for many other lower class people, poverty and the dole were equally unacceptable. The problem seemed uniquely theirs.

In America the usual stigmas were not apparent. Workingmen worked, dressed the part, even when they had no jobs. A gent or a toffeehead too could dress the part. He was allowed in. Wives and children dressed the part, too. Beatrix quietly dressed the part, as she and

Johnny agonized, silently.

The workingman's telegraph came to their rescue again.

"Doight, they're looking for a cabinet-maker in East Rutherford, New Jersey, at Diners' Manufacturing or some such name."

"Diners?"

"Doight, you should see them. Big dining cars the size of a pantechnicon, on great wheels that steer like a hay cart. When someone wants to open a breakfast teashop, they buy one of these diners, hire a lorry to drag it to a vacant property and park it parallel to the street. The wheels stay on so it can be moved, if needed. A mason puts in a foundation. Inside it's like a gypsy caravan, movable but permanent. It's fitted as a restaurant, all the patrons sit at a long counter and can look over it at the kitchen. I would be building counters."

Rod came home bubbling with enthusiasm over his junior high school teacher.

"I think she's smashing, Mudderkees, so pretty, with wavy black hair and red cheeks. And she was getting volunteers for the *Three Kings Pageant*. I couldn't sing in tune so I was not chosen for a king, but she'll let me do the class paper. It's for the seventh and eighth grades—what do you think of "Octo–Septo?"

"Fine. What's your teacher's name?"

"Padrofski, I think."

"That's a Russian or a Polish name, probably."

"Oh no! But she's so nice ..."

"What's the matter with Polish?"

"Well, you remember—garlic!"

"Don't be silly. Forget the smell and remember how you felt when you first came to North America. Remember your first impression, how you felt wearing short pants in Canada. You were a bit of a guy yourself, until we bought you a regular set of Canadian breeks!"

"Yes, Mother."

Beatrix's instinct and training told her that attitudes and gestures should precede understanding, and that preceded respect. Her children would have the gestures and the attitudes, and the attributes would follow or she would know why. This was the steel cable running through her character. When the children came up short with Beatrix there were no arguments. She had given Rod many a puffed right ear in response to his rudeness. Rudeness was an anathema, it broke the shell of civilization. Beatrix knew from her upbringing that behaviour was the key to relationships, and by extension, to being civilized. Behaviour had to be governed by polite and respectful manners. "Manners Makyth Man" was a motto she instilled early in her children. Her boys were to take their hats off in shops, houses, churches, when meeting friends, and they were to stand at a loose attention with their hats off when a funeral went by.

"Never let down your side. Never be rude."

She never broke with that, nor did mild-mannered Johnny. Once when Rod's parents imagined an insult to friends, Johnny got down on Rodney, who was going through a bad spell with the family and was unable to explain. Rodney paid the penalty, a hiding with a trunk strap.

While working on the diners, Johnny developed new woodworking skills, which he used to get a job with Kroehlers, a massive furniture factory. At Kroehlers, Johnny soon learned to use an electric screwdriver, the first power tool he had used. Johnny was amazed at the way Kroehlers framed the carcasses for overstuffed furniture.

"Doight, they just tack the wood frames together with staples. They haven't heard of mortises. I can't say a word or they'd fire me. And you should see how they use the screwdrivers, driving the long screws to hold the tabletops down. They're fine for heavy work, but the screwdrivers drill through a one inch board in a second if you miss."

Now Johnny had enough skill to make a living with his hands. Beatrix meanwhile strove to keep the ethical and behavioral standard that her father had set her to guard. Though she never mentioned her father when she told of her care of the children, the Minchin legacy was strong in her. Her sense of justice pervaded all she did with the family, and nobody had a sense of being picked out for favour. She was always there, strong and principled and there was never any sense that she was anything but Johnny's wife, mother to his children, James' daughter, England's banner. Disaster might dog her, but she dealt with life evenhandedly.

North America in depression was now to be their life. Job after job collapsed for Johnny. Month after month Beatrix dug deeper into her survival skills. Jacky's wages as a beautician in New York helped stave off penury, and the family moved with the jobs.

East Rutherford was a grimy city, flanked by the Jersey Marshes, the settling tank for the area's sewage, and surrounded by grimy cities – Paterson, Passaic, and Newark. They resembled Blake's dark Satanic Mills. There was no pleasant place for a walk to escape the noise, smell or sight of industry. East Rutherford offered first hand immersion into a slum. The family lived in a flat over the home of a Hungarian seamstress, a pieceworker, who used a sewing machine leased to her by her clothing maker.

The continuous roaring clatter of her machine, running up cheap women's clothes sewn together all on a tape, buffeted the air from breakfast to supper, and into the evening. Working class life in New Jersey was just survival.

A small crevice in the facade of dreariness came unexpectedly from an American, Reverend Nye, a Rhodes scholar who was the minister for a nearby Episcopal Church. When Beatrix met Reverend Nye, she discovered he shared some of her prejudices, and Rod, overhearing the conversation, spoke up about his own complaints.

"At school, they make me pledge allegiance to the flag and sing *America the Beautiful* each morning. It's just a bunch of lies. One nation with liberty and justice for all—I know it's not true. They have us put our hand on our hearts when the class says it, but I won't say it. I won't do my hand on my heart, either. Miss Padrofski gets upset, but most of the time she is facing the flag—they have a flag in the classroom, and when they say "with liberty and justice for all" we are supposed to put out our hands towards the flag. I hate the things they try to put on me. They are so false, so false, like their country."

Beatrix, aware that Reverend Nye had enrolled Rod in Confirmation class, broke in with a mitigating comment.

"Don't fret yourself, Rod. When the English sing *God Save the King*, foreigners have to put up with it, even in the theaters. And, especially, don't trouble Miss Padrofski. She's the key to your becoming an American."

"Can't I stay an Englishman?"

"You can stay anything you want to, even in prison. But, you want to be able to choose."

The minister took his leave, and Beatrix continued,

"Now come here, I want to talk to you. Are you listening?"

"Yes, Mother."

"Many years ago my father, your grandfather, told me some things. When I had expressed some egotistical snobbery, I suppose, or some intellectual arrogance, your grandfather told me that there are certain subjects that are open to discussion only with great circumspection. He used the word, 'circumspection', as he used all words, carefully. Subjects, such as other people's religion, patriotism, reputation, sense of humour, personal beliefs and business, family reputation, income, are dangerous territory. They are dangerous, first of all, because they are not logical and cannot be discussed accurately, and secondly, because points of view on these subjects are held jealously. So they are automatic grounds for disagreement. My father and I often discussed this because he suffered family criticism for his freethinking ideas. He went to Church of England services all the time, but privately he doubted many of church tenets and did not discuss them. He respected, but privately disagreed, with many of the sects he was familiar with, but he never doubted the individual commitment of their leaders. For him, Jews, Catholics, Jains and Sikhs were equally capable of holiness, just as those who pledge allegiance. One can privately evaluate the ideas for oneself but one is on shaky ground to disparage anybody else for holding to them. Remember that the person who thinks two times two is five is in error. But he is not evil, only in error. He is only mistaken. You cannot say he is evil for believing in an error!"

"Do you mean that Grandfather James would have called me down for calling the people in my classroom false?"

"Yes. They believe it, sincerely. You can try, from your lofty British perch, to convince them that you are right and they wrong, but you won't get far and won't deserve much of their time. Belittle American patriotism at your risk, Rod."

"All right. But I still don't want to swear those things they expect me to swear."

"That's all right. Live your life however you want to. But for my sake, don't limit your possibilities, and specially, don't irritate Miss Padrofski."

CHAPTER TWENTY-TWO

When Freedom from her mountain height
Unfurled her standard to the air,
She tore the azure robe of night,
And set the stars of glory there.
She mingled with its gorgeous dyes
The milky baldrick of the skies
And striped its pure celestial white
With streakings of the morning light.
Then from his mansion in the sun
She called her eagle bearer down,
And gave into his mighty hand
The emblem of her chosen land.
Majestic monarch of the cloud...
Child of the sun! to thee 'is given
To guard the banner of the free.

—Joseph Rodman Drake, 1795–1820

Evenings with Reverend Nye and his wife were a balm to Beatrix. She could live again in the world of books as they discussed *The Forsyte Saga* and Conan Doyle lore. They also found other light reading wanting.

The family joined Reverend Nye's Episcopalian congregation, and Rod became the trusted crucifer, carrying the cross during the service. Reverend Nye catechized Rod for confirmation and, when the moment of confirmation came, the bishop "laid on his hands."

"Mudderkees, I felt nothing!"

"Well Rod, he blessed you and that can do no harm."

"But I expected a flash of fire or a special feeling. Isn't he supposed to be an extension of Christ?"

"Yes, but think of how good you feel taking the cross at the head of the choir on Sunday and helping with the Eucharist."

"Yes, but where's the mystery?"

"Oh, it'll come one day."

But it didn't.

Another change was to come. Kroehlers cut their work force and Johnny knew he would be out of a job in a week or so.

"Johnny, we'll have to do something. Let's visit the Coynimans and ask their advice."

The Coynimans were friends whom Beatrix assumed knew about America. Coyniman was a plumber, and had traveled.

"California hasn't had the depression yet," he said. "Go to California, lots of jobs there."

Reverend Nye corroborated.

"Well Johnny, how can we do it? We've eaten your last paycheque, and the rent is due in two weeks."

"I know where there's a big second-hand Hupmobile for sale. Buyers for second hand cars, especially a big one with seven seats, are few. I could get it cheap and we could make a start for California. We'd need a few, precious few, bits of camping gear, a tent, a petrol stove, a couple of folding cots. We've mined the heart out of the life insurance—it can stand a few hundred dollars more. If we motor to California, the trip should not be too expensive. Although petrol is almost ten cents a gallon, we may never have another chance to participate in a trip across America."

"Yes. My father taught me, kiss bad fortune and smile at danger. It'll be a right good change from the slide we're trapped in here. We could draw down the balance in our bank account and get the money from England as soon as possible."

They were joining the great American Odyssey, trekking to California.

Johnny made a light frame to protect the fabric of the car roof. The belongings, largely clothes and bedding, were parceled and packed on the frame. A large bell tent with a centre pole was to be camp for Johnny and Beatrix at night, and their cookhouse when it rained. The three children would sleep in sleeping bags under the sky in dry weather and share the tent with their parents when it was wet.

Jacky and David rode in the Hup with Beatrix and Johnny. Rodney, a difficult fourteen year-old, was relegated to the car of a friend of Jacky's, Mac, who was driving tandem with the family. The caravan, which could reach the speed of forty-five miles an hour on downhill slopes, moved slowly across the continent.

CHAPTER TWENTY-THREE

There's a whisper down the field where the year has shot her yield
And the ricks stand gray to the sun,
Singing:—'Over then, come over, for the bee has quit the clover
And your English summer's done.'
You have heard the beat of the off–shore wind
And the thresh of the deep–sea rain;
You have heard the song—how long! how long!
Pull out on the trail again!
Ha' done with the Tents of Shem, dear lass,
We've seen the seasons through,
And it's time to turn on to the old trail, our own trail, the out trail,
Pull out, pull out, on the Long Trail, the trail that is always new.

—Rudyard Kipling, 1865 – 1936

Beatrix crowed, "We're pulling out on the long trail, what larks! At last doing something, something with some spirit to it!"

As the family put their misadventures aside, the feel of a holiday appeared out of their sea of worries. They soon left the city driving along Highway One, which connected

New York to Los Angeles, through countryside with long stretches of farms. The road was usually two lanes and sometimes only two narrow double tracks of concrete just wide enough for the car wheels. There were no highway police and few gas stations. Come suppertime, if a trailer court or private campsite was not found, the family camped in a wild site with no evident ownership.

"Are we looking for a wild camping place, or for a tourist camp?" asked Rod who preferred the wild campsites.

"I hope they have a toilet. The last gas station didn't even have one for the staff."

"Have you filled the emergency petrol can, Nacko?"

"Of course. We haven't had to use it since that eighty mile stretch in New Jersey."

"If we stop at a tourist camp, I hope they have hot water showers. The last one had no shower and the two before that had no hot water. I've learned to take a fast shower in cold water. Do you think we can chase Rod into the shower? He's getting ripe!"

Jacky was never far from criticizing her younger brother.

"Yes. He's Colonel Flannel, Shrinks from Washing. If we take away his clothes when he's in the shower, he'll have to change into a clean set."

"If he showers."

They sometimes waved at other cars traveling west, piled high with family possessions, and at exotically burdened farm carts carrying Okies and with their household goods: beds, an occasional piano or farm tools… and dust.

One old woman rode the tailgate of her family's cart, raving and gesticulating, plucking at her white hair and bonnet.

"Potty, poor old thing!"

"Not so poor. At least they're keeping her."

"Well Johnny, do you think this crew would put us out on an ice floe to freeze?"

"I don't think Jacky would. She'd share her fire and food with us, but the boys…David would arrange something, but I'm afraid that Rod would get sentimental and leave us with an eiderdown."

"You can't tell, can you Johnny? The world is so much chancier for us now. We're landless peasants!"

"We *are* landless peasants, and on the move, like the navvys in my boyhood. They worked on the railways, and camped wherever there was a cutting to be made."

"What's a cutting, Johnny?"

"Where a railway had to cut through a hill, navvys cut a notch using shovels and wheelbarrows to make the cutting. They had no machinery. They were called navvys because they navigated from job to job."

"Like us. Remember that woman from Northumberland, who had a navvy husband who worked in the south? They didn't own much—a kitchen table, chairs, bedding and cooking equipment. When the family had to return home, she turned the table over, put a blanket over the legs and piled everything on the blanket. She tied the bundle together and was able to ship it home, kitchen table and all, on a common carrier."

"We must have made at least ten homes, Johnny. We'll soon make another, but at the moment I'm enjoying our wandering. A good thing we have a couple of weeks left.

What did you think of that tourist camp owner who named their little boy Hell Bent? Do you think he was pulling our leg?"

"I'm still amazed at how different Americans are from our people. You'd think at least we'd have the English language in common, but here words and phrases have different meanings. Remember that wet morning we pushed straight out and stopped for breakfast in that little café? Fried eggs were 'straight up', porridge was 'mush', tea was hottish water, and a scone was a hot biscuit.

"I was hungry and a little discouraged trying to talk to them, but then, we're immigrants."

"Immigrants or no, I just couldn't stand the sight of those scones with white grease gravy all over them."

Beatrix groaned and shuddered at the thought.

"I don't feel that Rod is making much of an adjustment. He wasn't young enough to just leave it all and make a new life. The differences are all so much more clear to us old ones. When something, even a word such as scones comes up we don't want to shift to biscuits, but the children will have to change. If one of Jacky's men friends leaves his hat on in the house or, horrible to contemplate, leaves it on while eating, she won't adapt. She will have the hardest time. After all, you and I don't have to create a new personality to adopt the new culture, but the children will. If only we could provide for them.

"I suppose Doight, that we are working people now."

"The English are convinced that on the whole, working people are common, which I'm beginning to see in a different light now that we are part of them. In fact, I haven't heard the word *common* since we came to America. It really is a terrible word."

"You're right. There doesn't seem to be room here for many of these old country prejudices that are such a part of British life. Imagine not being able to eat with some people because they said 'tighble' instead of 'table.'"

As they drove along the edge of the Old South, Beatrix

deluged the children with images and quotations from *Uncle Tom's Cabin* and *Uncle Remus*. Beatrix watched for Bre'r rabbit in each briar patch, unaware that bre'r meant brother in the language of southern people. Beatrix's reading of the dialect was exotic.

She told the children about the Drinking Gourd, the map in the sky showing the North Star, which gave direction for slaves as they escaped at night. As they crossed a long iron bridge over the Mississippi they re–lived the stories—*Little Women, Hiawatha, The Deerslayer, Uncle Tom's Cabin, Huck Finn, The Virginian, Silverado Squatters.*

It was a library laid out for them.

In the Midwest, the highway petered out to a gravel road. After a couple of hours' driving on gravel, they stopped "on top of the moor", as Beatrix said, at a wayside store. There men were heavily dressed - misshapen in Wellington boots and heavy wind–breakers - resembling Eskimos.

"Would you tell us the name of that cone–shaped mountain on the horizon?"

"It must be Pike's Peak."

"On to Colorado!"

At Walsenburgh, as David and Jacky walked along the plank sidewalks of the main street, they noticed men who were wearing cowboy hats and jingling spurs.

"Young man, where do you come from?"

David was nonplussed by this six foot three cowboy who had accosted him on the street.

Jacky intervened, "We are from England, Sir."

"Well, young feller, are you from England too? You must be, with that white cotton hair."

Mr. Perryman then introduced himself to Johnny and Beatrix and, after he told them how he admired their incredibly blond son, he invited the family to stay on his ranch.

"Would you like to break your journey at our place? It's not far from here."

"Well, only if it's no trouble. We have our own food and camp gear. If it is not too much trouble."

Mr. Perryman, with his six-shooter in a tooled leather holster, guided them west into Colorado countryside. They drove passed fence after fence, the boys opening and closing the gates, for twenty miles into the foothills of the Rockies. For the Pains, this was a scene that was right out of western movies, shades of Zane Gray and Hoot Gibson! The Pain family knew this landscape - the distant vistas and movie cowboys riding across the dry valley with little pops of dust rising from each hoof beat. After an hour over rutted, corduroyed roads, suddenly a box canyon opened at their feet and there was the ranch at the foot of the cliff.

The Pains stayed for a week. Jacky and the boys rode saddle broncs into the country, and ate in the bunkhouse with Mr. Perryman and the cowboys. David's fresh beauty and foreign frankness fascinated Mr. Perryman, a gentleman rancher and owner of a large drug store. He would have kept the family longer, and asked to adopt David and keep him on the ranch. Beatrix and Johnny protested that they had to press on.

On one last ride before the family continued west, a bronc tossed Rod into a patch of nopal cactus. The spines stuck to Rod's arm and back. Johnny cut away the cactus spines to relieve the heavy weight of the cactus leaves, but Rod was still full of needles. Johnny pulled them out one at a time. David overheard Rod's laments.

"Take that for bullying me!"

In Colorado, Rod, Jacky and Johnny hiked the eight-mile trail down to the Grand Canyon, to the Colorado River, passing other tourists who rode mules down to the Canyon Ranch. The three Pains ate sandwiches and drank from the springs along Bright Angel Trail and the Colorado River.

Johnny thought of his brother, Henning, and how he had run the Canyon in a rowboat more than a quarter of a century before.

CHAPTER TWENTY-FOUR

*I lay upon the summer grass,
A gold-haired sunny child came by,
And looked at me, as loath to pass,
With questions in her lingering eye.*

*"Why do you read?" She said...
"I read a poet of old time,
Who sang through all his living hours..."*

*Beauty of earth—the streams, the flowers
And now I read him, since men go,
Forgetful of these sweetest things;
Since he and I love brooks that flow,
And dawns, and Bees, and flash of wings!"*

*She stared at me with laughing look,
Then clasped her hands upon my knees:
"How strange to read it in a book!
I could have told you all of these!"*

—Arthur Davison Ficke, 1883 – 1945, *The Oracle*

The distances of America were a vast surprise to the unseasoned travellers. Their sense of proportion and size had was challenged. America was thousands of miles across, with hundreds of miles even between rivers. England had fields, woods and a river every four miles; every inch had felt the print of human foot. In England, only ploughed fields, graves and garden paths showed raw dirt. Arizona, by contrast, did not fit these established notions. A person could be lost here! Beatrix had no fix on this western scenery. Here the dirt ran hot in the sun and wild to the horizon, with the occasional menacing candelabra cactus or spiked cholla. The western scenery was overwhelming.

Although the old Hup ate up the miles, there seemed no end to this western land.

In the Painted Desert, Beatrix wondered at a big fragment of petrified wood, older than the Stone Age, older than England. She felt she was traveling through a dream, waiting for the Silverado Squatters as she balanced this ancient piece of wood changed to stone.

The desert became so hot, the caravan drove at night the road lit by the dim headlights, which needed re–silvering. Here there were no white lines on the roads, sometimes only one lane, and sometimes three lanes - the centre lane was called "suicide."

As the family drove across America, one custom was inviolate – the Lipton tea break. Johnny would stop at five and light the gasoline camp stove. Lipton's, was one of the few luxuries they would not forego. Beatrix and Johnny felt that at each tea break they celebrated a little cheer for Britain with their loyalty Lipton.

One morning, the family woke in a Mojave Desert campsite to an unfamiliar aroma. Their neighbours, two desert veterans, were making coffee. The bearded, sun–dried men were dressed in denim with wide–brimmed felt hats, high boots, and holstered revolvers. Their donkey, Jake, was tied to a bush and a bag of water dripped slowly from his packsaddle.

"Why Ma'am, we're taking a break from traveling. We get up at four to miss the heat of the day. Old Jake there don't like carrying all our outfit in the heat while we're off prospecting for gold."

"Good gracious! Does it just lie around to be found?"

"Oh no, Missus, it jes hides and hides and we prospect for it. We look for sign."

"Sign?"

"Waal, it's like this. We look for rocks that jes look like every other rock, but has gold in them. That's sign."

"Do you often find it?"

"Not offen enough to bother us. No, we don' find it offen. Would yo like a cuppa coffee?"

"Thank you, yes. We have a bit of shop cake left from yesterday. Would you like some?"

"Yes, thank you kindly. What's shop cake?"

"Oh, bought cake. Thanks for the coffee. It's the first we've had in months. We usually drink tea."

"Tea! Well I'll be durned!"

The next day the family arrived at Cajon Pass, high above the Promised Land, California. As they wound down from the Pass, David suddenly exclaimed:

"Look, Mudderkees, orange groves! I can see the little oranges, just like the advertisements, bright like Christmas ornaments. Hurry Nacko, let's get down there!"

They coasted down the switchbacks to an orange grove.

"Do you think we could try one, Nacko?"

"Well, there are some on the ground. Don't pick any from the trees."

The rich sweet juice from the full, sun–ripened fruit ran down their chins. They nearly sickened themselves, eating so many oranges.

"We *have* left England!"

Their travels were almost over as they drove on into Los Angeles, the City of Our Lady Queen of the Angels.

"Rod, do you remember *Two Years Before the Mast?*"

"Oh yes, the California farmers left saucers of change by guests' beds to make them feel welcome."

"Haciendados, not farmers. They were sort of lords"

No one noticed when Beatrix said *haciendaddos*. Little remained of that early Catholic settlement and the haciendados who left the money for the guests.

The Pains bored on through from Pasadena to a low range of hills with farms.

Johnny said, "I'm following instructions, and haven't got you lost yet. We're on La Brea and will cross Manchester soon. Just be patient. After all, we've been on the road three weeks."

"Here's Manchester. Which way, Nacko?"

"Read the letter to me Doight."

"I wonder if the Coopers are expecting us as Mr. Nye promised."

"It would be a long way to come to not be welcomed."

Nye had told them about the Coopers.

"Salt of the earth, as British as you are. The Coopers were my parishioners for a long time but were tempted into California with jobs. They will welcome you as a message from England, with working class enthusiasm. I know you'll like them"

Although Beatrix had done her best to maintain a few clean clothes, the family was a travel–stained crew. The old Hup was dirtier, with its layers of desert dust.

"I'm really ashamed to meet these people. I know the

collar of my blouse is filthy and, as for you, Rod, we'll just have to hose you off before they let you in the house."

They turned into the driveway of a white stucco bungalow, its doorway outlined in curved plaster, a modest workingman's home.

The Coopers were all Mr. Nye had said, solid working people. They were a small family with the narrow sharp faces of Londoners, ready smiles and ready voices, anxious to talk to compatriots. They welcomed the Pains with such enthusiasm, as they had never expected. They were hardly in the door before the kettle was on for tea.

"Tell us the news of Mr. Nye, the dear!"

"What was it like, driving? We took the train."

"How was your trip? Did you see the Grand Canyon?"

"Where in the Old Country are you from? We're from London!"

"Father! They're from Maidenhead!"

Their old father had immigrated with the Coopers, and still had a minuscule pension coming from the Printer's Union, where he had worked as a ruler of blank ledgers for accountants.

"Yes, they sometimes need a lot of columns of different widths." The old man's accent was balm to their ears.

The Pains stayed with the Coopers for three weeks, camping in their tent on the back lawn. It was clear to Beatrix and Johnny that they would have to go to Los Angeles or Hollywood to find work, because Hawthorne had few jobs. In the meantime, Rod found work with an old vegetable peddler who drove his Model T Roadster to the vegetable wholesaler every morning, buying a few cases of fruit and vegetables to hawk from door to door.

"Mudderkees, I enjoy carrying a basket of fruit and vegetables from to door to door, and the people buy from me. I get ten percent."

"Come around here and I'll buy some."

"Yesterday, when we stopped for lunch, he picked out a bruised cantaloupe. He brought out his big penknife to share the melon, "You know it's ripe if it's bruised," he said. He spat on the knife to clean it, for he chewed tobacco. Made me feel funny, but I ate the cantaloupe. It was delicious."

"Or with tobacco sauce Rod!"

"No, it was the ripeness. The tobacco was extra."

The Cooper's kindness continued. They had friends in Hollywood, who might help, so the Pains drove over the golden hills to Hollywood with a letter of introduction to John and Pat Stover. John Stover worked in the motion picture studios and might know where Johnny Pain could find work.

John Stover was a kindly man from Pennsylvania, mild and religious, a Dunkard, a form of Quakerism. Every day, wearing a threadbare coat and shapeless felt hat, he rode the streetcar to the movie studio where he was a "special effects" man. His upbringing as a Dunkard had taught him compassion; John and his wife, Pat, took the Pains into their house.

Desperate, with their money and vacation at an end, Johnny and Jacky took the first job they could get, door to door selling. They were to sell deodorizers, pink naphtha crystals crusted onto a wire to hang in the toilet.

"So you don't like cold turkey?' their boss asked. They didn't understand their employer's dismissal at the end of a day's hawking.

After almost a month with the Stovers, Beatrix felt anxious.

"You know Johnny, it's wrong to whine when good

people are generous to you, but it's hard for me to be indebted to strangers."

"I know, Doight, but they are good people who want to help and, goodness knows, we need help. It won't be long and we'll find our footing, you'll see. I might find a job in the studio where Stover works, and we'll be able to find a place to live."

"You're right. I'll buck up. We are doing a bit for the Stovers, buying some of the food and doing the cooking. I hope it won't be long. Let's go to bed."

Beatrix felt shamed. For her, the family was lowered to the point of accepting charity, however graciously and generously given, from strangers. And to make matters worse, she had started a hard menopause. This was the lowest Beatrix had felt since her marriage.

CHAPTER TWENTY-FIVE

*Let me not to the marriage of true minds
Admit impediments. Love is not love
Which alters when it alteration finds,
Or bends with the remover to remove:
O no! It is an ever-fixed mark,
That looks on tempests and is never shaken;
It is the star to every wand'ring bark,
Whose worth's unknown, although his height be taken,
Love's not Time's fool, though rosy lips and cheeks
Within his bending sickle's compass come;
Love alters not with his brief hours and weeks ,
But bears it out even to the edge of doom:-*
    *If this be error and upon me proved,
    I never writ, nor no man ever loved.*

—William Shakespeare, 1564 – 1616

"I guess you know your mother is going through the change, Rod."

"Not really, Pat. What change?"

Rod saw his mother simply as *Mother*, never shaking or bending, never ill, whatever the storm.

"Oh, you don't know much. Your mother's body is changing naturally, from being a mother to never being able to have children again. It's a difficult change. You must help her as much as you can, and do things for her. She needs all the help she can get."

"What can I do?"

"Just be nice and don't fret. Don't fight with Jacky and David."

"I'll try."

The family stayed with Pat and John Stover until Nacko set up his cabinet shop near downtown Hollywood. The Pain family found a house to rent on Rosewood Avenue, close to the Stovers place, in a family neighbourhood. The cottage was Mission Style, derivative of Roycrofters. It was a style consistent with the evanescent, ephemeral quality of Hollywood, founded on sunshine and dedicated to the lightest of light entertainment. Here today and gone tomorrow.

Contractors built these houses on narrow trenches cut three inches into the ground and filled with concrete, barely enough to keep the wooden plate timbers dry, marking the outline of the house. Walls were three and a half inches thick, the roofs trussed with light planking. The outside walls, the weather walls, were wrapped with tarpaper and the lightest gauge chicken wire, and then stuccoed with gentle California arches, Mission Design. These houses, a week's work, sold for $1500. This was home for the Pain family, and a far sight prettier than the slum of East Rutherford.

"I can live with this," thought Beatrix, enjoying the modest attractions of the little house and the shade of old carob trees. People in the area lived hand to mouth. Vegetables cost one or two cents a bunch. A two-dollar bag of groceries was too heavy to carry home. With care, it would feed a family almost a week. Gasoline was 10 cents a gallon—but where was there to go? The local bank had collapsed, paying ten cents on the dollar to depositors.

Across the street, two old vaudeville stagers practiced on their unicycles. With a whoop they tossed boomerangs to each other, picked up bicycle frames and fitted them to the unicycles, riding onwards to grab front wheels and handlebars. With a cry of triumph they rode in tight circles, assembling the bikes as they rode. With another whoop, the unicyclists reversed the routine. David and Rod watched spellbound.

Jacky found a job, Rod and David were off to school and Johnny was setting up his cabinet shop. The sign for his new shop was hung from two posts, white with black letters, for a gentleman craftsman carving his way into carnivorous Hollywood.

JOHN PAIN

Period Furniture—Carving Lessons

Furniture Repair

Refinishing

His shop building was two garages, side by side with the connecting wall knocked out, open to passers by. An emaciated machinery salesman, Mr. Tweak, outfitted Johnny with a secondhand table–saw, turning lathe, band saw and a light drill–press. Beyond the light–weight machines, Johnny made do with hand tools - saws, planes, and chisels. Mr. Tweak continued to call but only managed to sell the occasional box of screws and sheets of sandpaper.

Johnny began to eke out a living, mending and refinishing furniture. His artistic talent and his quiet country manners were considered courtly in Hollywood. His unfailing gallantry to women and his good looks gathered a modest following of doctors' wives. He started to teach woodcarving.

The business had no money for wages. His apprentice, Arthur, worked for the experience and made woodcarving chisels out of files, heated red hot in Johnny's gas torch. The handles were turned out of wood scraps from the shop. Arthur sold the chisels to Johnny's wood carving students.

Beatrix managed the household, served tasty meals, washed the laundry by hand as she had no washing machine, and ironed with her new electric iron, a gift from Johnny.

"Rod, will you give me a hand?"

Rod had pulled the sheets with his mother for years, pulling the corners to stretch out the laundry wrinkles with a pleasing, irregular, jerking motion. It was a small chore they enjoyed together.

"No, not pulling, Rod. Would you just scrub this weeks' sheets, I have a lot to do, and I'm very tired."

Rod washed the bed sheets in the washtubs. When his knuckles got sore, he made some inch wide strips of inner tube rubber and cut holes in the ends, to slip over his fingers.

The family now needed all the cohesion it could muster. Beatrix knew they were *on their uppers,* having, as the saying intimated, worn holes in their shoe soles, they now walked barefoot under the shoe vamps, *on their uppers.*

"Johnny, I sometimes remember those days in London when we had all those servants, fancy meals, bespoke clothes and handmade shoes. We even had time to read and write."

"I hardly know what to think of it all, Doight. The song says 'the rich man in his garden and the poor man at his gate.' Why are we always at the gate?"

"Poor Ja. She's the one who gave up the most in the move to America. She would have been better staying in England with Dolly and Henry, with all they could have done for her."

"Her training isn't doing her much good. Nobody here is interested in France or anything French, and being British is a disadvantage."

"I can't for the life of me understand the antipathy. Going back to George III seems a bit extreme, but they do harp on the Boston Tea Party. I suppose that when there's a revolution there has to be bad blood, like a youngster leaving his mother and father, needing a row to legitimize the break. But, after two hundred years one would think they'd let bygones be. On the other hand, look at the Irish, and how we feel about them!"

"Well, I still hear 'damn Limey' more often than not."

"The boys have heard it too."

"I've always been proud to be an Englishman and I can't for the life of me understand why I should be ashamed of it."

"Of course, you mustn't be ashamed, Johnny. There's no cure for ignorance. After all, it was the British Empire that made this country. Maybe that's what bothers them. Perhaps we are all too proud, and of the wrong things."

"Pride seems to be all that we have left. I hope the boys will do better."

"We can't cut it much finer, Johnny. The other day, when I asked Rod to go to the shop for a can of tomatoes, he went to the nearest little shop. They charged 13 cents for the can, when a few blocks further the A&P store had the same can for 12 cents. When I asked why he hadn't gone for the cheaper one, he said that it was a long way to ride for one cent. I'm afraid I upbraided him, telling that I'd have walked that far to save a penny. He looked crestfallen."

"Riding eight blocks for a cent might be hard for him to understand."

"Poverty is something a parent wants to save the children from. But here we are in poverty, although I think we have kept them from thinking of themselves as poor, and certainly from thinking that because they were poor, that they were common..."

"This little cottage is the nicest place we've had since we arrived in North America."

"Yes. I hope we can keep it."

Jacky had the hardest job, as a waitress. She was paid out of ten-cent tips - a nickel was considered just too mean. She was too proud to be a pushover—to 'be available' or, as they put it, to 'get round heels', so she moved from job to job. Her worst job was a second-storey restaurant on Hollywood Boulevard with a downstairs kitchen. Every serving, plate, cup and saucer had to be carried upstairs and then carried back downstairs, dirty, on banquet trays. She needed all her strength then. No more cartwheels.

The small independence Johnny and Beatrix had scraped together to pay for the trip west had shrunk to nothing. It was 1932 and Beatrix realized she was the most employable person in the family.

"Johnny, with my experience during the war, I think I can get a job cooking."

"You can't! I won't have it! The idea. I'll get something more to do. I'll find a way. Oh no, you can't—you mustn't."

"Calm down, Johnny. It's only for a little while. Remember I worked during the war, and it was no disgrace then, and no disgrace now."

"I won't hear of it! You can't."

But she did. The employment bureau was not hard to find, and Beatrix described her experience convincingly. The fee for a job was simple—the job seeker paid the bureau her first two weeks' wages. The agency needed the fee as much as the job seeker - there were so few jobs to sell.

Beatrix was hired by a wealthy lawyer, Mr. Biby. The family would also take Johnny, letting him stay with Beatrix in her little cook's room in exchange for his polishing the two Lincoln cars once a week, on Saturdays, ready for church.

The Pains could no longer afford the Rosewood Avenue rent so Jacky moved her brothers, now eight and fourteen, into a small flat built on top of a double garage near the diagonal streetcar track that united East and West Hollywood. In the middle of their first night, David suddenly stood up in his bed, "What—what was that—what's happening?" Streetcar bells clanged ten feet from his head.

Johnny soon realized he needed to be at his shop on Saturdays.

"Doight, washing those Lincolns is taking too much of my time. Let's get Rod to do them on Saturdays so I can go to work in the shop."

Rod looked forward to his day at the Bibys, helping his mother. Beatrix was feeling the strain. Her job was to cook, clean the house weekly, take alternate Sundays off after clearing up Saturday supper, and be back to cook the Monday morning breakfast. She had not been taxed like this since Edinburgh.

After cleaning the Biby cars, Rod helped to clean the house.

Through the week, Beatrix saved thick cuts of roast, scalloped potatoes, slathers of hot gravy, and big cuts of pie with whipped cream. Beatrix called this *the brock*, the old Scots name for the broken meats from a wealthy table, divided among the servants. On the weekend, Rod could eat to repletion.

Although slavery and owning slaves were a distant part of United States history in the 1930s, Beatrix found that respect for the profession of personal service did not prevail in Los Angeles.

She agreed to wear cook's white, but balked at wearing a cap. For her, the cap was part of the uniform, which was symbolic of the working class in England. Beatrix wore a hair net but would never wear a cap.

CHAPTER TWENTY-SIX

Then Peggy O'Connor took up the job,
'Biddy' says she; 'you're wrong I'm sure'.
But Biddy gave her a belt on the gob,
And left her sprawling on the floor;
The war did soon enrage
'Twas woman to woman and man to man
Shillelagh law did all engage,
And a row and a ruction soon began
Whack fol the dah, dance to your partner
Welt the flure yer trotters shake...

—James Joyce, *Finnegan's Wake*

Although Johnny rarely talked about his Beatrix being in service, he felt twisted. He despaired, and turned time and again to his primitive memories of beleaguered British class culture, trying to make sense of his feelings as he learned the lessons of this new country, a country where people were supposedly equal.

Beatrix confided in Jacky.

"Ja, when I'm at work, it is not doing things for other people that jars on me. I've been doing that for a long time, for your father, my father, for Dolly, the wounded soldiers and so on. But it's the unknowing, insensitive way the Yanks have with servants that jars me."

"I know, Mudderkees! In restaurants, the boss owns you, the customers own you. They expect what they're not entitled to; they think they own your body! I quit the job on Hollywood Boulevard because the manager pressured me. When I said no, he said, 'There's the door. Pick up your tips.'"

"Exactly. Even after nine at night, the Biby family thinks nothing of ordering a glass of hot milk, after your duty is done. You are half undressed and you can't serve them in your nightgown. They even expect you to alter your day off to suit them. We would never do that sort of thing to a servant in England. There, except for the cook and the maid serving dinner, the staff was off after tea. In England, even horses had a day off every week and often retired to special pasture."

"Oh Mudderkees, I do hope you can stop this working out soon..."

"So do I, but there isn't much prospect. Your father's business is not prospering, though he does more than his best."

"He's up against the same thing. Americans don't understand the traditions we identify with."

"Of course, the people we've been meeting are nice, but the *everyone's equal thing* wears thin, especially when they are putting you down, paring you down, and don't care. The other day when Rod was cleaning the floors, Mrs. Biby was telling him how to wax the edges of the floor round the carpet. She said, "Just sit on the polish rag and scoot round. Here, I'll show you!" and she sat on the rag and scooted. Rod didn't know what to say..."

"Wouldn't have done to have laughed!"

"No, and another thing. When Rod was vacuuming the front hall, young Margaret came out of her bedroom stark naked, and paraded. Rod pretended not to see her. He packed up and came to my room, wanting to know what to do. I said, if she was ignorant enough to do that sort of thing in front of servants, she deserved to be ignored."

"Well, at any rate, she won't have anything to tell on Rod."

Beatrix spent her rare days off at the family apartment. Jacky and the boys' second story flat was in an area of light industry—a commercial sandwich kitchen on one side of the apartment building and, on the other side, a business owned by Mr. Harman and Mr. Ising, known as *Harmonising*. They made animated cartoons. The area was light industrial, but the Pains saw it as a slum.

Beatrix's jobs continued to be demanding. When her old friend, Doris Weatherstone–Smith, visited from England, Beatrix was allowed only two days off. Then the job with the Biby family ended and once again, Beatrix endured the indignity of job interviews.

"You have no idea of the different kinds of people they send me to for an interview, and that's after they have been screened by the agency. From their speech, I would guess many employers are illiterate, certainly illiterate of manners. One woman asked me my age, and then complained in front of me that the agency had better not show any more old women to her for hire."

"But you are getting such a good reputation as a special cook!"

"You don't know Ja, how many there are waiting in line and waiting for my job. I may have a good reputation as a cook but if I look less vigorous than some young Swedish pastry cook, where am I? And Nacko doesn't want to be separated from me, so I ask, but most employers don't allow extras, even husbands. The wages are kept rock bottom because there are so many others standing in line. Nobody gets more than the standard wage."

She realized how the family relied on her earnings for rent and food. Jacky had only sporadic work in restaurants, and Johnny's earnings from five or six customers were not enough. Beatrix had to work, and, in a work-scarce economy, she couldn't complain. To merely have a job, good or bad, was a blessing.

Jacky got on at *Old Vienna*, a German restaurant with a zither player and beer jelly on the menu. There the men were Europeans so she was left alone. Sometimes when she was tired or could not go home, she brought Rod and David in for a meal. Thirty-five cents for a whole meal.

Johnny was to suffer another blow, not huge, but it hurt, bitterly. Rod told his father, "Nacko, I've met this man who makes fishing rods, Mr. Kowalowski, I think his name is. He makes rods and reels for the sword fishermen, the men who fish for those huge game fish. They use really strong rods and compound geared reels so they can fight the fish for hours."

"He is a rod maker?"

"Yes."

A few days later Johnny took his beloved Greenheart fly rod, in sections, in the long bag with brown laces, to Mr. Kowalowski's shop.

"Not my line, Mr. Pain, but I might be able to get a little for it with one of the sport fishermen. They prefer bamboo fly rods, haven't heard of Greenheart!"

"It's the best in England, for fly rods and light lines."

"Put it together for me."

Johnny did, and handed it to Kowalowski, who whipped it a bit to see the action. "I'll give you twenty dollars for it."

"It's worth more than that. But I need the money."

Kowalowski started to disassemble the rod, pulling the little tube and centre pin joints apart. One was dry and stuck, and Kowalowski pulled. It came apart with a snap, the end joint of the fly rod hit the wall and broke. Johnny just took the pieces and walked out. He never fished again.

Johnny's wartime dress uniform, some tools Beatrix's Aunt Emmie had given him, and a few pieces of family silver were all that were left to remind him of the golden days he had left.

One weekend, Johnny and Beatrix stole away from Hollywood and drove two hours to a half–built cabin owned by the Stovers in the Santa Suzanna Mountains. They climbed a tall hill overlooking the San Fernando Valley, and sat on a boulder at the crest, each with an arm around the other, watching the sunset. They did not think they were observed. Physical demonstrations of affection or anger were hard for them to show. Part of their strength to just survive was used to show strength. The future held no target for them. Mustering private pride when humiliated, moving in silence when ordered around by people, toughened by the realization that any the job was a profound favour, all folded Beatrix into silent obduracy.

Beatrix found work in Limonera near Santa Barbara, with a family of lemon growers. The terms, or contract, gave her two days off a month, Friday night through Monday morning, as long as Beatrix cooked the meals ahead for Saturday and Sunday. On Friday evenings, after the supper was cleaned up, Johnny and she left for home and her family. When she returned to Limonera Sunday night, the dirty dishes from six meals waited for her.

When the lemon ranchers vacationed in their house near Twin Lakes in the Sierra Nevada Mountains, Beatrix went with them. There she befriended a chipmunk. Unfamiliar with North American mammals, she thought the chipmunk was a tiny squirrel. He took a long time to get acquainted, as chipmunks are notoriously shy and nervously alert, but she had time and patience. Every afternoon before making supper she courted him and, after many trials she made him her friend, naming him *Mr. Pastry*, after a favourite radio personality. He lived up to his name, eating pastry from her fingers.

Although she felt tired in the evenings, she always tried to read from a favourite book to regain strength for the next day. Before turning off the light, she often read the book of English verse, which her father had given to her.

"Well, Johnny—you are far away, though not from my heart. Here it is, Shakespeare always says something.

> *When icicles hang by the wall,*
> *And Dick the shepherd blows his nail,*
> *And Tom bears logs into the hall,*
> *And milk comes frozen home in pail,*
> *When blood is nipp'd, and ways be foul,*
> *Then nightly sings the staring owl,*
> *To–whit!*
> *To–who!—a merry note,*
> *While greasy Joan doth keel the pot.*

"And so to bed. I've keeled the pot! Goodnight, Johnny."

And the days ground on. Although people were decent

enough, most of the time they had no understanding of her.

"Make a nice meat loaf with pan gravy today, please Mary."

She had never given them her first name; that was for those who cared for her. Meat loaf! She despised even the thought of meatloaf; her body gave a spiral wrench of horror. She sympathized with the French chef, famed for his creations but unhappy working in England. He reportedly spat in the food every day.

In the 1930s, Los Angeles was the high church of materialism, where catering to fashion, appearances, and social attitude prevailed rather than the values Beatrix held so strongly—intellect, honesty, and the beauty of old things. She felt her life seemed to stink of Los Angeles.

A letter from Rod brought a rare moment of satisfaction. thanked her for *The Shropshire Lad*.

"Thank you so much, Mudderkees. You shouldn't have spent so much on my present, but I love it, particularly the lines:

> *Loveliest of trees, the cherry now*
> *Is big with bloom along the bough*
> *And stands about the woodland ride*
> *Wearing white for Eastertide.*

I wish I could write lines like that..."

Her heart rose.

Beatrix knew she was aging before her time, and the time ran hard. She had so little time with Johnny and the children in the rented place on Seward Street with its concrete garden. Her days just ground on. She felt David and Rod's schooling was a blessing; their achievements were hers. She read of the travails of others to lift herself to a short dream world:

Look at the stars! Look at the skies!
Oh look at the firefolk sitting in the air
The bright boroughs, the quivering citadels there...
The firefolk and the bright boroughs. Oh, if only!

"Oh Johnny! Look at this! A letter from the Old Country! My Aunt Fannie left me a legacy! That dear old thing remembered me."

"What a windfall. What will you do with it? Will you come home now?"

"Oh no. We are just keeping our heads above water, just barely. This money, we will plough into something real for the family, and for you and me. No gamble. Let's buy a bit of land and build a home on it."

On their day off they drove through the countryside, looking for a bit of country, in the middle of the huge Los Angeles. On the far side of the Hollywood Hills was the San Fernando Valley, a valley of dry sand, where a scatter of ranchers grew grapes and melons. Della Quadri, who was dividing up his large vineyard, sold seven tenths of an acre to Beatrix and Johnny. It seemed the right time for Johnny to close his struggling business.

"I hate to close it up, Doight, but those few doctors and their wives do not need enough cabinets and furniture to keep the shop open. I'll work for us, now, until we have the house built. I'll build us a home. I think I know enough to do it, and Rod and David can give a hand."

Beatrix felt a rush of satisfaction as the walls of their home went up. The Cape Cod design helped her think of home. Somehow she seemed to amount to something now. She always had been erect, but now it seemed her shoulders were more braced back.

Rod and Johnny set out early every morning, with a bag of hand tools and two shovels, a chalk line, and a set of plans Johnny bought at a reduced price from an off duty draughtsman. Johnny set the front line of the house to clear the spread of the two handsome chestnut trees. The boys dug the footing trenches, and the small hole for the cellar, cutting the walls of the sand as smooth and straight as they could. They used a shovel to mix concrete in a boat and carried it a bucket at a time to fill the space between the sand and the boards. After a week, a truckload of wood arrived. The driver levered the load to a balance point on the stern of the truck, and drove away letting the great stack of wood bang to the ground. Rod marveled that the length of each piece was different. It was then that he discovered why all the wood was of various lengths. Johnny had bought an economy load of random lengths.

Every stud and brace and window frame had to be cut by hand and passed up to Johnny to nail into place. They finished the house in three summer months and nailed a bush to the roof beam as a ritual. It was ready to paint, and the boys dug a cesspit to take the sewage.

They joked that they would name the home, as people in England did. *Armstrong* seemed to fit.

The building and the land used up the legacy, which, with a small mortgage, gave them their own place. The prospect of moving into their own country home overshadowed the years incomprehensible immigrant frustration.

One afternoon Rod asked offhandedly, "Mudderkees, what do you think of the Navy?"

"You know my feelings about war, Rod. There isn't anything good in it, but it is peacetime, and what else have you to do? There isn't much in the job market for you. What a pity we just couldn't afford the $250 to match that California Scholarship Federation award you were offered."

"The navy would be a job right now, and an opportunity within the year to compete for Annapolis and a degree."

"That is a good college, and being a Blue Jacket would be better than looming around the house with no chance of a job. I am glad you would have the prospect of a degree..."

"They said it was an open exam for everyone in the Fleet."

"I suppose you want my permission. You're only seventeen."

Rod went into the Navy, a somewhat unwilling recruit, with his hidden agenda.

"I know Mudderkees would like me to become a Naval Officer. She could raise her head with that."

But Beatrix kept her head down, and soldiered on. Though she claimed not to be a snob, she really needed a bit of glamour to offset the years of little or no pride.

"It's a good thing Rod writes regularly from recruit training. I'm as far from him as ever, but feel closer with his letters."

But the letters were not what she wanted to hear. They were tales of fights with his comrades, of the rigours of recruit training, short haircuts, and other demeaning experiences. Beatrix wanted to find something to make her proud.

"I've been too long without pride. I have had the satisfaction of keeping the family together, but for what? We have kept off the dole, but that's minimal satisfaction. I certainly would not tell anyone back at home what our circumstances are, however proud I might be to have kept off the dole."

Rod took the examination for Midshipman, an officer in the Navy, and passed, qualifying for Annapolis.

"Huzzah!" crowed Beatrix—"He is considered an officer and, in this strange land, a gentleman. But, isn't my Roddy a gentleman already? Why do they need an act of Congress to make that explicit? I guess they get a wide variety in their draft, and need to start them somewhere."

The mysteries of gentility in America still bedeviled Beatrix. She did not understand why America had to pass an Act of Congress to declare all officers as being gentlemen. She could not understand that this Act could create gentility for a farm boy recruit. She still felt that gentility was right for officers.

Her joy was short-lived. Rod was taken aside by his commanding officer to be advised that his appointment, otherwise complete, was canceled because his American citizenship was derivative, coming from Johnny's newly sworn citizenship, and not personally applied for or earned. This palpable fraud, as there was only one grade of citizenship, was not apparent to the family or to Rodney, though it obviously provided a place for some favoured applicant. That little bit of pride, gloss in a gloomy life toiling for others, was denied to Beatrix.

Rodney took an International Business School stenotype course, thinking that a life as a court reporter might serve when he completed his stint. To facilitate his training, Beatrix bought a Remington typewriter for him as a Christmas present, paying on time, five dollars a month.

CHAPTER TWENTY-SEVEN

Hierusalem, my happy home,
When shall I come to thee?
When shall my sorrows have an end,
Thy joys when shall I see?

There lust and lucre cannot dwell,
There envy holds no sway;
There is no hunger, heat, nor cold,
But pleasure every way.

—Anon.

"Johnny! I've a job offer, with a movie star. I'm moving up in life."

The employment agency had offered Beatrix a job cooking for a minor film star.

"What should I do? If I get a job in Hollywood, I'll be nearer to all of you. It would be better than being away. I wonder what working for a film star would be like? Would she have needs I'll not be able to meet? Miss James at the employment agency tries to match me up carefully, and takes two weeks pay as her fee. I'll try it, just to be back near you."

This was good news, especially for Johnny.

"I'll be so glad to have you closer to home. I can't tell

you how I hate having you away."

By this time Beatrix understood that the advantages of her own youth, all the luxuries and privileges, had indeed been *unearned*. Nowadays, she welcomed her meagre and hard-earned salary. It was better than unemployment. However, her employers treated her so casually she wondered if they appreciated her skills.

"They don't understand that being served is a privilege, not a right. They somehow exude a slave-owner attitude. One person I worked for expected me to pick up her handkerchief that she dropped after blowing her nose in it. It was no accident. When I ignored the handkerchief, she told me to pick it up. I knew she meant, 'Pick it up. There are plenty of servants out there waiting to replace you!'"

Beatrix wondered about working for Miss Bruce, a minor actress in Hollywood. Bruce's beauty was particularly evident to Beatrix, for whom beauty had always been denied. Beatrix later discovered that Miss Bruce had a team of professionals catering to her every hair, every nail, and every excretion.

Beatrix's heart went out to Miss Bruce's husband, a rich, unattractive young man with a waddling gait and flat feet. His favourite occupation was tending his collection of toy trains. He had also collected beautiful Miss Bruce as his plaything. They had separate bedrooms.

Getting little from his wife, he spent time with Beatrix, who at least catered to his appetite for food.

Beatrix was also expected to cater to Miss Bruce's fancies.

"Rod, you have no idea of how opaque she is to the niceties of life."

"What do you mean, Mudderkees—after all she's as talented as those WAMPUS babes."

Each year, WAMPAS, the Western Association of Movie Publicists and Advertisers, chose the thirteen most promising Hollywood starlets.

"I don't know how directors get anything from that empty flask. You should see what it takes in personal services and bottles of bleach to keep her image titivated. The list of her primpers is endless because she fires them as fast as she engages them: masseurs, hair stylists and hairdressers, toe and fingernail artists, bleachers and dyers, dressers and pressers and dressmakers, hatters and flatterers, a constant stream."

"What did she do that so upset you?"

"Well, it wasn't much, but just the way she did it. On that hot day last week, when Miss Bruce rang for me, she was stark naked, lolling by the pool on a chaise lounge, every hair showing. Though her robe was right there, she never pulled it over her nakedness 'Get me some orange juice, Mary.' she said."

"I don't see why that upset you, Mudderkees. I would have been all agog."

"Don't be dense. It was as though I were an automaton, with no sense of modesty, and that any modesties I had were non–existent. It was just so undignified, so immodest, so unthinking. I was furious. And I had to go squeeze oranges for that little trollop, that bought and sold bit of soiled goods."

Some imagined infraction soon caused Miss Bruce to fire Beatrix. But Beatrix, who almost immediately got another job, had to work a further two weeks for nothing. Beatrix learned her lesson. She realized how much she depended on Miss James to support her in a new position. Miss James had to guarantee service from those she placed, or she would not survive herself.

In the thirties, Hollywood films turned more and more to things English. Films were frequently historical romances written by Englishmen, and acted by English actors who had made Hollywood their home. Beatrix became a small part of this expatriate community when she became the cook and housekeeper for an English playwright, W.P. Lipscomb. He was hired to write the script for the Hollywood version of *Nell Gwynn.*

"Johnny, W.P. Lipscomb made his money writing about Nell Gwynn. What do you think of that?"

"You are in good company, at least. Nell Gwynn, why she almost parlayed simple skills into being Queen of England."

"Simple skills indeed! Here in Hollywood they call it the casting couch! Even though Nell was known as a charmer, W.P. is interested in the influence she had during that difficult religious time. Of course, nobody is really immune to real charm, and that is why I found Miss Bruce so unsatisfactory. She was a trollop like Nell, but no brains, no manners, no charm, nothing but casting couch skills."

"Oh Doight, you are hard on the poor woman!"

"Not nearly as hard as she was on me, Johnny, she cost me my self-esteem and a month's pay. She owes me a lot."

"Tell me about Mr. Lipscomb's parties."

"I've only done a couple of quiet evenings, simple English food, roast lamb and fresh mint sauce, and bread pudding to finish. Old George Arliss came, and C. Aubrey Smith, a real darling. After they enjoyed the dinner, they asked for me because they wanted to congratulate me for the English dinner. I felt respected. So different from my other employers!"

"I'm so glad. With war threatening in Europe, the economy is improving. I'm getting jobs as a carpenter now, and earning well. We'll soon have the mortgage under control and get you back."

"You hit that nail on the head, Johnny. Every penny we earned has gone for roof and food, and now there's a bit going for the main chance. It won't be long until we could be debt–free. I'm ready.

"Did I tell you that W.P. asked me to make Digestives?"

"The Peak Frean biscuits?"

"Yes, I have the recipe from an old Englishwoman. Very simple, not too sweet. They remind me of picnics in England."

"Me too, with a hard boiled eggs, mustard and cress sandwiches, cheese, and a cut of cake made with fruit or raisins. What could be better with a bottle of cold tea with milk and sugar, or a bottle of beer?"

"Sounds like heaven, Johnny."

CHAPTER TWENTY-EIGHT

Where the bee sucks, there suck I:
In a cowslip's bell I lie;
There I couch when owls do cry.
On the bat's back I do fly
After summer merrily:
    Merrily, merrily, shall I live now,
    Under the blossom that hangs on the bough.

—William Shakespeare, 1564 –1616

Beatrix Minchin, the debutante, and John Harrison Pain, county sportsman, were faint memories. The decline in their fortunes had taken such a long time they no longer thought of lost scenes and companions. They were two old lovers intent on their new house.

John was now an artisan, proud of his carpentry and woodcarving. The transition from country gentleman to member of a workman's union had not been smooth or easy. His cabinet–making and carpentry were learned without an apprenticeship in a tough mid–life accommodation under the pressure of making a living, and showed the late date of his self–instruction. His drawing and painting were more refined and genteel, reflecting that his earlier mastery of these crafts.

Beatrix could now be proud of her cooking skills. Her apprenticeship as a cook had been driven, as had Johnny's, by the need to provide money, food and shelter for the family. She felt the powerful need, the essential need, to make more for her children than was offered by the working-class culture in North America. Although the three siblings had never been sheltered from need, she succeeded in implanting in them an inner grace of civilized behaviour and an outer and visible symbol of love of literature, a validation of her father's scholarship and sense of humanity. Neither Beatrix nor Johnny achieved a prideful identity with the working class. They maintained their pride in a paper-thin independence, and they never went on the dole.

The depression was losing its power to depress people, giving way to the preparations for the war in Europe, a start towards prosperity. Beatrix's jobs were more available, higher paid, and more varied. Poverty was no longer the bondage it had been for them. They had been hard-scrabbling for many years. They were now able to afford not luxuries, but more soul-serving needs.

Hollywood became a hotbed for British War Relief. Jacky was in the thick of a home guard of British motion picture actors and writers who organized clothing collection for Great Britain at war, and entertainment for British student pilots in training at Lancaster, California, in a school Roosevelt had Lend-Leased to the British. As the world prepared for war, Beatrix began to feel her family was both a victim of and now sometimes benefited by the American attitude to the British. On one hand, Senator Taft discoursed on isolationism in order to exclude the United States from Britain's conflict. Meanwhile, Roosevelt was arranging for pilot trainees to pull planes across the border to Canada at the end of a rope. The British needed the American armaments—airplanes, ammunition and transport ships, known as *bottoms.*

Hollywood was a centre of rest and recreation for these pilots, and they were ready for the fun provided by the British Colony. They expected half their number to die in the air war.

CHAPTER TWENTY-NINE

"Here we are, in a strange Country, surrounded with dangers and difficulties... Our situation is critical and highly unpleasant; however we shall endeavour to make the best of it; what cannot be cured, must be endured."

—Simon Fraser, *On the Path of the Explorers*, June 15, 1808

Beatrix was finally able to come home to her Johnny and their home with two large walnut trees in front, their estate.

The house was truly finished and a garden established front and back. Rod was at Stanford University. David was on the *USS Mount Vernon*, and Jacky was in the Coast Guard. Johnny was training to be an air-frame builder for Hughes Aircraft. The whole family had worked toward getting Beatrix home. They had won.

Beatrix came out of the tunnel of her long dark journey. It had been a difficult grind. She and Johnny felt they had barely survived the interminable depression. It had nearly scuttled their plan to survive in North America.

"Johnny, I've been waiting to quote *Music Makers* to you. Finally it's right and right for us!

Beatrix

> *We are the music makers*
> *And we are the dreamers of dreams*
> *Wandering by lone sea breakers*
> *And sitting by desolate streams*
> *World losers and world forsakers*
> *Yea, we are the movers and shakers...*
> *For each age is a dream that is dying*
> *Or one that is coming to birth...*

"Our age and its dream died so that the children could get theirs! Now I'm really coming home; I won't have to go back to somebody else's home tonight. It's been so long, Johnny, since we were together, at night, at meals, at work, enjoying."

"Remember 'Ma, gimme a piece?'" Far too long it's been tallow and spread instead of butter and jam. You can't imagine, Doight, what it means to get you back, out of service. There was always the feeling that somehow I was failing you. After all, a fellow should be able to keep his wife at home!"

"We all did it, Johnny, we pulled together. It was lonely, particularly when I worked up in the mountains. Servants didn't have access to the telephone. I don't think I would have settled for immigration if I'd know what it meant. Do you remember the building superintendent telling you, 'We don't 'ire no toffs 'ere?'"

Johnny took his time, remembering.

"I was really upset. It was especially galling when I had to recognize that the tables were turned. We grew up in the class that did the hiring and firing. Now we were the outsiders. Outsiders without a clue."

"We haven't done much hiring and firing for a long time!"

"Doight, just to have you at home making our life like the one we had in Britain is so wonderful. Now we can do things for you. I can't tell you how much we have missed you."

"I missed you all the time but I was often so tired that I couldn't think!"

"It's getting pretty hectic around here, what with the chickens, turkeys, rabbits, eggs, British War Relief, and Jacky's friends. You won't rust, I promise."

"I'll be able to take the load off Jacky."

This was Johnny and Beatrix's second war and a lot different from the first, where it was sacrifice, sacrifice, always with the risk of the dreaded telegram. Rod and David seemed much less vulnerable than Nacko had been at the front in France.

Jacky, always the wild card who never properly rationalized her separation from her English roots, married Bill Mesland, a Dutchman, who was such a great help, but a bore to Beatrix, "so dense, so unaware, so gauche, so provoking."

"I can't see how Jacky puts up with him! His table manners are so awfully continental. When he pops the whole yolk of a cooked egg into his mouth in one gulp I could scream."

But Beatrix didn't scream, she just took on a hundred more chickens, gathering the eggs, candling, buffing and weighing them for the market. Her eggs, like her diction, were refined.

"Chicken Maryland tonight, Bill. Please bring me in a nice fat hen."

Bill would oblige, and eat a huge supper. Beatrix vacillated between appreciating him and being irritated.

The 'home guard' worked its way into a routine and Beatrix watched for the postman, her connection with her sons.

"Johnny, look at this letter from Rod—he has a professor who discovered the significance of the stirrup, of all things. Seems that the Romans beat the Scythians because the Romans had stirrups. Here's something new, he has a new lady friend, Frances Jaffer. From the way he writes she's more important than his other girlfriends. It's about time for him, I'd say. Wonder what she's like."

Johnny was unusually candid, "Well, time will tell. Billie Fisk was a bit of all right as far as I was concerned, but she left and Rod seemed to dry up. I hope he does well..."

Beatrix added, "Oh, I think he will. Rod has never played the field like David. Interesting to think of their differences. Rod liked to help in the house and had no interest in gardening, and David is so wonderful at gardening. I think he made more money at gardening than I did cooking."

"Well, Rod will be down with this new young woman soon."

"Hope so, the family seems to be at a standstill. Bill's only a so–so partner for Jacky."

"Don't remind me, Johnny. He's so provoking."

"I don't think he will last with Ja. He's so generous that it's hard to be down on him, but I don't think Ja will keep on with him. She'll find him wanting, you'll see."

"She's a reader like you, and Bill only reads the front page of the paper and the funnies. I hate to have friction in the family. Let's hope they just drift apart smoothly. But then, one never knows what she'll do. Remember those times with the German friends before the war. How Schum and Von Morehart roared at each other about

Hitler. And Ja was in the thick of it. I think I'd have liked Schum as a son–in–law, he has real quality."

"But he was a Jew, Johnny. Would that have bothered you?"

"Well the difference between the Jews and the Nazis is clear, and I'm for the Jews now. But that wasn't the way I was brought up."

"What was Rod's girlfriend's name, Johnny, Jaffer? It sounds a bit German."

"Perhaps."

When Rod did bring Frances Jaffer home, she and Beatrix got on well, exchanging books and ideas. Beatrix wondered how a 'girl' could be so well informed and yet feckless at housekeeping, until she remembered her own youth, when, as a twenty–year–old, she could not boil an egg or wash a sock.

"We're a pair!"

In 1940, Rod left Stanford to join the U.S. Coast Guard Reserve, stationed in San Francisco. He and Frances were married in Los Angeles.

"I was impressed by the Jewish ceremony." Beatrix was pleased, liking Frances and her mother, Celia. When Frances and Rod returned from a brief honeymoon in Palm Springs she asked:

"Been looking in the ink–pools, Rod?"

"Diving in, Mudderkees! I'm smitten."

CHAPTER THIRTY

'Do you remember me? or are you proud?'
Lightly advancing thro' her star–trimm'd crowd,
Ianthe said, and look'd into my eyes.
'A yes, a yes, to both: for Memory
Where you but once have been must ever be,
And at your voice Pride from his throne must rise.'

—William Landor, 1775 – 1864 Ianthe's Question

Beatrix's life had come many turns, each one putting new demands on her sense of humour, her diminishing strength, and her sense of self and self–esteem. And through it all glowed a memory of her father and his love of literature.

Beatrix wondered, *What would my father say to me now? What would I say to him? Kipling's 'If' would be a bit much as would be old Henley's 'Invictus'. Not to disparage the importance of the soul, but there were times when all I wanted was a better pair of knees while scrubbing a kitchen floor!*

Summers in the San Fernando Valley were hot and dry. When Frances visited her in–laws, she and Beatrix would sit in under the arbour in the shade from the Zinfandel grapevine.

"Come on Cesca, we'll do eggs." Beatrix called to Frances using the nickname Rod had given her, Francesca for Frances, shortened to Cesca, or Chesca, a conceit Rod derived from a small watercolour Johnny had painted of Francesca di Rimini.

"Why do eggs need buffing, Mudderkees?"

"Mucus on the eggs seals them against spoilage. If you washed eggs to get rid of the dirt on them, you would remove the mucus and the eggs spoil. So we use sandpaper to buff the eggs clean. It's mindless, easy work and then we need to candle and weigh them, ready for the egg cartons."

As they sat, the two women talked about the astringent details of their girlhood lives, of Beatrix's disappointment at having her attractive sister usurp her, of being preempted from promised treats by an unfeeling mother who arbitrarily substituted her pretty sister Violet, of being conscious of her plainness.

Frances told her of her mother's failings, of hiding her feelings of frustration, of her large aquiline nose. They both had lost their fathers too soon.

"I was nineteen when my father died and I was thrown back onto my mother and sister, Vi. And then I found Johnny."

Beatrix's voice had, to an American, a sort of cathedral sound, her direct manner cut across the American style of obliquity for manner's sake. She drove unequivocally to a subject she had wanted to discuss.

"You know, Mudderkees, I remember being anxious about my uncles and aunts and my mother, and particularly how my grandparents would react to the news that Rod and I were getting married. I had no way of understanding why they just kept quiet. But when Rod and I visited my grandparents, it was wonderful. They are really 'old country,' from Minsk on the Polish–Russian border. And they were tiny people, probably undernourished, but very proud. Not proud of Russia which treated them terribly, but very proud of being Jews. So you can imagine I was afraid of their reaction. But they received us in my uncle's kitchen and looked us over. My tiny grandmother looked up at Rod, who must have been more than a foot taller, and said:

"'Well, I could have had a Goy, when I was a girl!'"

"That did it. We were accepted in good faith."

"I'm glad to hear that. Old fears and prejudices die hard. I was concerned."

"They don't die hard, Mudderkees, they are continually reinforced. My father started, organized and built a golf course in Hartford, and then was denied a membership in it for being a Jew. You have no idea of how universal anti–Semitism is."

"I'm really sorry to hear that from you. I have wanted to tell you a story, a true story from my youth. My father belonged to a rather grand club in London. I think it was White's, a gambling club. A young man called Marks applied to join. The standard behaviour was to allow a Jew to apply, and then by democratic and secret vote, blackball him. My father knew this was going to happen, and let the club know that if Marks was not in, Minchin was out. The club, not wanting to lose a very significant and valued member, accepted Mr. Marks. Our families had a long friendship. The Marks owned a huge toy business, and you can bet we girls had a wonderful time with them. I remember wonderful Christmas parties with jugglers and Punch and Judy shows."

"And I remember seeing George Arliss in *Disraeli* and realizing that he was accepted in England."

"Well, yes and no. He became a Christian, and was always seen as 'our Jew', a prideful expression of British civilization. But really, as the token Jew, he proved how prejudiced we were! Prejudice is so well camouflaged in Britain. Jews, Catholics, and what in our secret language we call 'Non-Conformists' meaning 'all the rest, all not Church of England', all live with and under prejudice. It's just more overt here in America."

"You've got me there, Mudderkees. We are generous with our promises of democracy, but often miserly in living up to them."

"I can tell you one thing, Cesca, that the people at the bottom here have neither freedom nor power and, what's more, little respect. You have to be at the bottom to see how the people treat you."

Beatrix told the story of being told to pick up the dirty handkerchief.

"It was hard to keep a job and harder to get one then. Yes, I picked it up."

"She deserves and has your scorn."

As Beatrix limped to the chicken pens to gather more eggs, Cesca wondered what had bastioned her mother-in-law against the grinding indignities and years of heavy work. Her matter-of-fact manner masked years of being pressed down. Where did she draw her strength from? In spite of all the things that had happened to her in her life, she had a strong, satisfactory sense of who she was. It wasn't because she was an aristocrat, but because she had been an aristocrat, she had been given a great deal of strength to deal with all the things that had happened. She had somehow survived the melting pot.

"Let's finish this lot, and have some tea."

Every afternoon at 4:30, no matter what was going on at the ranch, everything would stop for afternoon tea.

"What makes you so confident, Mudderkees?"

"What do you mean, confident? It doesn't take much spunk to buff eggs!"

"No, I mean confident in life. You had such a great upbringing with your father—I know I'd have loved him—and so much came your way. But then you lost him, and fell into your mother's clutches. For you and Nacko, things went well until the business failures. That brought an end to the good things your heritage had promised you. And here you are, seeming to have bent with the storm and not been destroyed. How do you do it?"

"Well, my father was so wonderful. He always found the principle that would guide you in every event. I remember a poem about an Englishman who found himself among Moslem brigands, in India where there had been much hatred, between Moslems and Christian. He was caught alone and disarmed and told to accept Allah or be killed. He responded: 'Give me until sunrise, then, to pray and get ready.' Even in the face of certain death, he maintained his presence of mind and morality.

"The poem goes on, relating the Englishman's thoughts. He remembers his upbringing, his family, school, his triumphs and delights, and then he sees the gold of the dawn behind the eastern mountain, and then a tiny sliver of brightness. He turns to the brigands and says he is ready. He kneels, and a sword swept. At the end, he only had his principles to hold him together. I had a much easier problem – to work with and for the family, and I had all their help and my father's principles were always there."

"I think I have principles too, but holding to them is the point. But you *look* like principles, even when you limp out of the chicken house."

"Well it doesn't do to slump around. We always had the boys stand up straight. The man in the poem was erect, and knelt on his own terms.

"My father was very tall, over six feet at a time when most people were shorter. He was slim and straight until he died. He carried a Malacca walking stick to keep from putting his hands in his pockets, which would have seemed slouchy to him. I suppose I try to be like him."

In the summer of 1945, Beatrix became a grandmother. Rodney David Lincoln Pain was named after his father, uncle, and Abraham Lincoln, an icon to Frances. Beatrix supported Frances as she could, as Rodney and Frances worked out their uneasy relationship. Years later, Frances and Rod's divorce created a split between Beatrix and her daughter-in-law. A generation later, Frances, a feminist poet, revised her impression of Beatrix, and generously shared her memories for Beatrix' biography.

CHAPTER THIRTY-ONE

*I travell'd among unknown men,
In lands beyond the sea;
Nor, England! did I know till then
What love I bore to thee.*

*Among thy mountains did I feel
The joy of my desire;
And she I cherish'd turn'd her wheel
Beside an English fire.*

—William Wordsworth, 1770 – 1850

"Doight, remember the pictures Rod took in 1937, when he was up in Washington State on the battleship *USS Idaho*? They were pictures of the countryside - a facade of woodland, a dense wall of fir trees along a road and a delicate tracery of white dogwood blooms. I would love to see the dogwood.

"Now we are independent we could live in the woods or the country again. Our Social Security pension would buy just as much in Washington as it does here in California. Johnny, I'm sick of the sun, the second-hand car lots, the concrete crassness of Wiltshire Boulevard. And we'd be closer to Jacky."

"When?"

"How long to pack up your tools?"

Jacky, who lived in a cottage floating on cedar logs, a wanigan, moored in Seattle's Lake Union, helped Johnny and Beatrix find a small acreage with a modest cottage. Johnny started gardening and, despite his age, tried to start another commercial garden. Wearing referee's leggings to keep flying rocks from bruising his shins, he followed a gas driven cultivator, breaking the soil for a berry farm.

In 1947, when Rod and Frances expected their second child, Rod brought two-year old Lincoln up to visit. Beatrix had her way. She taught Lincoln to use the "wee pottee."

Beatrix had spoken of a cousin, her Uncle Harry's wayward son, who had run away to Vancouver, Canada. In time, Beatrix found her cousin's address, and when they met in Vancouver, she learned that her uncle, who had a good voice, became the choirmaster in a Vancouver church.

His grandfather, Beatrix's uncle, had been his father's nemesis, as he had been to Beatrix Mary, who visited her uncle's rectory on Christmas and summer holidays. At the family dinners, the maid passed the dessert and Beatrix was served plate of quivering jellied pudding. She found the shaking jelly disgusting and left it. Aunt Adeline, Uncle Harry's wife, admonished her:

"Beatrix, eat your pudding!"

"I can't. I don't like jelly!"

"Well, it has been served to you, so finish it up like a good girl."

"I just can't, Aunt Adeline."

"Very well, it's no dessert for you until you finish it

up."

For three days the jelly was put in front of her. It began to gather dust. She watched the others enjoy their new confections but she continued to refuse. On the fourth day the wobbly jelly again appeared, but without dust. It had been washed.

Charley had made a black and white reproduction of the miniature family portrait of the whole James Minchin family, including James Innes at twelve, and his older brother, Harry. Beatrix had it reproduced in black and white, and sent it to the San Diego family.

This was the only time Beatrix saw her cousin.

The longer Beatrix and Johnny stayed in Washington the more they longed to see their grandchildren. The time she spent with her grandson Lincoln was a reminder of how much she missed her other grandchildren, David's expanding family. They decided to return to California.

Johnny and Beatrix regretted leaving Jacky, and the dogwoods and fir trees of Washington State. With David's help they moved back to southern California, to San Diego, and settled into a modest cottage, and another tool shed, and another garden, soon so stiff with the year-round flowers of California that people stopped on the street to admire.

Beatrix rejoined St. James church and her old friends.

Living more and more in the past, Beatrix asked Johnny to read her passages from George Borrow, to remind her of their halcyon days in the New Forest. She rarely asked Johnny to read, but she felt she wanted to revisit the halcyon days of their honeymoon when she and Johnny circled the New Forest in her light gig, meeting the Forest Folk, the gypsies.

> ...*There's the wind on the heath, brother; if I could only feel that, I would gladly live for ever....*

"Those lines give me a catch in the throat for the old country, that sense of the places where we were alive. It feels as if it's all gone!"

"It's not gone, Johnny, it's still there, we could go and see it again!"

"I guess we could. We are no longer bound down by the depression and the children are all launched."

In 1969, forty years after immigration, the family was no longer under the wheel of poverty. The children were professionals: Jacky, who followed her parents back to California, was a respected civil servant working for the United States Marine Corps in nearby Fallbrook. Rodney was practicing dentistry in San Francisco and David, law in San Diego. They had finally escaped the dilemmas of the old, and the new land had reluctantly accepted them. Beatrix and Johnny had succeeded in a way totally outside the English possibilities.

Beatrix was no longer demeaned by her circumstances or her family's circumstances. If she could see her relatives again, she could even boast a little of their North American adventure, of how they had 'made it', and with 'worn out tools' too! But what could she say of the years between that her relatives could understand?

"And what have you been doing, dear, all these years?"

Could I say 'I was a servant, I cooked and cleaned for people who paid me wages?' I doubt they would understand.

Would they think that 'common is as common does'— Would they understand that I called myself Mary so my employers would never connect me with Beatrix, or know my situation? I wonder if they would they understand that I had to choose this path, to keep the family from penury and the dole.

Would that make sense to them? And what difference would it make?

Before they left England, Henry and Dolly had offered more help, and she and Johnny had turned it down. And then like Plato, they had drunk the bitter cup, for them, the immigrant cup.

But Beatrix had one more, bitter cup to drink.

CHAPTER THIRTY-TWO

John Anderson, my jo, John,
When we were first acquent,
Your locks were like the raven,
Your bonnie brow was brent;
But now your brow is beld, John,
Your locks are like the snow;
But blessings on your frosty pow,
John Anderson, my jo!

John Anderson, my jo, John,
We clamb the hill thegiver;
And monie a canty day, John,
We've had wi' ane anither;
Now we maun totter down, John,
But hand in hand we'll go,
And sleep thegiver at the foot,
John Anderson, my jo.

—Robert Burns, 1759 – 1796

Her bonny Johnny, her right arm and quiet, loving companion of sixty years, was dying. He was dying of lung cancer—his lungs scarred by the phosgene gas of World War One and a lifetime of smoking.

Beatrix cared for Johnny at home. As she tended him, she looked for solace in her little book of verses.

Beatrix

> *A little while I yearn to hold thee fast,*
> *Hand locked in hand, and loyal heart to heart;*
> *(Oh pitying Christ! those woeful words, "We part")*
> *So ere the darkness fall, the light be past,*
> *A little while I fain would hold thee fast.*
> *A little while, when light and twilight meet,—*
> *Behind, our broken years, before, the deep*
> *Weird wonder of the last unfathomed sleep,*
> *A little while I still would clasp thee, Sweet,*
> *A little while, when night and twilight meet.*
> *A little while I fain would linger here.*
> *A little while I still would linger here.*

She coddled Johnny and catered to his simple wants - his tea, well sweetened, and a piece of bread and butter - as his body failed. She kept him with her until she could no longer.

When he sickened, he was carried to the hospital. Beatrix visited daily, with a thermos of his favourite sweetened milk and tea, where he waited, quietly introspective. "One does not give tongue." The good foxhound is mute, even when hurt.

That quiet man who accompanied Beatrix through all their tribulations and their sometime joys, the silent teacher of wood and garden skills who had left his sons and grandsons tool–ready, the builder of gracious homes, gorgeous gardens, and honest furniture was gone from the family, gone from the gardens, gone from his old tools, and thrice gone from Beatrix.

~~~~~~

Again a new life rose before Beatrix.

Jacky drove from Fallbrook to visit her mother every

week. David, his wife Helen and the grandchildren visited most often, taking Beatrix out in her wheelchair. Beatrix found a new friend, Mary Eunice, who joined her in challenging St. James Episcopal Church or, as she called it, "the Republican Party at Prayer."

"Mudderkees, how can you stand all those snarkey sybarites in Saint James?"

"David, I strike at their soft underbelly, like Churchill. Their weak spot is their dedication to the moneyed class. San Diego is not a liberal city, and there are lots of places to make a stand for labour unions or the brown minorities."

The pair of Episcopalian radicals had many adventures together, witnessing for their libertarian ideas. Mary Eunice's son pushed Beatrix with her placard in a picket line at Lindbergh Field Municipal Airport to support an open–hiring policy, and protest the *whites only* rule. They won, and the open merit policy persists to this day.

CHAPTER THIRTY-THREE

Let me go forth, and share
The overflowing Sun
With one wise friend, or one
Better than wise, being fair,
Where the peewit wheels and dips
On heights of bracken and ling,
On Earth, unto her leaflet tips,
Tingles with the Spring.

—William Watson, 1838 – 1878

"Rod, David and I have talked about my making a trip back to England."

Rod's friend was explicit.

"Don't wait, Rod. Take your mother back now. My mother had waited all her life to go Ireland. She had her tickets and, two weeks before her trip, she fell and broke her hip and was dead in a month. Don't wait, go right away."

Beatrix wrote to Johnny's niece, Marjorie, to Mr. Lewis who was Tom Worley's successor, to the lawyer who had cared for her affairs through all the years, and to her friend, Doris Weatherstone-Smith. There were so few left. When circumstance had bitten the family, neither Beatrix nor Johnny had wanted to parade their ill fortunes, so she forsook nearly all the family connections.

Beatrix wondered what difference it would make now, what her friends and relatives in England thought? What difference did it make that she had been 'in service' and wore the same old clothes for years? ...that there had been so little to be proud of for so long that ordinary pride had all but disappeared from her vocabulary?

David bought the tickets on a charter flight from Lindbergh Field in San Diego. Jacky, David, and friends were there to see Beatrix and Rodney off, quipping 'flying down with costly bales.' Beatrix's knees could not climb the twenty steps of the portable boarding ladder so a forklift with a freight pallet was commandeered from the freight depot, rigged to engage the wheelchair and lifted the two travellers to the airplane.

"Mudderkees, what do you think of the forklift operation?"

Her arching, bell-like voice, so much a heritage of her English youth, was now slightly muted by the out-of-doors and the adventurous start of her journey.

"Of course, I think this forklift is momentous"

"I hope you'll get such special treatment across the ocean. Do you want me to ride on the forklift with you, Mudderkees?"

"I'd love you to."

The forklift wafted them up and Beatrix waved her good-byes.

"Will they have a forklift at Prestwick, Roddy? If Mr. Lewis sees me arriving on a forklift, he'll say, "What will those crazy Americans think of next, fork-lifting old ladies of eighty-two!"

"What do you think of all this, Mother?"

"It's very exciting, like Robinson Crusoe seeing the footprint in the sand—very dangerous, but with lots of possibilities. Let's play some cribbage."

After cribbage and two cups of tea, Beatrix slept on three seats abreast. Rod give up his seat and stood all the way to Chicago. Again Beatrix slept through much of the long journey of the prop–driven plane to Ireland. When Beatrix woke, she asked to be wheeled to the washroom where she stayed long enough to concern Rod.

"Would you check on her, stewardess? She's eighty two, and this is the first time anyone in our family has returned to England since we left almost forty years ago. We never expected we'd return home."

"How wonderful. Oh! She wants something."

"I can't find the damn thing. Rod. Would you find the confounded eyebrow pencil? It must be at the bottom, underneath all the stuff Jacky put in."

Rummaging around, he found it and she locked herself back in.

"It's important for her to have her eyebrow pencil, stewardess. She has sort of disappearing eyebrows without it.."

"It's wonderful that she still bothers with eye–brow pencil."

"Okay Rod, you can push me back to my seat."

The happy pair watched as western Ireland appeared, cutting deep into the Atlantic, rimmed with rocks and foam, and then the Isle of Man!'

"There it is, Mudderkees! The Fields of Home just like the song! Can you see the hedge–rows and the trees?"

"Oh! It's so wonderful! I had given up thinking I would ever see it again."

"We're over the downs, now, the chalk country. Oh, look Mudderkees, the Great White Horse."

Beatrix climbed onto Rod's knees and looked down at the Horse.

"It is, it is! The Wantage White Horse! Why, Father and I went by it, just last week, on the train. He never tired of seeing it and neither did I….. Did I say 'with Father last week?' I must have been dreaming. It was more than seventy years ago!"

"Was it near Wantage School, Mudderkees?"

"Oh yes. We visited it and thought it was very old. The cut chalk doesn't seem to grow grass, and so the Horse stays white. We climbed up to it once when the village had a ceremony where the young men dress up and 'scour the White Horse,' scraping off anything that sticks to the chalk."

It was not long until the Thames came into view—

"Rod! The Houses of Parliament! Oh Rod, we are coming back. We are back! I never dreamed I'd see it again!"

She had gripped his arms in the joy and tension of the moment.

The sun shone on the buildings and the river, belying sooty memories of London. As the plane made a big curve towards the airport, Beatrix drank in the sight of landmarks. But then a traveller's concern replaced the joy of the experience. "I doubt Mr. Lewis will be there to help us through customs. We had no way to contact him to let him know of our four hour delay in Chicago."

"Well we'll just have to rustle for ourselves then."

"To Great Russell Street, rustle to Great Russell Street."

Their reluctant cabdriver seemed to lack resolve even to take a fare with the wheelchair. At the Great Russell hotel, the lobby was as dark as old wainscot and dim electric lights could make it, and the ride in a creaking and wobbling lift, a birdcage elevator, was just as they expected. An ancient lift attendant bounced the car gently to match the levels of the shiny brass threshold. "Home, Mudderkees, the 'Hunters Home from the Hill'! What larks, Mudderkees, what larks!"

The old words from Dickens washed sweetly in Beatrix's ears. As she collapsed onto the bed, she had Rod take off her shoes and hoist her legs so she could lie straight.

"I must take—" and she was asleep. Half an hour later she woke, looked bewilderedly round, gathered herself and asked Rod to ring for tea and some buttered Hovis.

"Rod, you can't get a decent cup of tea or a proper slice of bread in America, but you always can get a cup of bad coffee!"

"I just don't understand the customs here, Mother. The toilet is down the hall. And along the hall there's a huge bathtub, with a big brush to wash the tub between customers. It has a snorkel tap that just dollops water in, no high pressure here, just generous and quiet. We're going to enjoy big baths with unlimited hot water, Mudderkees. There is no washbasin in our room, but there's a clean towel and a water pitcher on the rack."

"Not a pitcher, Rod, a ewer. Check to see if there is a slop jar under the washstand."

"Oh, Mother you will never believe...it's Royal Doulton!"

Their howls of laughter drew the maid, who saw nothing to laugh about. The Irish chambermaid kept their huge Rockingham teapot perpetually full and hot. The

Hovis was fresh and tasty.

"Remember The Alderney and the King's Royal Slice of Bread?"

"—and told it to the Alderney," she chanted. "The dedom, the domdom."

Mr. Lewis called and arranged for afternoon drinks. Marjorie would send a driver to get them in three days. Beatrix and Rod set out looking for lunch, feeling completely at ease as they meandered through Soho.

"Let's go into that little Italian restaurant. I'd love some Dover sole."

It was elegantly cooked, and followed with Italian cheeses and a bottle of Chianti.

"What did Mr. Lewis say when he called?"

"He wanted to know how we were progressing, and asked if he could do anything. We're going there for supper and a trip up the River."

"It's so reassuring to find that the river is still in their lives just as it was when I was a girl." They walked home, dawdling to enjoy vistas, to enjoy clutches of Londoners, to hear the remembered cadences, the swing of Cockney, even from people with brown faces.

"There's certainly a lot of brown faces, and they have the jobs the Cockneys used to do, Rod!"

"I suppose the pecking order is working, 'get the Lascars to do it'."

"I'm not so sure of Lascars, Rod, they seem to be working willingly! I suspect it is not only willingness of the immigrants, but a bit of 'side' on the part of the old Cockneys—getting too fancy for the heavy work."

"Soho isn't just French, Italian and Jews. They seem to be the minority now. In that little Italian restaurant the waiter was East Indian."

"The menu wasn't East Indian, Mudderkees!"

"I loved that bit of sole, so fresh."

"Do you remember when Nacko and Ja were sailing on the Norfolk Broads, and helped set a seine net, and mailed a big packet of fresh fish to us. It arrived at Ye Meads in less than a day. We sat down to yesterday's catch!"

"The trains were really quick. Rod. Let me ask that policeman the way to Picadilly Circus."

"Constable, which way to Picadilly Circus?"

"I'm a Traffic Warden, luv'. Just over to your right. Not two minutes' walk."

"Sorry Warden. I thought you were a policeman. Do bobbies no longer wear a helmet?" Beatrix remembered the *Peelers* of her childhood.

"Oh no, luv'. Just a hard–top cap."

His Cockney 'luv' was a blessing.

The precious days slid by.

"I'll see Marjorie today. She's sending a car. Will you be all right?"

"Oh yes. It's better you see her at first. We can see her together later."

This visit with Marjorie, Johnny's niece, was to open a Pandora's box of memories. Marjorie's parents were long gone, and Marjorie now past sixty, seemed elderly.

Beatrix prepared to open Pandora's box gingerly. "After Johnny and I left for America, did your mother and father stay in the old house on the Parade in Aldershot, with the huge holly hedge with the hollows where the children played?"

"When Dad left the Army we moved to a country place, much nicer."

"When your mother died. Nacko was heartbroken.

Pooge raised him. I still remember his grief, separated from all of you and not able to share his sadness."

"She died of dropsy. They tried to drain the fluid from her ankles. She suffered so at the end."

"Tell me what you have been doing, through the war."

The little bed-sitting room, with pretty chintz slipcovers, had pictures of Marjorie's parents, Arthur and Pooge, and her brother, Peter. All gone, though they were all there in their silver picture frames, polished winking bright.

"Johnny was very fond of you, you know."

"But he never wrote—"

The tea was cooling in the cups, and Marjorie freshened them from the cosied pot.

"Do have a biscuit, Aunt Beatrix."

"Marjorie, in America, if you said 'have a biscuit', it would mean 'Have a scone.' You have no idea how different everything is, even with the same language."

Marjorie seemed to collapse

"Oh! Aunt Beatrix, Aunt Beatrix. It's hard. You are the last one left. It's been so long and all of mine have died!"

Much to Beatrix's surprise Marjorie knelt, put her head in Beatrix's lap and sobbed. Her aunt sobbed with her, and smoothed her gray hair.

Marjorie's voice was as it had been long ago, a young woman's voice broken for the moment from meeting her aunt, and broken from her memories of a dead soldier sweetheart. To break the intensity of the moment, Marjorie rose awkwardly and sat down.

"Marjorie, when did you drop your braids?"

"My braids? You must mean my 'plaits!'"

"Johnny loved them."

"But he never wrote!"

"He hardly ever wrote, you're right, except to me in the war, the First War, that is. He often talked of you..."

"It was a hard time, and I'm glad my parents weren't around to suffer the Second War. It would have been a huge burden for my father. I played songs for the Tommies at the canteens. I loved the playing, even on the uprights, however out of tune."

"Could you give me a bit? I remember you played *Traumerie?*"

"The arthritis stopped my piano playing, after the war."

CHAPTER THIRTY-FOUR

*The year's at the spring,
And the day's at the morn;
Morning's at seven;
The hill-side's dew-pearled;
The lark's on the wing;
The snail's on the thorn;
God's in His heaven—
All's right with the world !*

—Robert Browning, 1812 – 1889

When Beatrix left Marjorie, she was glad that there were few friends and relatives that they had to visit.

"It was both wonderful and sad to see Marjorie. It's a 'golden echo and a leaden echo,' Rod. Wonderful to see them, to hear their voices, but not their words. They seem to be old fashioned, stuck in some fold of time in a way that we have moved beyond. I feel like a parent visiting the new house of a recently grown child, being careful of what I say, not to seem stuck up."

"But they are wonderfully kind. I'm glad they're mine and I'm theirs."

"To me, Rod, this trip seems sort of like a honeymoon, something that will never happen again, but is wonderful right now. I'm glad to be able to talk it over with you."

"I know I'll never forget it, Mudderkees."

Both of them relished the scenes and the kindnesses, relished them together with the bitter sweetness of last time—never again.

Next day they were off to Regent Street. Rod misjudged the traffic and started to push the wheelchair off the pavement, meaning to cross the many lanes before the traffic bore down on them. He tried to pull back, sensing a disaster, but the first vehicle, a taxi, screamed to a stop. The driver held out his hand to the next lane of traffic, stopping that lane and the hand signals stopped the traffic lane by lane, and the couple were waved across.

"I felt like the goose with her goslings that they stop traffic for. So kind!"

"Fine goose, fine gosling!"

"Shades of Churchill.

"Mudderkees, what would you say we go to your birthplace, to the big house with nursery at the top?"

"Of course—it wouldn't be a full trip without a return to my first home. If we take a cab, we'll be able to find the way to Eight, Westbourne Gardens Park."

It was harder than they thought, but finally they turned the corner. There was the neighbourhood tuck shop, and then Number Eight, dark, erect, and rather narrow with a generous front door. Four stories up, nursery bars were still fastened across the windows.

"Mudderkees, an East Indian family lives there now."

"I hadn't expected that Rod, but it is some sort of retribution. After all, Father made a career out of serving them."

"Shall we go in, Rod?"

"No, I think you would be devastated if it was cut up

into apartments."

"Alright. It is such a thrill to see the outside, just as I remembered. And there is the park. I'm ashamed to say it was locked to the public, only tenants could go in and sit there undisturbed. We had so many amenities and, now I've come to think, deserved so few."

They went to a ticket agency to book tickets for Torquay.

"We would like two first class tickets to Torquay for the day after tomorrow, and return two days later, please."

The elderly manager of the travel booking shop was straight out of *Alice in Wonderland,* fresh from the Dormouse's teapot. He grumbled:

"These little transactions—losing money—same effort as for a round the world ticket."

"Don't you have printed Great Western tickets for Torquay?"

"No—no—just for steamship companies, such as P&O. Now I will have to write up your ticket longhand to allow your change of trains. What a bother."

"I see this ticket has the wrong dates. We would not be able to present it with items crossed out. Anybody could have altered it."

"Oh, bother! All right, I'll do another."

Later Rod and Beatrix discussed the experience. "Mudderkees, judging from that experience, the Empire is crumbling. The centre is not holding, not even the edges!"

"Don't worry—all will be well in Torquay. I'm so looking forward to Doris, Una, and Vera."

"I have a vague memory of being bullied by Doris. She always seemed to feel that I had a dangerous streak that had to be headed off, at all cost. And I remember she made remarkable blancmange, in different colours."

"Coloured blancmange! She must have been fooling you. It's all the same white recipe with different food colouring. She did that to keep you and Pamela quiet."

"Wonder if I'll get a chance to see Pamela. She was like a sister to me. We never contended. She was my first naked Venus, you know. You show me yours and I'll show you mine—you first. We only wanted to look."

As they rambled, Beatrix spotted Hambly's.

"Rod, this is Hambly's, used to be called the *Biggest Toy Shop in the World*. When I was little, we were allowed to stroll through on special occasions, not to touch. We were well behaved! Did us no harm and, I suppose, hardened us up a bit for life to come. Everything was something of a sermon, with admonishments for good character or good breeding or some such thing. We even had Sunday books for children - *Happy Sundays for the Young and Good*, bound in hard blue black rather like a prayer book, with little stories of how one nasty girl was kind to a cripple, even though she didn't want to be kind at all. I hated it."

In Hambly's, Beatrix and Rodney went upstairs in an old birdcage elevator, piloted by an ancient, working his brass control pillar. Beatrix asked how long he had worked there.

"Since before this here lift, Mum."

"I'd have thought you would want to be retired. I was more than ready."

"Yes Mum, me too, but I likes a little extra bit of money." He brought the elevator car to an exact stop, flush with the level of the floor, his control making smooth, oily clicks as though he were on the bridge of the

Queen Elizabeth. Beatrix and Rod reveled in the toys, particularly the magnificent dollhouses, with the front walls that opened, showing inner rooms, complete with electric lights.

"There are no dolls. I suppose girls nowadays would have their own dolls, those Barbie dolls."

Beatrix had fixed ideas about Barbie dolls, which she judged meretricious and tasteless with their 'chocolate box faces.' Despite her own lack of good looks, Beatrix had never developed a charitable attitude toward other women's faces.

At the same time she adored plain Eleanor Roosevelt, "Who never puts on. She moves with kings, and does not lose the common touch."

In England, the common touch meant being in touch with commoners, to be with them but not of them, walking alongside, but not playing with them. Gentility for Beatrix was to walk through the world of people with no display of dignity, but never to lose it. Back in England she began to lose her sense of outrage at being miscast by fate in North America, of being a servant and rarely respected.

Later that day Rod was lost. "Are we back in Soho, Mudderkees?"

"Yes, and this is where St. Anne's, Soho, used to be. They had some of the most magnificent music in all of London. Nacko, his sister Bimba, and I used to go with friend to enjoy the singing through Lent. We'd bring a picnic with us and stand in line for hours and hours. Pity it was bombed out.

At Trafalgar Square they could not find a place to sit where they could address postcards. Beatrix remembered the nearby St. Martin's in the Fields.

"This is a Wren church, Rod." Beatrix said as they

entered. "I understand that when they built the church, the contractor cheated and put rubble inside the panels, instead of concrete."

"Didn't seem to have done any harm."

After a short nap, Beatrix woke exclaiming.

"Evensong! They'll soon be lighting the candles! The priest won't be long now."

"Mudderkees, he's Chinese."

"Well I never! What a change—I've never heard a service in Chinese."

"Will you take mass even if they have fortune cookies?"

"Don't be irreligious, Rod. It's such bad manners."

Rod subsided. He did not like to be unintentionally bad mannered, or caught at it.

The service completed, the priest prepared to exit, and genuflecting to the altar, he tripped and fell, recovered, and hobbled out.

"Do you think he'd go straight to heaven if he'd broken his neck while he did Evensong?"

"Shut up Rod! You are really irritating!"

The intensity of Beatrix's rare outburst hissed in the silence.

The next day Beatrix suggested they go to Liberty's and look for some gifts for those at home.

"Duty presents always used to be lawn hankies with rolled edges and an embroidered initial. What would you think if someone made you a present of an initialed white linen hankie?"

"I'd find someone with the initial R, and give it away."

"Crepe de chine painted scarves have taken over. You'll never again see so many scarves in one room."

The couple ranged through Liberty's interior. The rug and carpet room resembled a Kasbah, and the leather room was full of clothing and animals clad in natural leather, including a fat pig made of pigskin.

They bought a length of bright paisley, with memories of the time when Beatrix's mother had cut up the antique Paisley shawls for a fancy dress and incurred James' anger.

"The Cheshire Cheese is close by. I'd love a glass of beer and some roast beef. If you tip the waiter, he'll put you in the same chair that Samuel Johnson, or was it Boswell, sat in."

"I'm sure he would, Mudderkees, and Boswell sat on all the chairs there, too!"

"What do you expect, to eat his meal? Don't be such a Pecksniff!"

"Sorry, Mother. I didn't mean to be a hypocrite."

The Cheshire Cheese was crowded, and the waiter asked if they had a reservation.

"No reservation? We book a month in advance, mostly from America."

"Could you fit us in? We're here from California and haven't been here in thirty five years," said Rod, offering the waiter a half crown. He thought they might take the place of a party, which, he said, he expected to be late.

"Waiter, we'd like a rare cut, extra thick." Another half crown tip disappeared.

"Rare is the only kind we have, Sir."

The Yorkshire pudding was generous, covered with the gravy. They left, feeling well treated and ready for a rest.

The next morning they had tea and Hovis in bed.

"Don't forget to give the maid our laundry, Rod."

"They do it right in their day–room on this floor."

"Let's look for some bookshops today. There should be some on Charing Cross Road."

En route, they spotted a chapel.

"Look here, Mudderkees, a Welsh chapel, and the next sermon is 'True Religion is the Most Joyous Thing in Life', Richard Jones, M.A.B.S. Would that be Master of Biblical Studies?"

"I was raised to think that chapel was not the real thing, that in some way they could not be truly godly if they weren't Church of England. How could they talk with God if they were playing at being religious in their chapel? Now I know better. The Chapel boys in the RAF were as good as the gentry. They offered a life just like anyone else."

"It's all one to me, Mother."

"What do you mean? Oh I know what you mean, that it's tommy-rot, and I know you don't believe that."

"Of course not, Mother, I'm a believer."

"And better be, too, for your own good."

She nodded and, as though to drive home her homily, she unexpectedly declaimed:

> "The Rommany chi
> And the Rommany chal
> Love Luripen
> And dukkeripen,
> And hokkeripen,
> And every pen
> But Lachipen
> And tatchipen."

"What on earth are you saying, Mudderkees?"

"Mine to tell, yours to ask!" she said and she never explained the peculiar verse. Rod felt as though he had been secretly admonished for his skepticism about RAF flight officers.

Shortly after, they branched into Litchfield Street, stiff with bookshops and art.

"Rod! Do you remember our Beardsley prints, the racehorse prints, the great horse *Hambletonian* with a jockey up, silks, yellow topped boots, and an ostler holding the bridle? I used to think that Father had bred that horse. His own horse in India was *Queen of the Night*. She was brought to his tent every night for her lump of sugar."

"What a picture Mother. I'd give a finger to see it in the flesh."

"I frequently see it in my dreams."

At Smiths, 'The Snuff Centre', Beatrix and Rod lingered to sniff the spicy breeze.

"Do you remember Grandmother taking snuff, Mudderkees?"

"Of course. In her day, women did not smoke, but used to take snuff like mad. I never liked it."

"Have you noticed the sound of women's feet click click clacking on the pavement as they walk by us?"

"I hate that noise. Too much like they are trying to make a *rary show* of themselves. I wish they would change into something more suitable, and quieter."

Beatrix was true to her unspoken social dogma, both for little and grand issues. Never make a big noise or trouble. Never push yourself forward or make yourself the centre. Never be loud or obvious—be quietly courteous and unobtrusive. *Be*, a personal rule of conduct for everything. Be gentle, in the sense of gentlewoman, beyond being ladylike.

Here she was in modern London, re–experiencing the city of her childhood. Her years in service had changed nothing inside her except her awareness of unkindnesses piled on servants during the depression. Her philosophy had not changed. She still moved through the people of the world as she met them, on her terms, unassailably herself. Although adversity had altered her, it had radicalized Johnny. He had become a union man through and through, a Technocracy supporter, who, until his death, had a spectral view of Management.

"Have you ever seen a place like this, Mudderkees? It looks like an automat that sells pork pies."

"Sounds good to me. All those books made me snappish."

The young policeman with a walky–talky advised them to try the Black Angus.

"Why are you stationed outside the church, Constable?"

"We've had some skinhead trouble here and I'm to see that nobody is bothered."

"Yes Well good day, Constable."

"Good day, and have a nice hols."

There was something so amiable and reassuring about the policeman. It had been an age since she had a hols, but here she was, luxuriating in her hols and treasuring these little encounters.

CHAPTER THIRTY-FIVE

Mrs. Gamp...performing a short series of dangerous evolutions with her umbrella, managed to establish herself pretty comfortably.
"And which of them smoking monsters is the Angworks boat, I wonder?"
"Goodness me!" cried Mrs. Gamp.
"Which boat did you want?"
"The Angworks package," Mrs. Gamp replied.
"I do not deceive you, my sweet, why should I?"
"That...in the middle," said Ruth.
"And I wish it was in Jonadge's belly, I do."
— Charles Dickens, 1812 – 1870, *Martin Chuzzlewit*

As they waited for the train to depart for Torquay, Rod admired the decorated steel arches in the train station, a monument to the great engineer–designer Brunel. It was a Victorian cathedral dedicated to the steel industry and railroads. In the centre, the huge clock with four faces hung from high steel spans over the concourse. Their train waited at the platform, protected by steel lattice barriers. Carriage doors opened and banged shut.

Rod loaded Beatrix and her wheelchair into a first-class carriage. The stationmaster's whistle sounded and, as last-second passengers ran to get aboard, the first gentle tug broke the train's connection with the busy station.

Beatrix savoured every vibration of this classic experience, sensing the purposeful chaos on the platform and checking the time on the great clock. She embraced the scene, relishing the good–byes, the porters, the stationmaster with his watch, sprinting latecomers, and at the first tug, the ungainly carts pulling free of the luggage vans. The train started its accelerating glide, past the walled back gardens.

"Sit back and enjoy all the noises of so long ago, Mudderkees. The rattling, clicking, and chattering over the points. Such delightful clatter."

"Tell me when we get near Taplow, Rod. It will only be a second, I know, but it's a second I've dreamed of so often."

"Me too. I have a picture in my head of the Stationmaster's cottage, of the station with the pretty wooden bridge joining the two platforms. Remember the crowd of business types with their bowler hats, tightly rolled brollies, and Daily Mails?"

"Not much chance of that any more. There are hardly any bowlers, even in London. Besides, the business types live in London now."

"Oh there's the tea man!"

"Could we have two big cups, please, and may we order sandwiches?"

"Sorry Sir, no special service to the carriages, only serving in the saloon carriage."

"I don't think we can make it all the way through the corridors with the wheelchair. Do you think they'd bend a rule for us? My mother is just returned from America, her first time back in over thirty years."

And they broke the rule. The tray arrived with big

white china cups and teapot, sardine sandwiches with sprigs of watercress, dressed with linen napkins.

"One pound, five and six, Sir."

"Here's for your trouble, thank you so much. This will make Mother's day."

"Thank you, Sir."

"How far to Taplow?'

"Only a few miles, a few minutes."

And suddenly it came tearing along. Bath Road running alongside, hurtling, no pause for the bridge, a snatched view of the station cottage, rattle, and Taplow was gone.

"That was so quick we almost missed it! I'm glad we watched for it, Rod. Now I'm looking forward to Torquay. I wonder if Doris will still be the snob after thirty-five years? I always suspected the Weatherstone of Weatherstone–Smith was a reaction to the commonness of Smith."

"I did too, but then, I didn't have to deal with the name Smith.

"It really is a pretty commonplace name. We'll see."

"So much has passed by in the intervening years and yet so much is unchanged. For example, it's still a surprise to see the brown faces with the same expressions I'd expected from white Cockney faces, and genuine Cockney speech from those brown lips!"

"Our relatives haven't traveled down the challenging paths we have: poverty, different jobs, different food, American democracy, handling one's own problems without a family to fall back on. They were challenges."

"I'm sure people here faced similar challenges, Mudderkees! But of course the English are insular, they are born to be insular. Look! There's a man ploughing a field with a team, ploughing clay, with a heavy team, too.

You'd never see that any more in North America.

Mother, sometimes I feel just stuffed with memories of things now quite gone, like blacksmith shops and cobbler shops. I remember watching the cobbler in Taplow soling shoes, dishing the sole leather to fit the shoe, tacking it to the upper, stitching it round by hand with awl and needle, then cutting it with the funny crooked knife with the special blunted crook on the end. He polished the edges with little burnishers he heated in an alcohol flame. Sometimes I think I could just reproduce craft after craft from having watched them as a boy."

"You inherited that from Nacko. There wasn't anything he couldn't turn his hand to as though he had been trained to it."

"What do you feel now, Mudderkees, now we are deep in the country we used to know best?"

"Relief, Rod, relief from that feeling of having to be different. In England I am me without having to change anything. Here is where my heart belongs, my words are right, my looks belong, and where my father is buried. I could die here, content, but I want to see and feel a little bit more. I don't think I could have waited much longer, but the length of the wait has made it all the sweeter. How do you feel?"

"Much like you. You know I have been restless in the States. They don't seem to like me and I don't generally like them—they have an approach to life that isn't mine. So it is wonderful here. The sights are smooth to my eye; the towns have a human dimension that never jibes at me. I'm happy with the size of it, without any superlatives."

"This is Norman country, Rod. We just passed Windsor Castle. Would you get the wee book from my bag and read a bit to me, something that says 'we're here,' that would fit us into the countryside?"

"What do you think would go well?"

"Something light. I feel carefree here. Give me a bit of *The History of Mr. Polly.*

"You tried to get me to read him, but I never did. I just heard the scandals—here it is. 'Herbert George Wells, 1866.'
Just before you were born—that's nice."

"It was about two o'clock in the afternoon, on hot day in May, when Mr. Polly, unhurrying and serene, came upon a broad bend of the river to which the little lawn and the garden of the Potwell Inn run down. He stopped at the sight of the place and surveyed the deep tiled roof, nestling under big trees—you never get a big, decently shaped tree by the seaside—its sign towards the roadway, its sunblistered green bench and tables, its shapely white windows and its row of upshooting hollyhock plants in the garden. A hedge separated the premises from a buttercup yellow meadow, and beyond stood three poplars in a group against the sky, three exceptionally tall, graceful, and harmonious poplars.

It is hard to say what there was about them that made them so beautiful to Mr. Polly, but they seemed to him to touch a pleasant scene with a distinction almost divine. He stood admiring them quietly for a long time."

As she rode through the familiar counties, Beatrix listened thirstily, the words blowing through her, the familiar pronunciations, phrases of her own countryside, the very trees and meads of her girlhood. She heard not Rodney, but Johnny and her father, all restored for the moment. Her silent tears graced the moment, pain and pleasure mixing as the serene words wove on.

"*The green tables outside were agreeably ringed with memories of former drinks, of a couple of Toby jugs and a beautifully coloured hunting scene framed and glazed...but these were the mere background to the really pleasant thing in the spectacle, which was quite the plumpest woman Mr. Polly had ever seen, seated in an arm-chair in the midst of all these bottles and glasses and glittering things, peacefully and tranquilly and without the slightest loss of dignity, asleep. Many people would have called her a fat woman, but Mr. Polly's innate sense of epithet told him from the outset that plump was the word. She had shapely brows and a straight well shaped nose, kind lines and contentment about her mouth, and beneath it the jolly chins clustered like chubby little cherubim about the feet of an Assumptioning Madonna...*"

Beatrix had composed herself and heard the old tale with continuing delight—

"*...she awoke with a start, and it amazed Mr. Polly to see the swift terror in her eyes. Instantly it had gone again.*
'Law! She said, her face softening with relief.
'I thought you was Jim.'
'I'm never Jim,' said Mr. Polly.
'You've got his sort of hat.'
'Ah!' said Mr. Polly, and leant over the bar."

Beatrix was listening to the conversation with a critical

ear,

"I'd wager she would have dropped the aitch in hat, Rod."

"Not here, she must have been country. Wells wouldn't have made a mistake like that. After all, aitches are like calling cards, like the K in somethink."

"I've noticed it's there, even in the second generation. Some American children of British parents slip back into the 'somethink' and never realize it. Go on, it's so rich..."

'What can I do for you?'
'Cold meat?' said Mr. Polly.
'There is cold meat,' the plump woman admitted.
'And room for it.'
The plump woman came and leant over the bar and regarded him judicially but kindly, 'There's some cold boiled beef,' she said, and added 'A bit of crisp lettuce?'
'New mustard,' said Mr. Polly.
'And a tankard!'
'A tankard.'
They understood each other perfectly."

"There's a wonderful line coming up now, Rod, where that old magician brings up friendship between consenting adults, no romantic nonsense."

"Here it is...

"They smiled like old friends.
Whatever truth there may be about love, there is certainly such a thing as friendship at first sight. They liked each other's voices, and they liked each other's way of smiling and speaking ..."

"There it is, the old magician, creating such a wonderful scene, creating such wonderful people, in a few words."

"Some have it and some haven't, Mudderkees. Take Scott, he paints a wonderful picture, but the people are bloodless."

"I have to admit that, but you know Aunt Dolly read Scott's *Quentin Durwood, Ivanhoe,* and the rest, every year.
She never let go of her childhood fantasy, I suppose. She was really more intellectual than that."

"I'll tell you, I could read *Kidnapped* every month, let alone every year."

"*Kim,* for me."

"Isn't Wells marvelous? He listened and wrote it all down, to the nuance!"

"The great American authors, such as Edith Wharton and Mark Twain, relish dialects. But without the class system, there is no way to love the way the people speak. I can't exactly put my finger on the difference, but for Huck Finn to say *ain't* doesn't have the verbal play that the *'it the side of 'is 'ead* seems to have. Somehow the Cockney carries a deeper meaning, that *sumpthink* carried the strength of the class system, and the mutual appreciation implied by it—difficult stuff to unravel."

"Part of it is respect, without a put-down."

"I can bear witness to that. Somehow Americans don't understand that it's not a slave relationship, that it's not proving anything."

"Let's talk about pleasanter things."

"I should say. Have another cup of tea!"

The steward refilled the pot, hot with the loose leaves of tea swirling in it, as they rode the train like royalty through the southern marches to Torquay.

Mr. Pace, the local cab driver, delivered them promptly, having shared the latest West Country lore and gossip.

"Oh Trix, how wonderful to see you, and Roddy, too. He's grown. Do come in. Thank you, Mr. Pace, that will be all for now, thank you. Roddy, do be careful of your mother over the door step!"

Rod sighed. He had been a 'pot of poison' to Doris, who, until now, had outweighed, outmaneuvered, and called him down. He had not seen Doris for thirty-five years, except during her short visit to celebrate his parents' golden wedding anniversary in 1965.

"Let's have some tea, we've prepared a little high tea in case you were hungry from the trip. It's so far to London, but then, it's not as far as California."

"I think it's farther to London, Doris. You have no idea the adjustments Mother and I have had to make..."

"Don't be wicked, Roddy. I know you of old, and hope you've learned to behave yourself. If you can't find a chair, you can lean on something."

"Thank you, Doris. I'll manage."

"Trix, dear, you can see the wee place we have here, with no extra bedroom for Roddy. We have arranged for Mr. Pace to take him into Torquay to get a hotel room after we have had tea. That'll be alright with you, won't it, Roddy?"

"Of course Doris. After all, I don't want to spoil your visit with mother. I'll amuse myself in Torquay. Just tell me when you want me to come back."

"I've arranged all that with Mr. Pace."

"I'm so happy to be here Doris, I've been dreaming of this for years."

"Roddy doesn't speak American!"

"No, he has been away to university so much ...
"Mudderkees says she thinks it's my Minchin blood!"
"Well it's nice to see that you haven't become a Yank. Trix, how many of your family are left? You must have seen the death of your brother in the paper."

Beatrix was not ready for Doris' being fixed in a time that she, Beatrix, had measured in other lifetimes in North America.

"George, yes, that was a long time ago. He'd be well over a hundred now. I had news of his death from my sister Dolly."

"Oh, is she still alive?"

"Oh no. Dolly lived to be eighty. You see dear, I'm eighty-two, Dolly would be about a hundred and five now, and George would be ten years older. He was born about 1850."

"I can't believe it—you must be, of course, I'm seventy!"

"I've kept my wits."

"I can't imagine you not keeping your wits!"

"A lot of people don't! My brother George went dotty."

"Isn't it dreadful how people go dotty?"

Rod had to meddle...

"Doris, I don't think it strange. Why should everybody just keep his wits to please other people?"

"Oh Rod, you're pulling my leg..."

"But some of us keep so sharp!"

When Doris remarked ironically that Roddy was a real optimist, Rod replied, "Mr. Pace is a real pessimist. He is both interesting and nice, as well as a misery. He filled us in on the way over here."

"Be nice to Mr. Pace, Roddy, because he has his car service and he's an excellent chap. He has two or three cars for his taxi service, and uses the big one abroad. He takes it to Spain and Lord knows where. He speaks other languages, as well."

"Would you like a bite to eat, Mother?"

"I know you want a bite!"

"I'll wait till everyone has some."

"What would you like? I have a little bit of poached salmon. Do you like that?"

"Salmon is such a luxury. There's not much salmon left in Britain, is there?"

"Not at this time of season, I'm sorry to say. This is American."

Beatrix felt urged to play a good card. "Although there was grouse on the hotel menu last night, I had roast beef."

Doris could not allow the beef bid to pass. "I'm not fond of it because we get this funny meat. We are going through a bad spell a bit, just a bit."

"Don't let Mr. Pace's talk make you pessimistic..."

"No, no Beatrix, he's really dreadful."

"Well he does go on and on, and I don't know why he has to, he has such a nice wife. She's just charming"

"He made me laugh when he was gold-plating Harold MacMillan and his miserable cabinet. He simply felt there was nothing wrong with the scandal..."

Rod, feeling the politics of the group were quite out-of-hand, added, "Of course these things had nothing to do with whether the men were good prime ministers. Mr. Pace would rather have a prime minister who was a complete jerk as long as he was a good minister."

"Oh Rod, you are a pot of poison, just like you always were. You haven't changed a bit."

"Thank you, Doris. You haven't changed much either. But the country is in a dreadful mess and needs a cure."

Mr. Pace arrived to take Rod off to town.

Later Beatrix told Rod of her adventures with her old friends.

"Rod, it was just wonderful to be with old friends, though sometimes they are hard to bear. They seemed rigid, their snobbishness seemed molded in them."

"But such good nature. Do you think we were like that before we left for North America?"

"I know we were. One can never understand slavery until one has been a slave."

"It was difficult to listen to them berating Mr. Pace for being what he was, and so palpably using him, even using him for the characteristics they derided – his affability and interesting points of view, which were quite open-minded."

"You wouldn't have believed the trip they took me on. We all crushed into their tiny Mini so I could see Bideford, which I remembered from *Westward Ho* and *Stalky and Co.* It was pretty, but in the books it was much more primitive. As I remember, *Westward Ho* was too Victorian for me. Sentimental morality, I think."

"Me too, I just had to skip through most, looking for the things I imagined were there, reading fifty years ago. Funny how one's judgment changes with time."

"Yes—now I'm hard to please with long moralities, like Dickens."

"Why do you think you used to read moralities, and now you don't like them?"

"I think life has taught me that moralizing about people is not as important as describing them. I'm not a Victorian any more."

"Doris and her family are very kind, but aren't they Victorian?"

"Yes, they took me out on the moors, so wild and green. And their lavish hospitality; they offered me food – food, from morning until bed-time, and then Ovaltine."

"Those Yorkshire girls really like to eat."

"It seems to me we always compared Yorkshire eating habits to our south of England austerities."

"Did it ever strike you, Mudderkees, that our family was really puritanical. One piece of plain bread before you could have any jam, no gluttony, and really, not too much fun?"

"Of course I have, but I don't regret it. The Minchins were all Roundheads you know, none of that longhaired, Loyalist ranting and roistering stuff for us. We were plain moralists, doubting the value of too many creature comforts."

"Give me the comforts and the Loyalist way, every time!

"I hated to leave because I know I'll never be back. That's hard. In some ways it is almost better not to see them. But one has to, and suffer with the joy."

Her face brightened, the blue eyes misting. It was as though she had been welling up for this moment, her return, her memories, the "have a nice hols, luv," Mr. Polly, the iron bar in the nursery window, St. Martins, Picadilly. They crowded into her mind and she spoke her apotheosis.

"When Father died, I died too. But then I found Johnny, and he took me away from all that to the New World. We had the family and all the troubles of making a living. He was always a countryman, best with a casting rod, good with animals and best of all with plants. He was a good companion. He was my arms and my legs, he was my everything. And we made it together. You children were educated. When Johnny died, there was only one thing left to do, to return home and make sure of the place I came from. There is something about closing the ring, which makes all the intervening things right, makes them testify to your having done all those long, tiring and tiresome days of toiling. It makes sense of it all, and now the rest of you can go on, in America. We started you in America, and you won't have to come back to find out that it was the right thing to do!"

She cried quietly, as they held hands.

EPILOGUE

O Celestial gift of divine liberality, descending from the Father of light to raise up the rational soul even to heaven...Undoubtedly, indeed, thou hast placed thy desirable tabernacle in books, where the Most High, the Light of light, the Book of Life, hath established thee, to those who knock thou openest quickly. In books cherubim expand their wings, that the soul of the student may ascend...

—Richard de Bury, 1281–1345, *Philobiblon*

Beatrix did not glance up when Rod came into her room in the rest home where she lived after her stroke.

"Hello Mudderkees. It's Rod, come to take you for a walk!"

The friendly Mexican attendant had tied her thin hair with a ribbon that matched her blue eyes, her last comely feature. Rod took her in her wheelchair into the bright San Diego sunshine along the river, into the shade of the willow trees. They stopped by the shimmering water.

"Mudderkees, do you remember how we used to picnic in a farm field, where we were rained out? Jacky turned cartwheels round the picnic, and the cows came to check us out."

She made no response; her face was as blank as a

sleeping baby. These conversations, though one-sided, comforted Rod, who enjoyed the memories, and the telling helped him ignore his mother's unresponsiveness.

"Mudderkees, do you remember when you took me to Bray Lock, where you were to play bridge with Mrs. Prideaux? You tied a string to a long twig, hung a bent pin on the string, and a lump of bread on the pin, and set me to 'fishing', so you could get a half an hour free to play bridge. Do you remember?"

As he sat down on a bus-stop bench, Beatrix turned to him, her bluer than blue eyes intense, and spoke in the voice of a child.

"So nice to have known you!"

Beatrix died not long after. Although she had not been active as a parishioner for years and had not been at St. James since her stroke, her funeral was crowded. Rodney played his bagpipes, *The Flowers of the Forest,* a last poem for a lady of poetry.

***

ISBN 141200482-9